SCIENC NOW

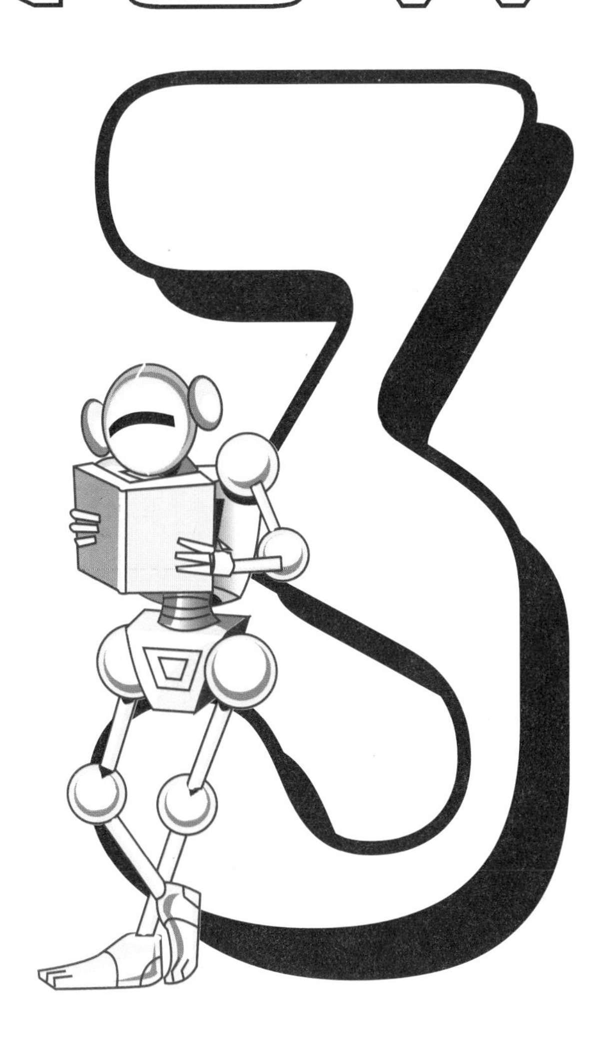

Ann Fullick

Ian Richardson

David Sang

Martin Stirrup

Heinemann

Contents

Heinemann Educational Publishers,
a division of Heinemann Publishers (Oxford) Ltd,
Halley Court, Jordan Hill, Oxford, OX2 8EJ

OXFORD LONDON EDINBURGH
MADRID ATHENS BOLOGNA PARIS
MELBOURNE SYDNEY AUCKLAND SINGAPORE TOKYO
IBADAN NAIROBI HARARE GABORONE
PORTSMOUTH NH (USA)

First published 1996

ISBN 0 435 50689 7 (hardback)
00 99 98 97 96
10 9 8 7 6 5 4 3 2 1

ISBN 0435 50688 9 (softback)
00 99 98
10 9 8 7 6 5 4 3

Designed and typeset by Plum Creative

Illustrated by Olivia Bown, Norman Clark, Nick Beresford-Davies, Dave Glover, Jeremy Gower, Martin Griffin, Donald Harley, Jack Haynes, Tony Kenyon, Lynda Knott, Sarah Lenton, John Lobhan, Dave Marshall, John Plumb, Steve Smallman, Andrew Tewson, Shirley Tourret, Tony Wilkins and Joanna Williams

Cover design by Miller, Craig and Cocking

Cover photo by Tony Stone Worldwide

Printed and bound in Great Britain by Bath Colour Books, Glasgow

Acknowledgements
The authors and publishers would like to thank the following for permission to use photographs:

p 1 T: Rex Features. p 1 B: Science Photo Library. p 2 T, M: Mary Evans Picture Library. p 4: Science Photo Library. p 5: Science Photo Library. p 7: Science Photo Library. p 8 T: Wellcome Trust. p 8 B: PA. p 9: Science Photo Library. p 10 T: Science Photo Library. p 10 B: BBC. p 14: Science Photo Library. p 16: Zefa. p 18 TR, TL, BL: Roger Scruton. p 18 BR: Rex Features. p 19: PA. p 20 T: Rex Features. p 20 B: Allsport/P Rondeau. p 21: Advertising Archives. p 22 ML, MR: PA. p 22 BR: Peter Davies. p 23: Rex Features. p 25: Advertising Archives. p 27: Roger Scruton. p 30: Sally and Richard Greenhill. p 31: OSF/Zig Leszczynski. p 34: Sally and Richard Greenhill. p 35: Rex Features. p 36 T: Courtesy of General Infirmary of Leeds. p 36 M: Popperfoto. p 39 L: Mary Evans Picture Library. p 39 R: BBC Natural History Unit/ Brian Lightfoot. p 40 T, TM: OSF/Daniel Cox. p 40 ML: Ardea/Starin. p 40 MR: OSF/Starin. p 40 B: OSF/Stan Osolnski. p 41: Mary Evans Picture Library. p 42 T: OSF/Johnny Johnson. p 42 B: Roger Scruton. p 43 T: Bruce Coleman. p 43 B: Roger Scruton. p 46: OSF/Stan Osolnski. p 48: Roger Scruton. p 56: Roger Scruton. p 57 T: Roger Scruton. p 57 M: Peter Gould. p 58 T, M: Peter Gould. p 58 B: OSF/Laurence Gould. p 59: Rex Features. p 60: Peter Gould. p 63: Peter Gould. p 64: Roger Scruton. p 69: Science Photo Library. p 70: Roger Scruton. p 72: Peter Gould. p 74: Peter Gould. p 75: Peter Gould. p 77: Peter Gould. p 78: Peter Gould. p 79 L: Roger Scruton. p 79 R: Science Photo Library/NASA. p 82 T, M: Roger Scruton. p 82 B: Peter Gould. p 83: Peter Gould. p 84: Peter Gould. p 86: Peter Gould. p 87: J Allan Cash. p 88: Peter Gould. p 89: Peter Gould. p 90 M: Holt Studios. p 90 B: AAA. p 91 T: OSF/E R Degginger. p 91 M: AAA. p 92: Science Photo Library/John Mead. p 93 T: Popperfoto. p 93 M: Beken of Cowes. p 95 T, TM: Peter Gould. p 95 BM: Roger Scruton. p 95: Courtesy of Standard Firework. p 97: Paul Jackson. p 98: Peter Gould. p 99: Peter Gould. p 100 T: Science Photo Library. p 100 M: Peter Gould. p 101: Peter Gould. p 102 T: Science Photo Library. p 102 L: Tony Stone. p 102 MR: Roger Scruton. p 102 BR: Peter Gould. p 103: Peter Gould. p 104 T, TM, MR: Roger Scruton. p 104 ML: Peter Gould. p 105: Peter Gould. p 106: Collections/Alan Le Gasmeur. p 107: Peter Gould. p 108 T: Performing Arts Library. p 108 ML: Roger Scruton. p 108 MR: Christian Him. p 113 T: Roger Scruton. p 113 M: Peter Gould. p 116A: Science Photo Library. p 116B, C: Roger Scruton. p 118 T: Collections/Anthea Seivelong. p 118 M: Meg Sullivan. p 119: Roger Scruton. p 120 M: Roger Scruton. p 120 B: Colin Willoughby. p 122: Peter Gould. p 128 T, B: Peter Gould. p 128 M: Science Photo Library/Keith Kent. p 130: Science Photo Library. p 132: Ace. p 133: Peter Gould. p 138 T: Peter Gould. p 138 B: Science Photo Library/ Matt Meadows. p 140: Roger Scruton. p 142: Roger Scruton. p 145: Colorsport.

The publishers have made every effort to trace the copyright holders, but if they have inadvertently overlooked any, they will be pleased to make the necessary arrangements at the first opportunity.

How to use this book

Welcome to **Science Now!** We have tried to make the book as easy to use and understand as possible. Here are a few notes to help you find your way around.

The book has ten units. Each unit covers one of the big ideas of science in biology, physics or chemistry. Biology units are green, physics units are red, chemistry units are blue.

What's in a unit?

The units are organised into double-page spreads. Each spread has:

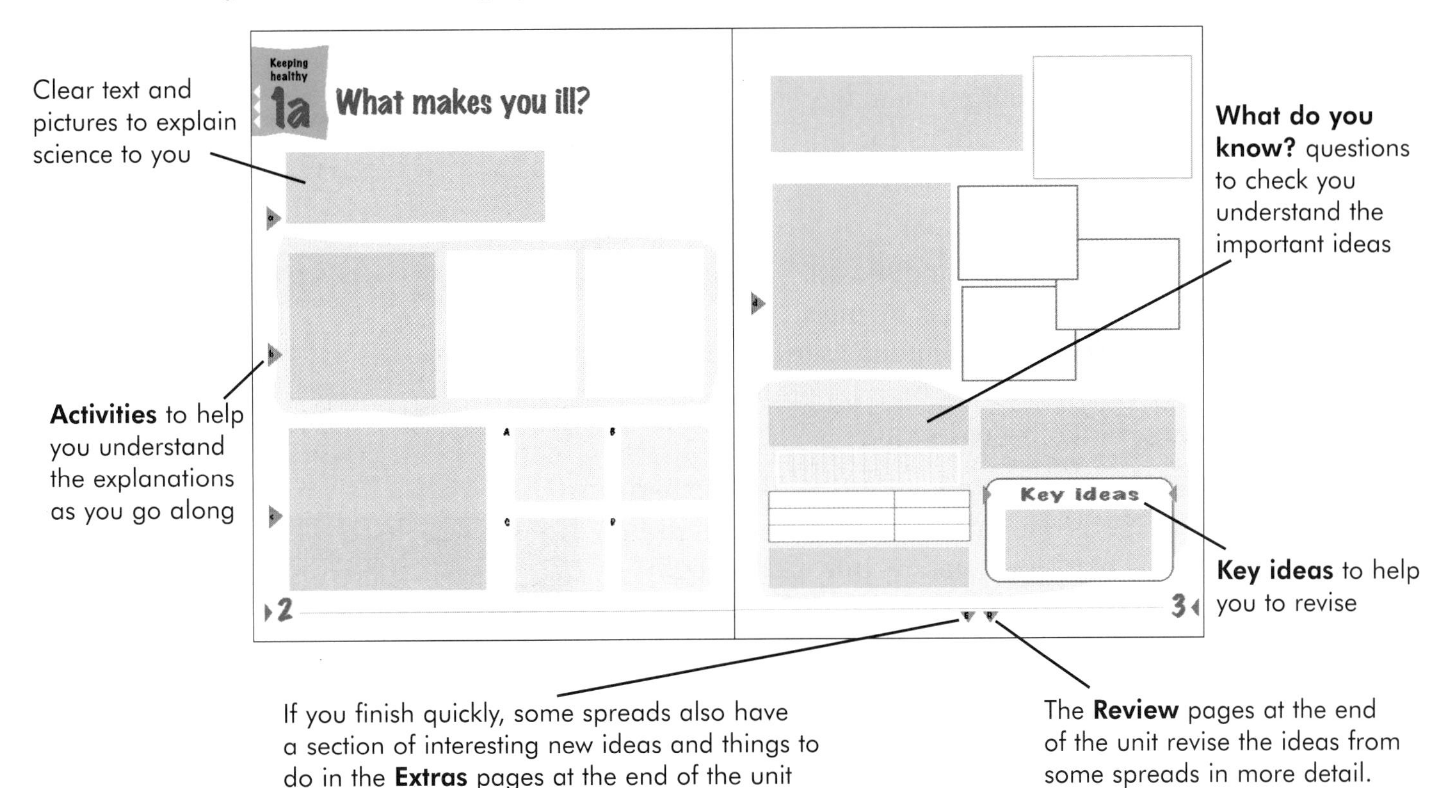

None of the activities needs special equipment or preparation. All the practical activities for the course are in the photocopiable Activities and Assessment Pack which goes with the book.

Glossary

At the back of the book you will find a list of important scientific words and their meanings, so that you can remind yourself quickly of what they mean. If you want any more information you can look at the pages whose numbers are next to the words.

We hope you find **Science Now**! useful in your course. Above all, we hope that you enjoy it!

1a What makes you ill?

Time off sick

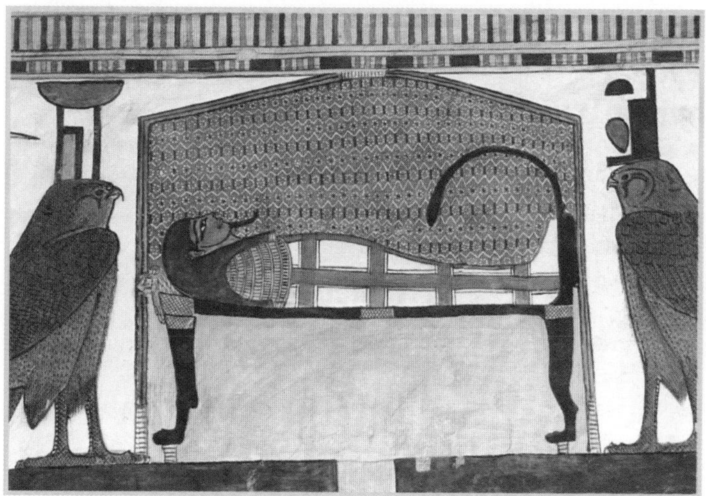

People have always needed time off to be ill! Human remains that are thousands of years old show signs of diseases that people still get today. But it wasn't until the nineteenth century that people had a scientific understanding of diseases. Before then, we had some very strange explanations for feeling ill.

Five thousand years ago, the ancient Egyptians used many remedies for diseases. They thought diseases were caused by their many gods. Treatments always included sacrifices to the gods, and substances like mouldy bread, poppy seeds, crocodile dung and honey were used.

The ancient Greek Hippocrates thought that disease had nothing to do with gods. He said there were four liquids in the body – blood, black bile, yellow bile and phlegm. Disease happened when the fluids were out of balance. This idea lasted until the seventeenth century.

Bacteria and viruses

During the last 300 years, people have discovered **bacteria** and **viruses**. These tiny living things can only be seen under a microscope – they are called **micro-organisms**. They cause all sorts of diseases, from tonsillitis to tuberculosis.

Now we understand the causes of diseases better, we are better at treating them.

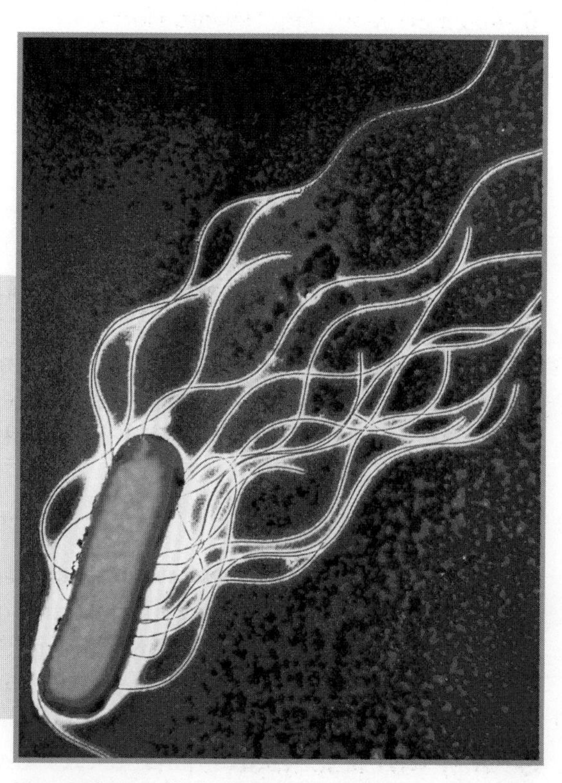

This Salmonella bacterium causes food poisoning.

1 Antoni van Leeuwenhoek invented the microscope in the seventeenth century. In 1683, he was the first person to see bacteria, although he didn't know what they did.

2 In the nineteenth century, Louis Pasteur showed that it was micro-organisms in the air that caused broth to go bad. He realised that similar micro-organisms (germs) must cause disease in people and animals.

3 There was a cholera epidemic in London in the mid-nineteenth century. Dr John Snow realised that everyone who got cholera in his area got their water from one particular pump. He thought that the cause of the disease must be in the water. He had the pump handle removed and stopped the spread of the disease.

4 Antiseptics – chemicals that kill bacteria – were introduced in hospitals in 1865 by Joseph Lister.

5 In 1890, Professor Beijerinck discovered viruses. He filtered bacteria out of a fluid, but found it still caused disease in plants.

6 About 60 years ago, Howard Florey and Alexander Fleming discovered that some fungi made chemicals which killed bacteria. Antibiotics had arrived.

◄ Louis Pasteur

Victorian water pumps like these spread cholera. ►

◄ Antiseptics were sprayed during operations and saved many lives.

Alexander Fleming – one of the discoverers of antibiotics. ►

What do you know?

1 Copy the following table. Complete it to show the different ideas about disease that people had at the time.

Time	Ideas about disease
ancient Egyptians	
ancient Greeks	
nineteenth century	

2a What was the important discovery made by Fleming and Florey?

b Why was it so important?

3 The development of medicine has improved our lives dramatically. Imagine you are taken ill with a serious bacterial infection. Compare the treatment in the time of the ancient Egyptians with the treatment you would get today.

Key ideas

Human ideas about the causes of disease have changed over many years.

Many diseases are caused by tiny organisms called **bacteria** and **viruses**.

1b Bacteria and viruses

We've all heard people say things like this, but how much truth is there in them? Very little, because diseases like colds and chills are caused by bacteria and viruses.

Out of sight

a How many different illnesses can you remember having? Make a table like this one to describe them.

Illness	Parts of body affected	How you felt
cold	nose, throat	tired, headache, stuffed up

Many illnesses are caused by bacteria and viruses. They can make us feel unwell, and even kill us.

Bacteria – the good and the bad

Bacteria are the smallest of all living organisms. They come in lots of shapes and sizes. If you put about 100 of the largest bacteria in a line, they would just about stretch across this full stop.

Bacterial cells don't have a proper nucleus. They can reproduce by simply splitting in half.

b Bacteria are living things. What do all living things do?

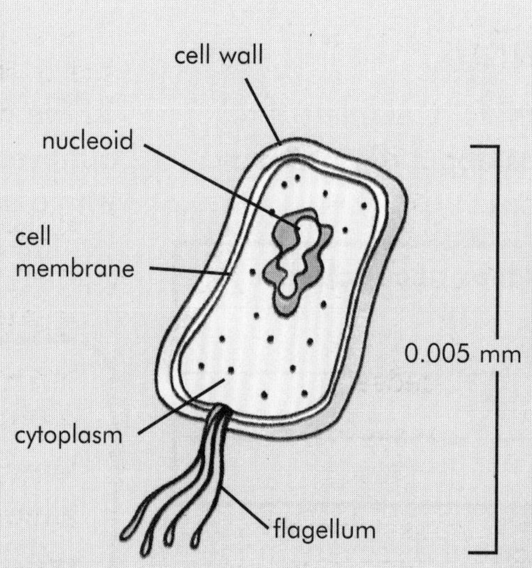

A bacterial cell

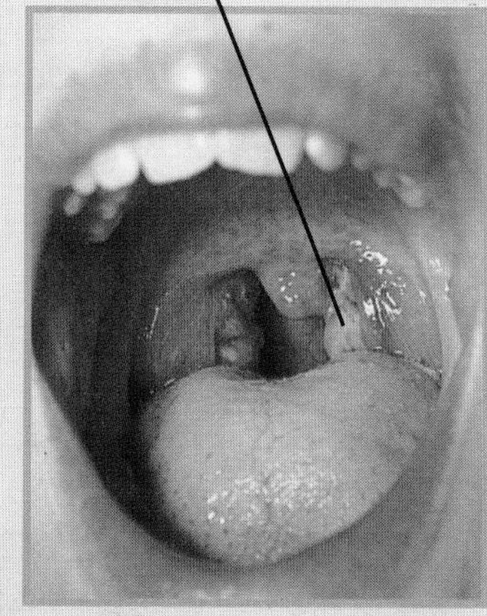

Tonsillitis is caused by bacteria.

Bacteria cause tuberculosis which destroys the lungs, and leprosy which destroys the flesh. They also cause food poisoning and spots. Bacteria cause diseases in other species of animals, and also in plants.

However, there are many different types of bacteria. Most bacteria are either harmless or useful to us.

- Bacteria help to break down the bodies of dead plants and animals.
- Bacteria in our gut and on our skin help to keep us healthy.
- We use bacteria to make cheese, yoghurt, wine and vinegar, as well as for treating human sewage.

Viruses - just the bad?

Viruses are incredibly small, about 0.0001 mm long. They can reproduce, but only when they are inside the living cell of an animal or plant. Viruses don't respire, move themselves, feed or excrete. They are not really living organisms, but they are not quite non-living!

Under a very powerful microscope, viruses are seen as strange shapes made of protein. All viruses cause diseases in living organisms. Diseases caused by viruses include colds, 'flu, chicken-pox, measles, polio and AIDS.

A single sneeze releases millions of viruses into the air for other people to breathe in – and catch your cold!

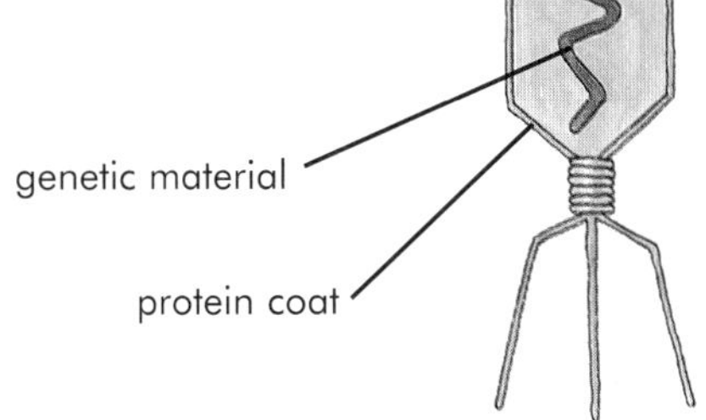

What do you know?

1 Write out these sentences, putting the correct pairs together.

Viruses	chicken-pox, colds and polio.
Bacteria cause diseases like	using a microscope.
Viruses cause diseases like	some cause disease.
Many bacteria are useful but	always cause disease.
Micro-organisms can only be seen	tonsillitis and tuberculosis.

2 List three ways bacteria are useful to us.

3a Draw and label diagrams of a bacterium and a virus.

b Explain why a bacterium is a living organism but a virus is not.

Key ideas

Bacteria are very small living organisms without a proper nucleus. They divide by splitting in two.

Some bacteria cause diseases, many are useful.

Viruses are much smaller than bacteria and they all cause diseases.

Viruses cannot do most of the things living organisms do. They can only reproduce in the living cells of plants and animals.

1c Body defences

Bacteria and viruses can get into your body through your body openings such as your mouth and your nose, or through cuts in your skin. Once inside they attack the cells of your body, and quite soon you begin to feel unwell. But you don't stay ill for ever, because your body has its own natural defences against the micro-organisms which cause disease.

First line of defence - don't let them in!

Your skin covers and protects most of your body tissues. Micro-organisms that get in through your mouth are dropped straight into the acid in your stomach.

The easiest way for micro-organisms to enter is through your respiratory system.

The hairs in your nose filter the air you breathe in. Your respiratory system produces a sticky **mucus**, and many microbes get stuck in this. The mucus is removed by special cells called **ciliated epithelial cells** which line the tubes leading to the lungs. The **cilia** on these cells beat backwards and forwards.

The cilia move the mucus carrying dust, bacteria and viruses up and away from the lungs. The ciliated epithelial cells have lots of **mitochondria** to supply energy for the beating cilia.

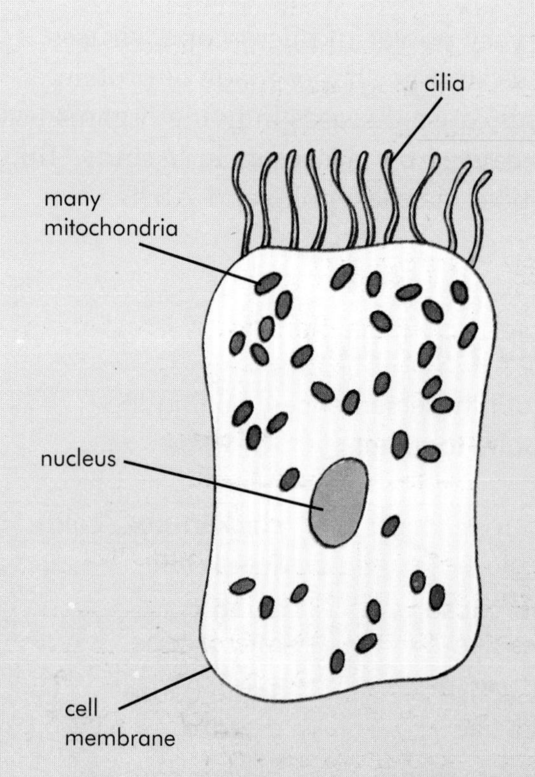

The ciliated epithelial cells are well suited to the job they have to do.

a The cilia in your respiratory tubes are beating all the time, but you don't usually notice them. You see the results of their work when you have a cold. What happens then?

Breaching the defences

When you cut yourself, your body is open to attack. Your body copes with this danger by forming **scabs**. These stop you bleeding, stop micro-organisms getting in, and protect your new skin underneath from any further knocks.

Second line of defence – zap them!

When bacteria or viruses do manage to get into your body, your blood takes over the defence. Your body has an army of **white blood cells** which swallow and destroy the bacteria or viruses.

When you get an infection, your body makes lots of extra white blood cells. They are made in special **glands** in your neck and other places around your body. When you are ill, you often have swollen glands. They are busy making white blood cells to fight off the micro-organisms causing your illness.

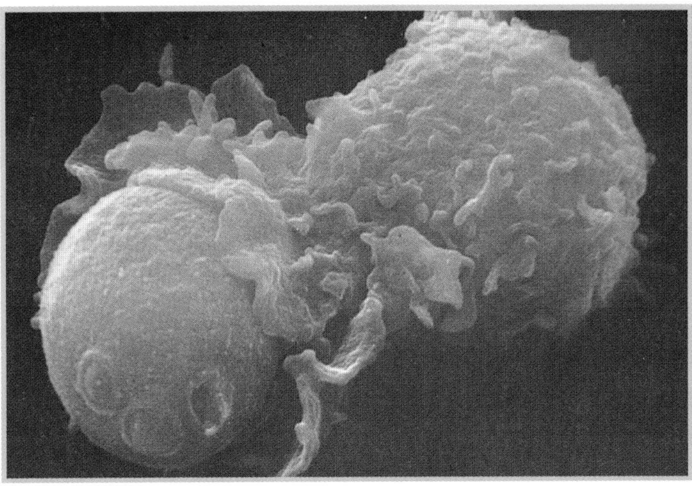

A white blood cell destroying a disease-causing micro-organism

What do you know?

1 Copy and complete the following sentences. Use the words below to fill the gaps.

skin scab defences
ciliated epithelial cells

The body has several ________ against disease-causing organisms. The ________ prevents them entering the body. ________ ________ ________ move them out of the respiratory system. A ________forms over a cut to keep micro-organisms out.

2 How do white blood cells destroy bacteria and viruses?

3 Why is it easier for bacteria and viruses to get into your body though your respiratory system than through your gut?

Key ideas

Disease-causing organisms enter the body through openings like the mouth and nose and through cuts in the skin.

The skin prevents the entry of micro-organisms over most of the body.

In the lungs, **mucus** traps micro-organisms and **cilia** beat to carry it away.

Scabs form to prevent micro-organisms getting in through cuts.

White blood cells destroy bacteria and viruses inside the body.

1d A helping hand

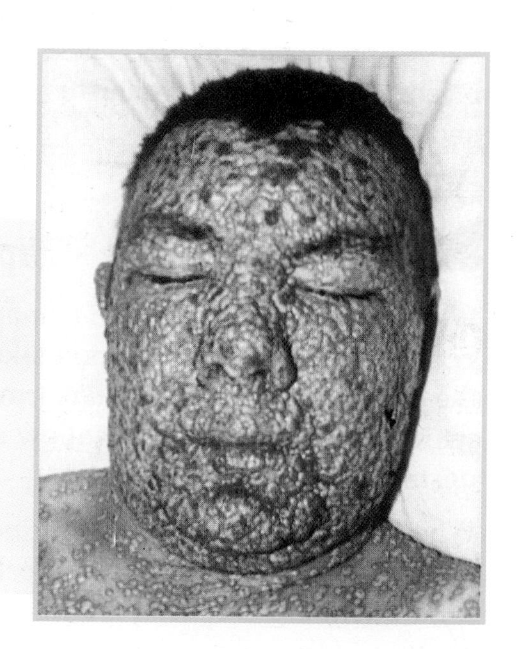

Our natural body defences deal with most of the disease-causing micro-organisms that we meet. But sometimes we need a little extra help to overcome them.

This man is suffering from smallpox, a terrible disease which has killed millions of people in years gone by. Today the disease no longer exists, thanks to **immunisation**.

a What diseases have you been immunised against?

Immunisation

When you have met a micro-organism, your body learns to make the right white blood cells ready to destroy it very quickly the next time you meet it. That is why you don't usually get diseases such as chicken-pox twice.

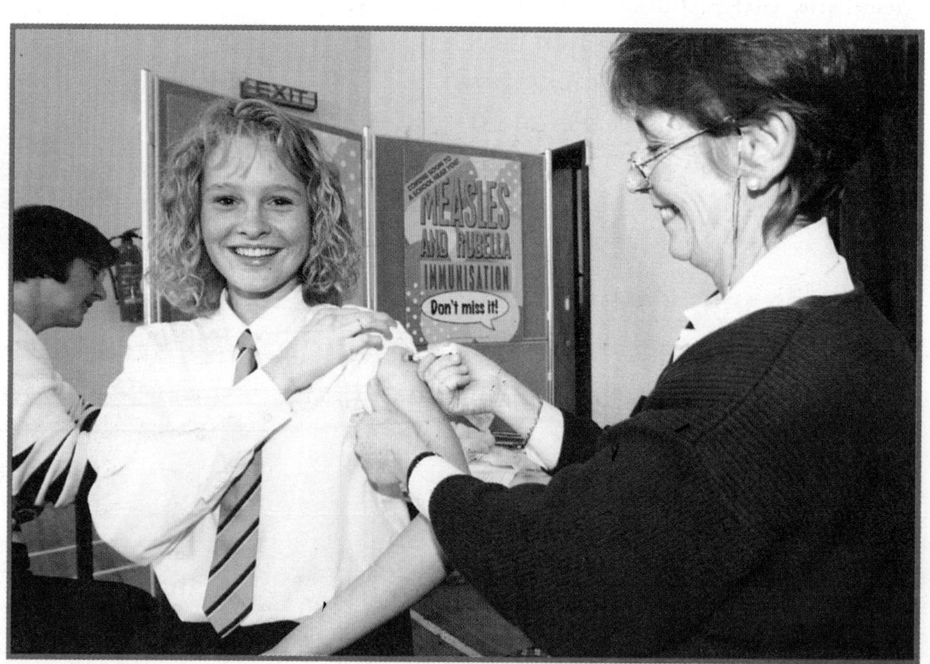

Almost every child in Britain was immunised against measles in 1994 to stop a massive outbreak of the disease.

Some diseases can kill. Others, like measles, can leave you permanently damaged. Immunisation lets your body meet these dangerous micro-organisms in a safe way. Then, if you ever meet the real thing, your body will be able to make the white blood cells needed to destroy it before you become ill.

Most of us are immunised against a whole range of diseases when we are young. These include tetanus, polio, diphtheria, measles and mumps. The immunisation usually involves an injection, which can hurt at the time, but is a small price to pay to avoid dangerous diseases.

Killing bacteria all around

We can't be immunised against everything. Apart from the cost, we would all look like pincushions! However, we can try and avoid picking up micro-organisms in the first place. **Antiseptics** are chemicals which kill bacteria.

You have probably used antiseptic cream on a cut. Antiseptics are also used wherever there is a risk of bacteria spreading. Hospitals, dentists and vets use lots of antiseptics.

Antiseptics can kill bacteria, but they don't have any effect on viruses.

Once you're ill

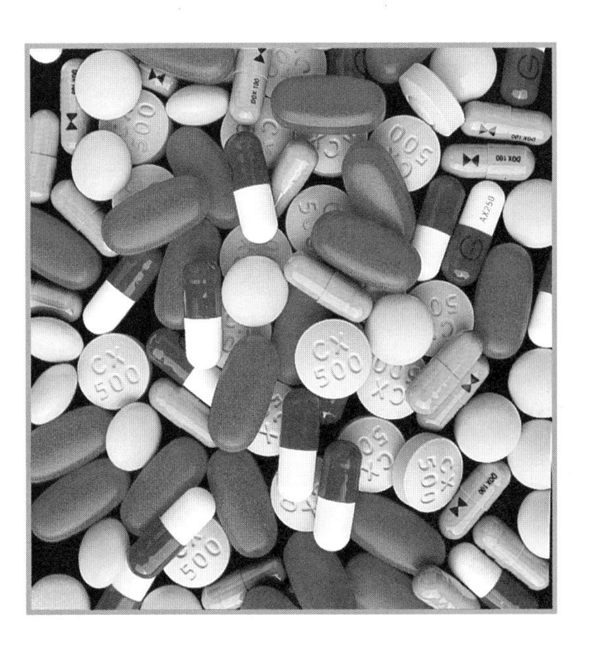

In spite of precautions, we all get ill from time to time. Medicines called **antibiotics** can help us get better. They kill bacteria more rapidly than our white blood cells can kill them. Antibiotics are the best way of treating diseases caused by bacteria.

b Your doctor will give you antibiotics if you have tonsillitis, but not if you have 'flu. Why is this?

Unfortunately, it is much harder to tackle diseases caused by viruses. When drugs are developed that will destroy viruses, it will be another big step forward in the fight against disease.

What do you know?

1 Copy and complete the following table. Use the words below to fill the boxes.

antibiotics **antiseptics**
immunisation **viruses**

	chemicals that kill bacteria
	organisms that are not affected by drugs
	drugs that cure bacterial diseases
	a way of protecting people against dangerous diseases

2 Why do you think it is important to immunise babies against diseases like polio early in their lives?

3 Antiseptics and antibiotics have greatly reduced the number of people dying from bacterial diseases in the last 100 years. Why have deaths from viral diseases not gone down too?

Key ideas

Immunisation gives your body a chance to meet dangerous micro-organisms in a safe way. If you ever meet the real thing, your body will be able to make white blood cells to destroy the bacteria or viruses before you become ill.

Antiseptics are chemicals that kill bacteria and so stop infection spreading.

Antibiotics are drugs that kill bacteria in the body, but do not affect viruses.

EXTRAS

1b Acid or bacteria? – the ulcer question

Ulcers happen when stomach acid begins to eat into the wall of the stomach.

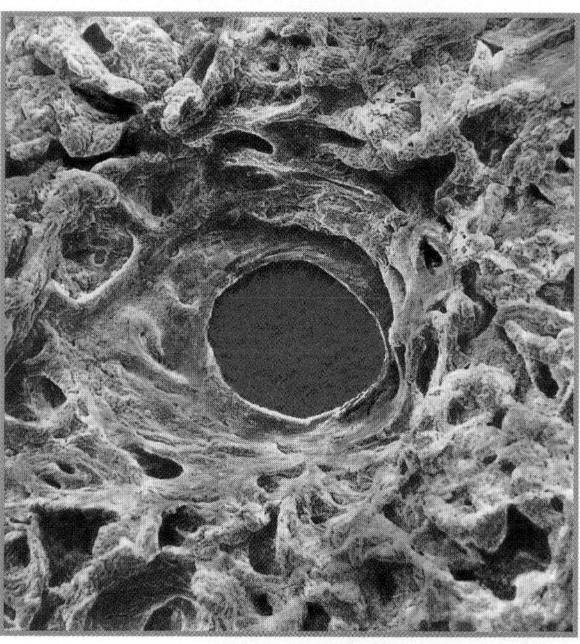

In Britain, about 5 million people suffer from ulcers, either in the stomach or in the first part of the intestine. For many years doctors have believed that ulcers are caused by extra acid made in the stomach when people are under a lot of stress. Patients were given expensive drugs to reduce stomach acid levels, sometimes for years, to stop the ulcer returning.

About twelve years ago in Australia, two doctors called Barry Marshall and Robin Warren found bacteria in tissue taken from stomach ulcers. Scientists had believed that no bacteria could live in the acidic juices of the stomach. But Barry Marshall became convinced that the bacteria *Helicobacter pylori* caused ulcers.

He started treating his ulcer patients with cheap antibiotics to kill the bacteria. He found that they got better fast. Their ulcers didn't come back, so no more treatment was needed.

Many doctors are now using antibiotics to treat ulcers successfully. However, there are still some doctors who either haven't heard of the new idea, or refuse to believe it.

1a What is the traditional explanation of the cause of stomach ulcers?
b What is Dr Marshall's explanation?

2 New scientific ideas are often ignored or contradicted for years before being accepted. Why might the main drugs companies not have accepted Dr Marshall's explanation of ulcers very quickly?

3 Barry Marshall now thinks he has discovered a link between *Helicobacter pylori* and stomach cancer. Bacteria have never before been linked to cancer, but the idea is being taken seriously.

What sort of evidence would be needed to show a link between *Helicobacter pylori* and stomach cancer?

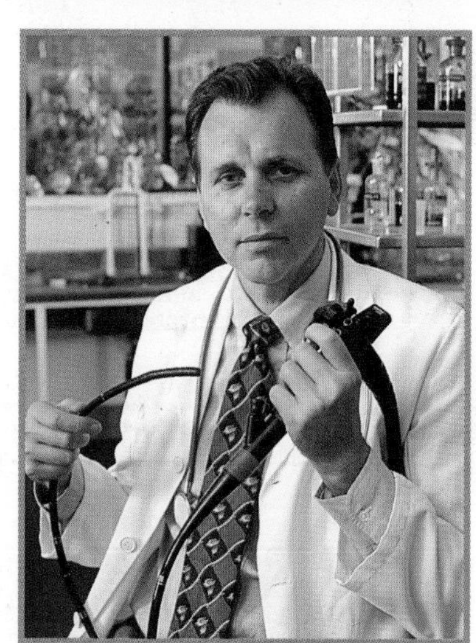

Doctor Barry Marshall was so sure of his ideas about ulcers that he drank some '*Helicobacter* soup', infecting his own stomach. He then treated the ulcer symptoms which appeared with antibiotics, and cured himself.

1d Patterns of disease

Any illness you get is miserable for you personally, but on a national scale it isn't very important! But sometimes, lots of people get the same disease at about the same time, or lots of people in one area become ill. When that happens, scientists can learn a lot from studying the patterns of disease.

At the end of the First World War, in 1918–19, there was an outbreak of 'flu which killed more people than the entire war had. In America alone 20 million people had 'flu, and 500 000 of them died.

Today, computers are used internationally to record cases of diseases and see if the number of cases is building up to a high level. Then steps can be taken to prevent the spread of the disease. In this country, elderly people can be vaccinated each winter against the type of 'flu most likely to be around.

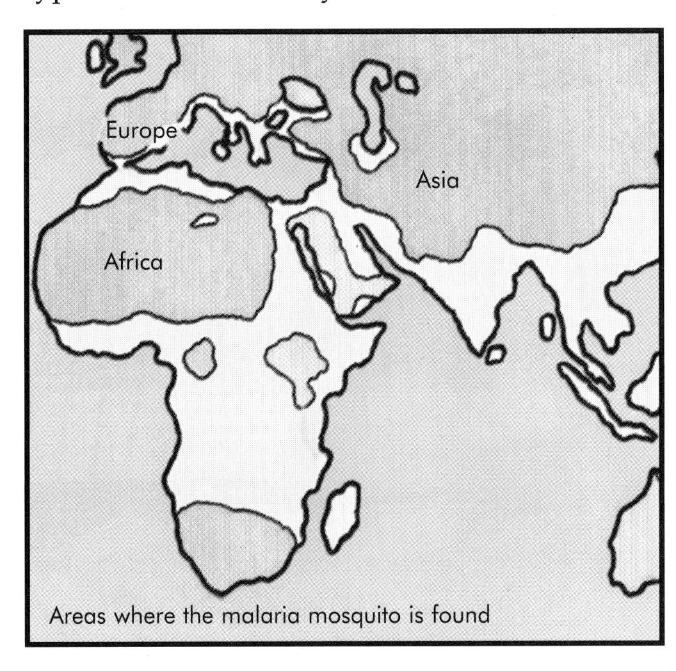

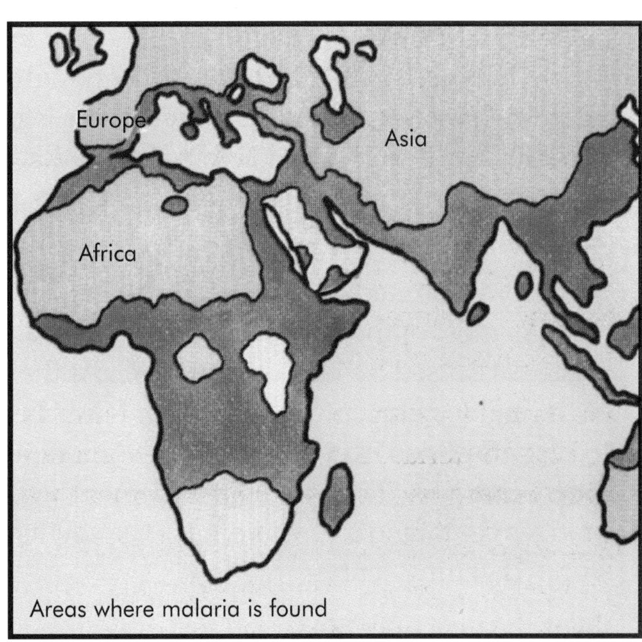

Malaria affects more people in the world than any other disease. By looking at where malaria is found and the spread of a particular mosquito, the link between the two can easily be seen.

1 In 1994, scientists predicted that there was going to be a measles epidemic in Britain which would have killed about 50 children. This didn't happen. Why not?

2 Anywhere in the world where there is war or famine, diseases become very much more common. Why is this?

3 Some people claim that children who live near nuclear power stations are more likely to suffer from cancer than children living anywhere else. How might a scientist investigate this claim?

REVIEW

1a Food can make you ill

As people began to understand that bacteria and viruses cause diseases, they were also finding out that diet affects your health too.

Many people had so little food they couldn't eat a balanced diet. Children often did not grow properly because of lack of protein. Many children had **rickets** – their bones did not form properly because they did not have enough vitamin D or calcium in their diet. Their legs bent outwards and they could hardly walk.

Sailors did not eat a healthy diet, because sailing ships took months to cross the oceans and could only store a limited amount of food. On a long voyage, most of the crew could die from **scurvy**, a disease caused by lack of vitamin C. At the end of the eighteenth century the British Navy began to carry limes on every ship and the sailors were given lime juice. Fruits like limes, lemons and oranges contain lots of vitamin C. The sailors stopped getting scurvy.

Over the years people found out how important other substances are in the diet, such as iron, carbohydrates, fats and fibre.

1 What do you think we mean by a balanced diet?

2 Make a list to show the main types of food and why they are important in your diet.

3 We all like different foods. If you are planning meals for a family, why is it important to think about more than just what everybody likes?

1b Cells and microbes

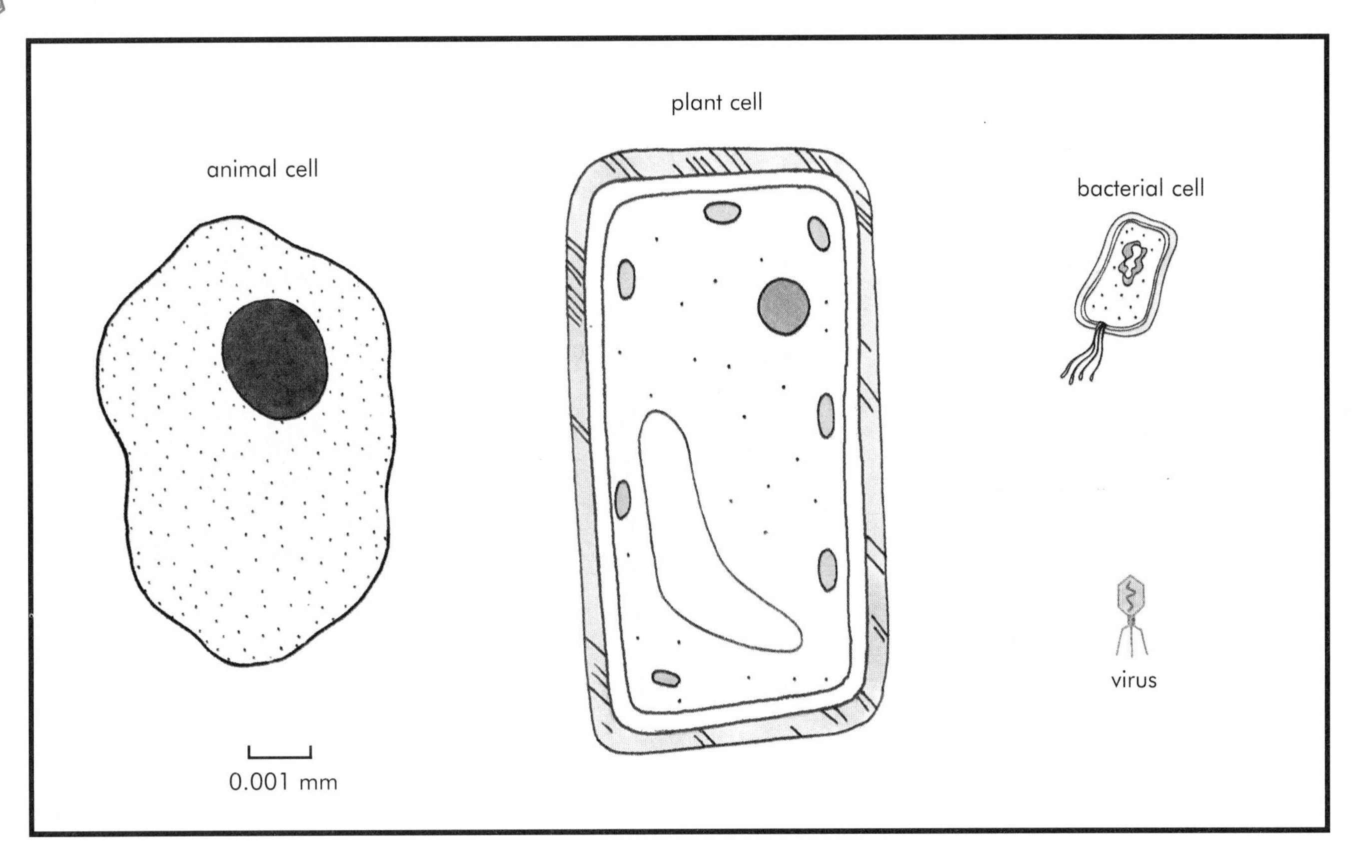

1 Bacteria and viruses are not made up of the same sort of cells as animals and plants. Copy and complete this table to show how micro-organisms are similar to and different from plant and animal cells.

	Bacteria	**Virus**
How is it like an animal cell?		
How is it different from an animal cell?		
How is it like a plant cell?		
How is it different from a plant cell?		

1c A lack of energy

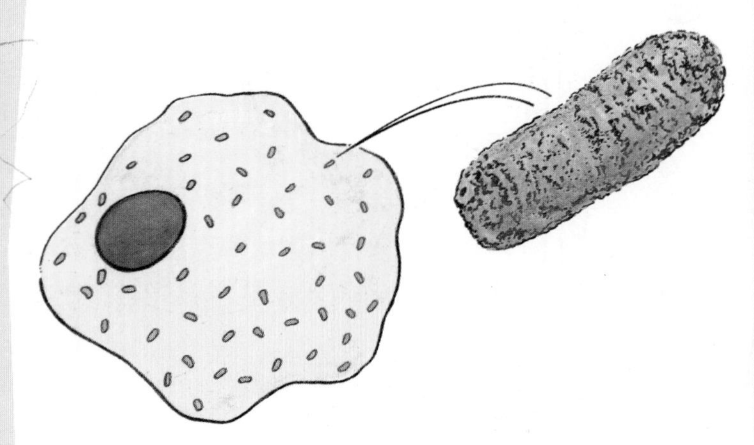

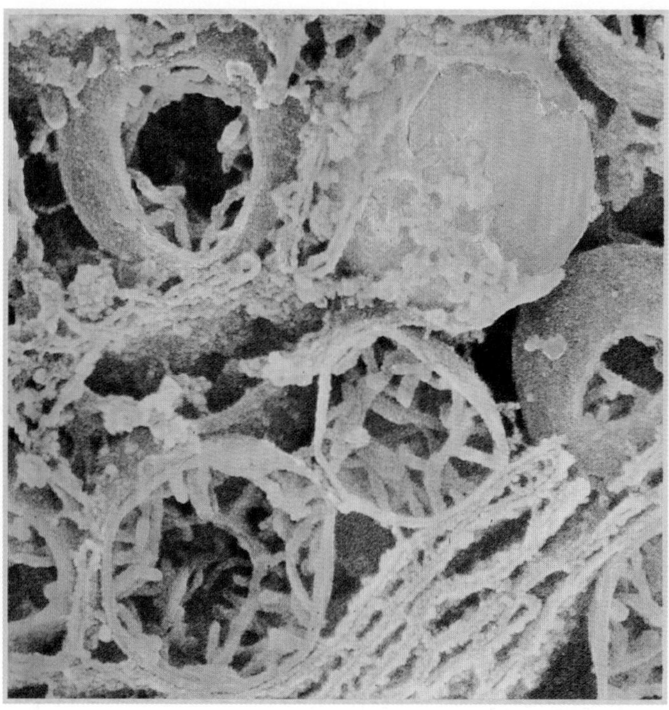

Mitochondria, shown green in this picture, are found in every cell in your body.

For you to be healthy, all the cells of your body must be working well. If your cells are in trouble, so is the rest of you! All of your cells have **mitochondria**, and this is where **respiration** takes place:

glucose + oxygen ⟶ energy + carbon dioxide + water

This equation summarises what happens in respiration, but lots of different chemical reactions take place in the mitochondria. Sometimes these reactions do not work properly, and so the mitochondria cannot supply enough energy. This causes **metabolic diseases**, which are usually very serious indeed.

1 List these structures in order of size, starting with the smallest:

nucleus mitochondrion cell

2 What is the job of your mitochondria?

3 Some poisons work by stopping respiration in your mitochondria. You quickly become paralysed and then die. Why do these poisons kill you so quickly?

1d When organs go wrong

When bacteria or viruses get into our bodies, they can make us ill. Usually our bodies, sometimes helped by medicines, destroy the micro-organisms and we get better. But microbes can cause serious damage to the major organs of our bodies, which can be permanent.

If your lungs are attacked by micro-organisms, the delicate alveoli can be destroyed. It gets hard to breathe and you can't get enough oxygen.

Gut infections can cause stomach ulcers. They can irritate the lining of your gut so much that it doesn't digest and absorb food properly.

Infections in the reproductive system can block the Fallopian tubes in women and stop sperm production by the testes in men. These infections can make you **sterile** (you can no longer have a baby).

Infections of the skeleton can make your joints very swollen and painful. This makes it difficult to move your bones.

1 Copy this drawing of a male human body. Label the main organs mentioned here, including what they do in a healthy body.

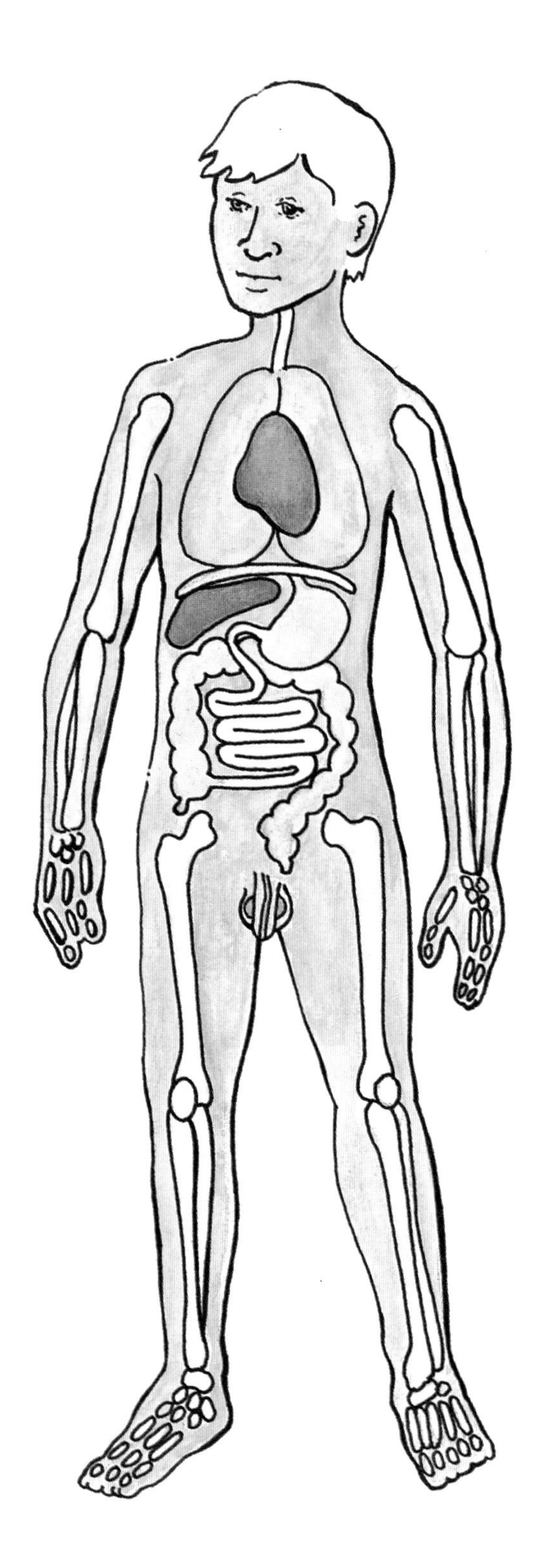

2a Growing up fast

Adolescence

Puberty is a time of great physical changes. But growing up is more than just the physical changes which can be so confusing and embarrassing for a few years. Your mind has to grow up too, keeping up with the new body you are living in. These emotional changes combined with your physical development are known as **adolescence**.

a What main physical changes happen to boys and girls during puberty?

All in the mind

Puberty prepares our bodies for reproduction. But for most of us, even if biology tells us that our bodies are ready to reproduce, our minds are not ready at all!

The changes in our bodies as we grow up happen as a result of special chemical messages sent around our bodies at puberty. These chemicals are known as **hormones**. The hormones that cause our bodies to change also affect our minds.

All change

As we grow up, we change a great deal. Friends of our own age (our **peer group**) become increasingly important, though our family is still important too. Then an individual partner can suddenly seem more important than all of our family and friends put together.

Some people find it very difficult to grow up and away from their parents. Others find it hard to stay close to their parents, and to ask for family support when friends let them down.

It might help to remember that some of our most confusing feelings are just the result of overactive hormones! But both physical and emotional changes are important biologically. They prepare us for adulthood and for the time when we choose a partner and produce a family of our own.

When we are very small, our close family are the only people who matter to us.

As we go through adolescence, our family remains important for love and security, but the views of our friends matter a lot too.

When we choose our partners, it can seem as if no one else is very important.

Once we have our own children, it is good to have close links with our partner, our friends and our family. We need all the help we can get!

What do you know?

1a What does puberty mean?
b What does adolescence mean?

2a Why do you think it is important for a baby to feel very close to its family?
b Why do you think friends and the opinion of the peer group are so important to adolescents?
c When people have small children, why do you think it helps to have close links with:
i their partner **ii** their parents **iii** their friends?

Key ideas

Your body goes through physical changes at **puberty**.

The combination of physical and emotional changes are known as **adolescence**.

Adolescence prepares us for adulthood and for producing our own family.

It's your choice

2b Peers, pressures and drugs

When you were a small child, you had very little choice about what you took into your body. Your meals, drinks and snacks were all organised by adults. But as you go through adolescence, the choice about what you give your body becomes yours alone. There can sometimes be pressure from your peer group to choose the same as they do. Some of the most important choices you will make involve drugs.

Introducing drugs

a What is a drug?

A **drug** is a chemical which has a specific effect on your body. You have probably used a number of drugs in your life already. Many drugs are used by doctors to help your body overcome diseases. Lots of drugs, like painkillers and indigestion tablets, are sold at the chemist's shop.

Tea and coffee contain drugs, and so do cigarettes and alcoholic drinks. All these drugs are legal and are in common use.

There are other drugs that are not legal. To make the right decisions about drugs, you need to know what both legal and illegal drugs do to you.

Caffeine – an everyday drug

Every time you have a cup of tea or coffee, you are taking in a small dose of a drug called **caffeine**.

Caffeine **stimulates** your body – it makes it more active. This is why a cup of tea or coffee will help you wake up in the morning, or pick you up if you are feeling tired during the day.

Caffeine is legal, socially acceptable and widely enjoyed. But caffeine affects your mind, and your heart rate and blood pressure too.

b

1 Which web do you think was spun by a spider high on caffeine?

2 How did caffeine affect the way the spider spun its web?

A

B

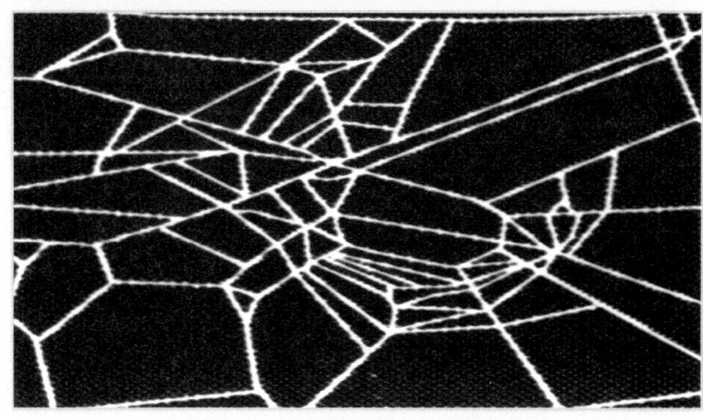

One of these webs is normal. The other was spun by a spider which had been given caffeine.

Addiction

Like many other drugs, caffeine is **addictive**, particularly if you take in large amounts. When we become addicted to a drug, we cannot manage without it. We need to use more and more of it to keep us feeling normal.

If you have to work hard or concentrate late at night, it is easy to drink lots of coffee to keep you going. Then, when you use less coffee, you have headaches and feel tired. If you don't drink coffee you will soon overcome the addiction and feel normal again, but it is easier just to make another cup!

Caffeine is not seen as a dangerous drug – there are no health warnings on jars of coffee. But it easily becomes part of our lives, showing us what can happen when we use other, more damaging drugs.

What do you know?

1 Make two lists headed 'Advantages of drinking tea and coffee' and 'Disadvantages of drinking tea and coffee'.

2a What is a drug?
b List three legal drugs which you have used over the years.

3a What does being addicted mean?
b Do you think drugs are the only things to which people can be addicted?

Key ideas

During adolescence you are faced with increasing choices about what you take into your body.

Many drugs are legal, but some are illegal.

Caffeine is a commonly used drug which stimulates your body and can be **addictive**.

2c Legal but lethal

Illegal drugs and their dangers make headlines. But some of the most dangerous drugs are legal. Many more people die each year from using the drugs nicotine and alcohol than from all of the illegal drugs put together.

Dying for a fag?

One day in school you are given the following instructions:

1. Collect some dried leaves, roll them up in paper, set fire to the tube and then breathe the smoke in deeply.
2. Breathing this smoke means you will smell unpleasant, age more quickly, be much more likely to die of lung cancer or heart disease while you are still young, and it could kill your unborn children.
3. You must smoke these rolls of leaves up to 60 times a day.

Most of you would refuse to smoke the leaves. All these things are true for cigarette smoking, yet millions of people do it. Why?

Cigarette smoke is made up of many different chemicals. One is a drug called **nicotine** which stimulates the body but narrows the blood vessels. It makes people feel calmer and more able to cope.

Cigarette manufacturers are keen to advertise at exciting occasions. If people are persuaded to start smoking, they will find it very difficult to stop.

If you start smoking, your body becomes addicted to nicotine. Gradually, as your body gets used to the drug, you need more nicotine to have the same effect, so you smoke more cigarettes.

Alcoholics anonymous

Alcohol is another legal drug which is used a lot. It affects your brain, and a little alcohol can make you feel relaxed. But more alcohol can make you aggressive, lose control, pass out and even die.

Alcohol is a very poisonous and dangerous drug. Like nicotine, it is addictive. People who cannot cope without alcohol are called **alcoholics**.

Many heavy drinkers die from alcohol-related diseases. It damages the liver and brain, among other things. Non-drinkers can suffer from alcohol abuse too. Drunken drivers kill innocent people in road accidents. Drunken husbands are more likely to beat their wives, and drunken parents to damage their children.

People have drunk alcoholic drinks since the earliest human records. Evidence suggests that regular small amounts of alcohol might help prevent heart disease. However, too much alcohol causes only damage.

a When the dangers of drugs are discussed by politicians and concerned adults, nicotine and alcohol are often ignored. Why do you think this is?

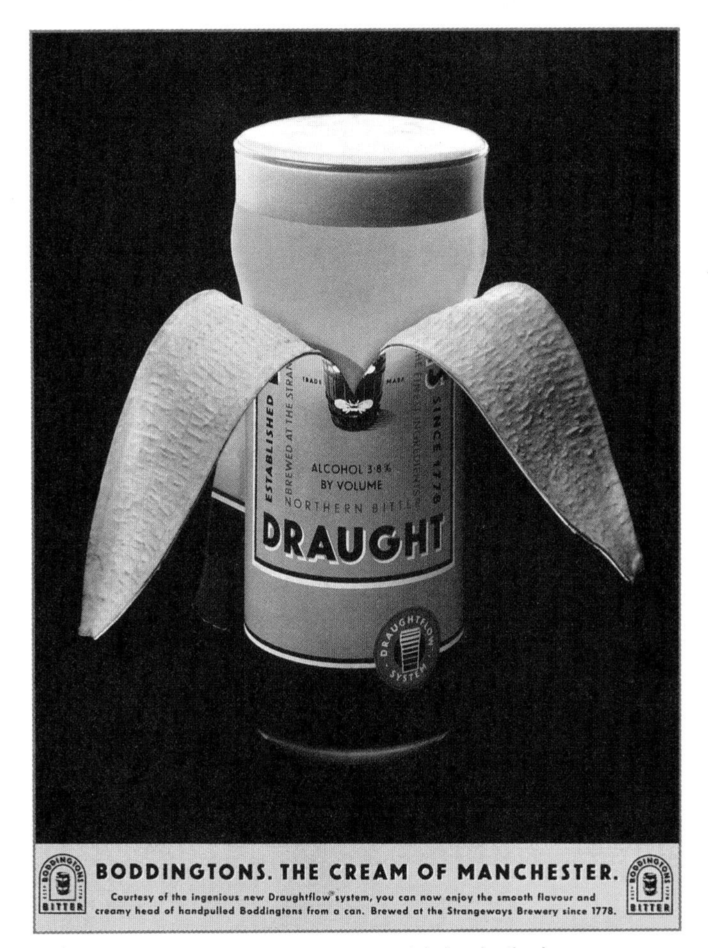

Advertisements encourage us to drink alcohol, but unlike cigarette advertisements, they don't mention that it is a dangerous drug.

What do you know?

1a Use the information on these two pages to make a list of the damage smoking can do to you.
b Why do people continue to smoke, knowing that it is bad for their health?

2 Addiction to nicotine can have a very bad effect on your own health. It can even be bad for other people to breathe in your cigarette smoke. But alcohol is a much more damaging drug for society in general. How can alcohol damage people who don't drink it?

Key ideas

Cigarettes contain **nicotine**, an addictive drug.

Alcohol is an addictive drug which damages the liver and brain. Its abuse causes much human misery.

Nicotine and alcohol are both legal drugs.

It's your choice

2d Illegal drugs

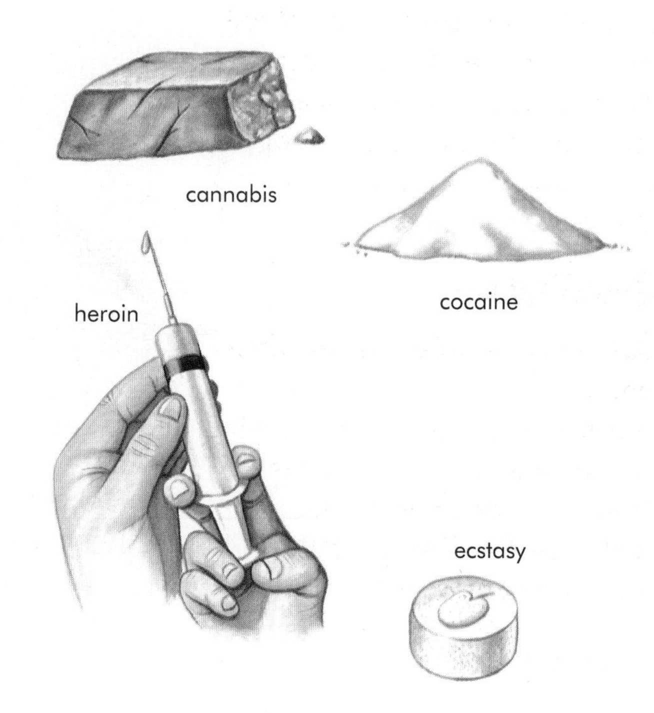

It is against the law to use some drugs. Some people still choose to put these illegal substances into their bodies.

Changing your mind

Many illegal drugs have a powerful effect on your mind. Some produce vivid hallucinations, like waking dreams. Others give an overwhelming sense of happiness and power. Once people have experienced the 'high' a drug can give them, they want it again and again. They cannot cope without the drug.

This total addiction causes many health problems. Once addicted, it is very difficult to stop using the drugs. You have **withdrawal symptoms** when you give them up, which make you feel extremely ill.

Sudden death

Most illegal drugs can cause massive heart failure and death. This can happen the first time you try a drug, or the hundredth time.

Daily Mail, Saturday, December 2 1995

FATHER'S EMOTIONAL TRIBUTE TO THE BIRTHDAY GIRL KILLED BY ECSTASY

Leah was like a little ship, dashed on the rocks of life

Left: Leah lies in a coma after taking ecstacy.
Above: Paul and Janet Betts arriving for the funeral.
Right: Her grieving friends from college.

Leah Betts died after taking a single ecstasy tablet at her eighteenth birthday party.

A question of money

Illegal drugs are very expensive. Addicts often become involved in crime to pay for their drugs. Many addicts live in poverty, spending all their money on drugs and not eating a balanced diet or keeping clean.

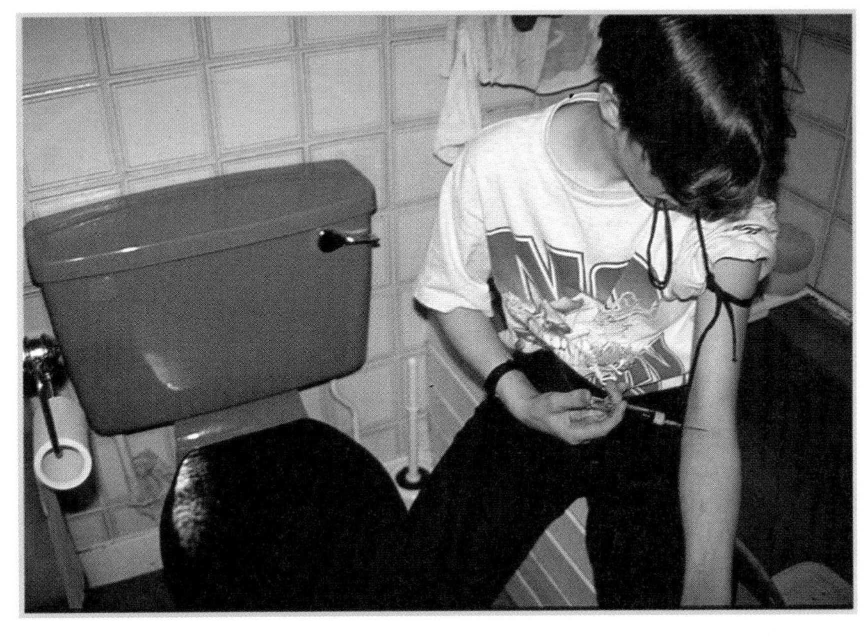

Shooting up

Addicts who inject drugs often end up sharing needles with other drug users. Blood carrying micro-organisms can be passed from one person to another on dirty needles. For example, hepatitis, a serious disease of the liver, is common amongst drug addicts who inject themselves.

Glue-sniffing

In recent years there has been a rise in another form of drug abuse. The solvents used in glues and aerosols can be breathed in to give a 'high'. However, the solvents are poisonous. Glue-sniffing causes brain damage so that you cannot remember properly or think clearly, and the damage can be permanent. Solvent abuse can also cause total heart failure and death.

What do you know?

1 Copy and complete the following sentences. Use the words below to fill the gaps.

injecting **illegal** **health** **cocaine** **possess**

Many people use legal drugs. Some also use ________ drugs. It is against the law to________ drugs such as ecstasy and ________. Illegal drugs damage your ________. ________ drugs is particularly dangerous.

2a Which part of your body do almost all drugs affect?

b How can drugs kill you very quickly?

c In what ways can drugs have a longer term effect on your health?

Key ideas

It is against the law to possess illegal drugs.

Illegal drugs can damage your health directly because of the way they affect your body. They can affect your health indirectly because of the lifestyle you become forced into.

Solvent abuse (glue-sniffing) affects the brain and can cause instant death.

EXTRAS

2c Don't drink and drive!

Alcohol has a rapid depressant effect on the brain. Just a small amount of alcohol will take the edge off your reaction times, blur your vision and affect your ability to judge speed and distance.

Once you have had a drink, your liver breaks the alcohol into harmless compounds. However, this takes some time. People driving the morning after a heavy drinking session are often stopped by police because of their dangerous driving, and found to still have high levels of alcohol in their bodies.

There is a legal limit for the amount of alcohol you are allowed to have in your blood when you drive a car. The limit is 80 mg of alcohol per 100 cm^3 of blood. The amount of alcohol in your blood can be calculated after measuring the alcohol present in your breath or in your urine.

1 Alcohol affects people's judgement, so that they think they are capable of driving far better than they really can. Why is this so dangerous?

2a What is the increased risk of having an accident when your blood alcohol is just below the legal limit if you are:

i particularly susceptible to alcohol

ii not very susceptible to alcohol?

b What is the increased risk of having an accident in the most susceptible group at 110 mg of alcohol per 100 cm^3 of blood?

c What is the increased risk for the least susceptible drivers at 150 mg of alcohol per 100 cm^3 of blood?

d The legal limit of alcohol in the breath is much lower than the legal limit in the blood. However, the legal limit in the urine is higher than the legal limit in the blood. Suggest an explanation for these facts.

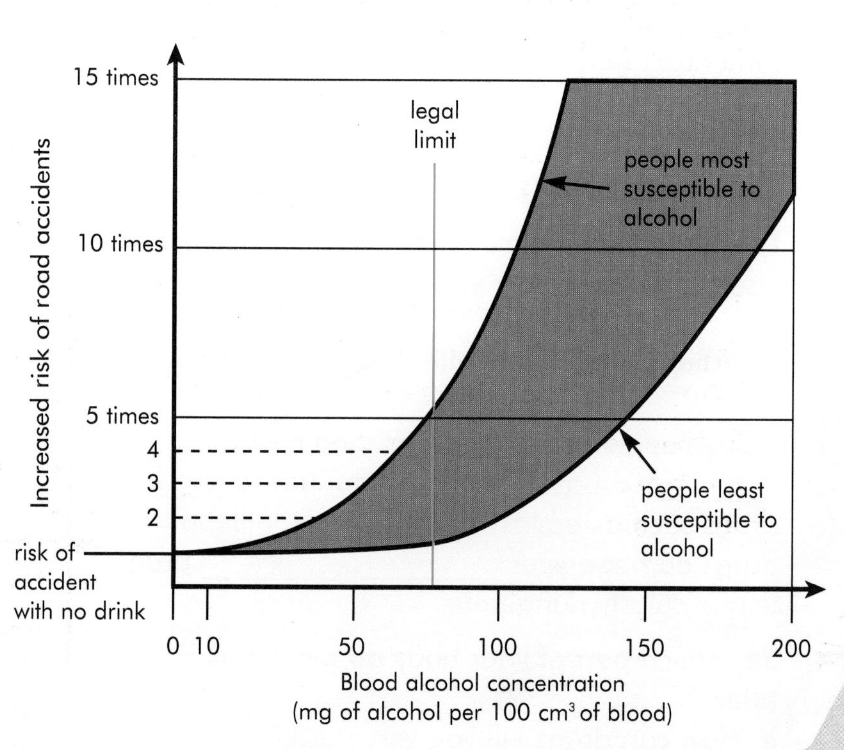

Giving up is hard to do

Over the last 20 years, society has become increasingly concerned about the use of illegal drugs. There have been a number of different approaches to the problem of drug abuse.

There are special centres where addicts are supported as they withdraw from using drugs. They are helped to prepare for a drug-free life. But there are not many of these centres, and often people cannot keep away from drugs once they return to life outside.

In the case of heroin, addicts can be prescribed a heroin substitute called methadone. This is supposed to be less addictive, and it is pure. This means that the people using methadone do not run the risks of using contaminated heroin. However, they are still addicted.

So far, science has not come up with a drug that can overcome the cravings of a drug addict. In spite of the public outrage about the problem, there is relatively little money available to support research. 'Hard' illegal drugs like heroin are responsible for the deaths of several hundred people each year. In comparison, over 100 000 people die from using alcohol, and another 100 000 from smoking-related diseases following addiction to nicotine.

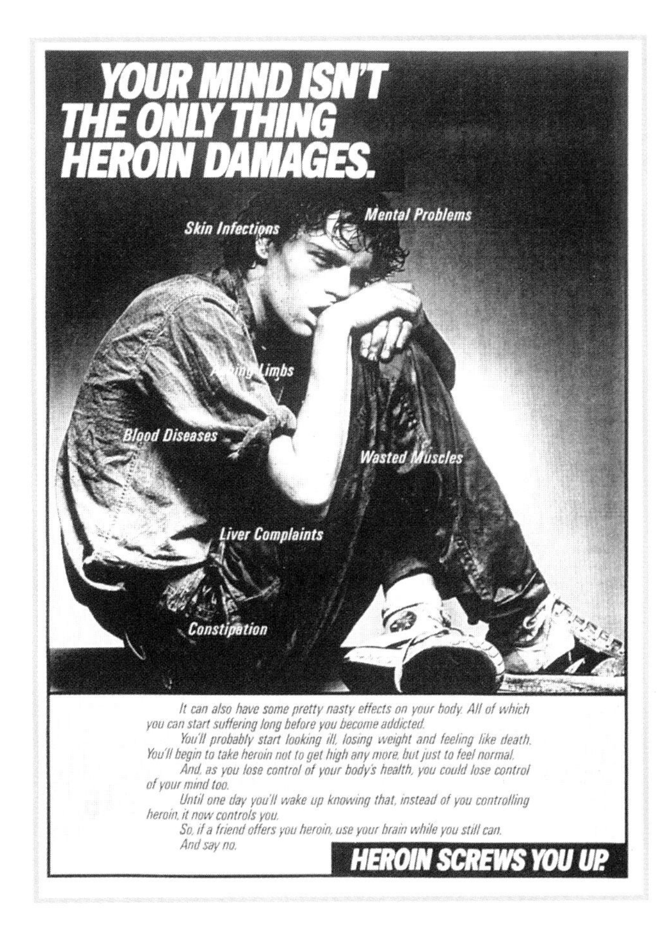

1 The success rate for programmes designed to help people give up drugs is not very high. Why do you think this is so?

2 Why do you think scientists have not produced a drug to overcome the craving for drugs?

3 Based on the information you have here and anything else you can find out, prepare a short speech:
either arguing for increased funding for research into drug addiction
or arguing that it is not right or ethical to target resources at anti-drugs programmes when alcohol and tobacco are the major killers in our society.

It's your choice 2

REVIEW

2c Just one cigarette?

Your lungs are very important. It is here that your body gets the oxygen it needs from the air, and also where you get rid of the waste carbon dioxide made by your body. The lungs are made up of tiny, thin-walled air sacs called **alveoli**. The exchange of gases between the air and the blood takes place in these alveoli.

If you smoke a cigarette, the drug nicotine gets into your blood in the same way as oxygen does. But each cigarette you smoke also leaves a trace of sticky black tar in your alveoli. The black tar builds up until your lungs are a grey colour. The tar can make it difficult to get enough oxygen, and it can also cause lung cancer.

Once the nicotine is in your blood, it is carried all around your body. If you are pregnant, it gets into the blood of your baby too.

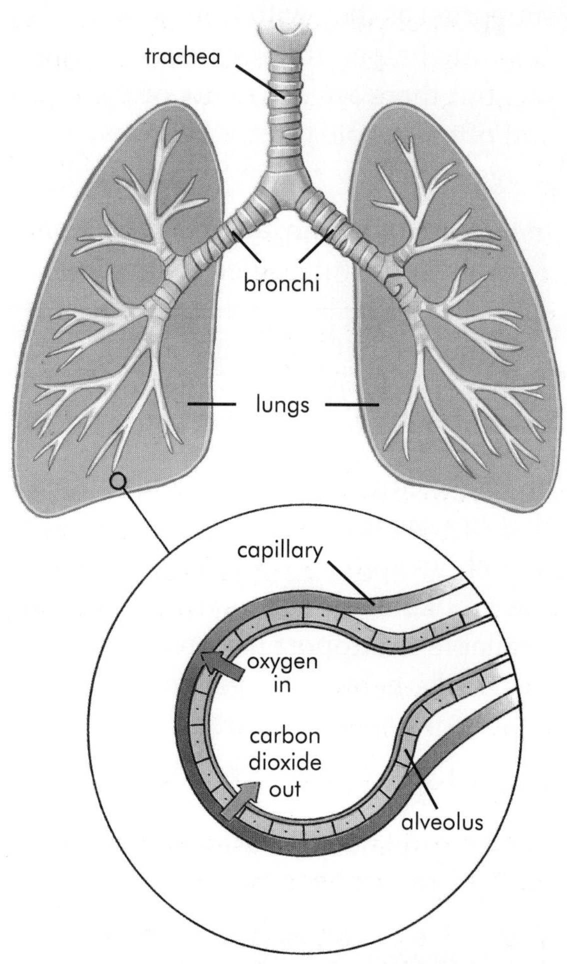

1 Why are your lungs so important to your body?

2 What effect does a cigarette have on the alveoli of your lungs?

3 If you smoke a lot of cigarettes, your body may get short of oxygen. Why does this happen?

4 If a mother is a heavy smoker, her baby may be born addicted to nicotine. These babies are often very miserable and restless for the first few days of their lives.
a How has the baby got addicted to nicotine?
b Why is the baby so miserable for the first few days of its life?

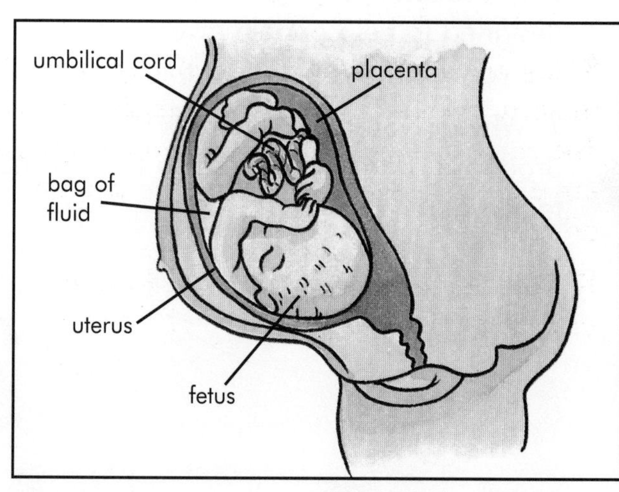

Going to your head

An alcoholic drink has a measurable effect on our bodies. People often say that a drink has 'gone to their head'. They are quite right – the alcohol has gone to their head, and also to every other part of their body. When you swallow a drink, it goes down into your digestive system and then into your blood.

Most of your food is digested by enzymes as it travels through your gut. The digested food is absorbed into your blood through the villi of your small intestine. This takes several hours.

However, alcohol is a small molecule and doesn't need digesting. It starts to cross into the blood as soon as it reaches your stomach. The blood then carries the alcohol to every part of your body. It isn't long before the drug reaches your brain, and you start to get drunk. Your liver slowly gets rid of the alcohol (which is a poison) from your blood.

Each of these drinks contains the same amount of alcohol. It doesn't take much to have a noticeable effect on your behaviour.

5 Make a table to show the jobs done by the main parts of your gut.

6 How long does it take to digest a meal?

7 Where is digested food absorbed into your blood? What happens to it then?

8 Alcohol is absorbed into your blood more quickly than food. Why?

9 If you drink alcohol on an empty stomach, the drug will be in your blood in 20 minutes. The same amount of alcohol drunk while you eat a meal takes much longer to have an effect. Why?

10 Very heavy drinkers often die from a disease of the liver. Why is this?

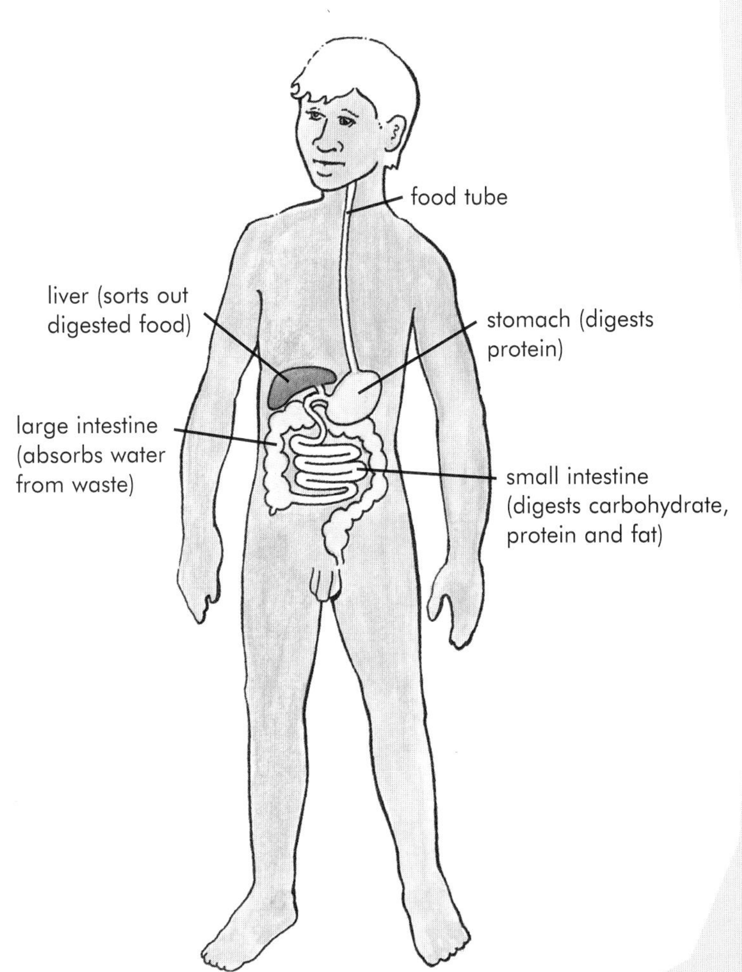

Variety of life

3a A world of difference

The world around us contains millions of living organisms of different types. These examples show the great **variety** of organisms on the Earth.

a Divide them into the two main groups of living things – animals and plants. Where will you put the fungus?

diatom

manatee

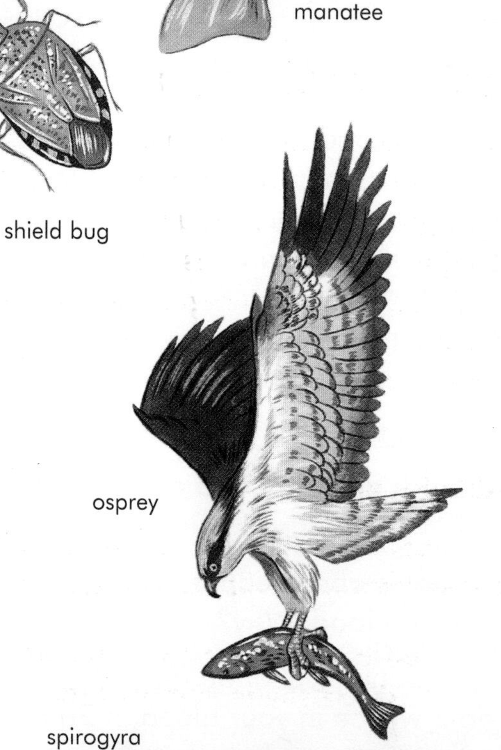

spirogyra

Grouping living things

Living organisms are grouped together or **classified** by looking at the differences between them. Animals are relatively fast moving, they move their whole bodies and they eat food to get energy. Plants can make their own food by photosynthesis, and usually move only parts of their bodies very slowly.

Living things are classified into smaller and smaller groups. Eventually each organism fits as a member of a particular **species**.

What is a species?

All the members of a species can breed with each other. They produce offspring which can also reproduce. If two animals or two plants cannot successfully reproduce and have fertile offspring, they are from separate species. For example, horses and donkeys look quite similar.

b List the similarities and differences you can see between a horse and a donkey.

Horses and donkeys can mate and produce offspring, which are known as mules. Mules are very useful animals for carrying loads and working for people. However, they are not **fertile** – they cannot reproduce. This tells us that horses and donkeys are two separate species.

Each species has its own characteristics, which are passed on from parents to offspring. Oak trees produce acorns which grow into oak trees, dogs produce puppies which grow into dogs and jellyfish eggs hatch into larvae which eventually become jellyfish.

We easily recognise all of these as cats. They have the **characteristics** of cats, such as pointed ears and long thin tails.

What do you know?

1 Copy and complete the following sentences. Use the words below to fill the gaps.

fertile **differences** **species**
classification **reproduce**

We can use the ________ between living organisms to put them into groups. This process is known as ________. Each animal and plant belongs to a particular ________. The members of a species can ________, giving offspring which are also ________.

2 How do we know that horses and donkeys are separate species?

3 What sort of differences might you look at if you were trying to identify:

a a type of tree **b** a type of bird?

Key ideas

The living world is **classified** into different **species**.

Members of a species can breed successfully with each other, but not with the members of another species.

The **characteristics** of a species are passed from parent organisms to their offspring.

3b The same but different

These people look very different. They have different heights, different weights, different colouring and different hair, but they are all members of the same species. As well as variety between species, there are also differences within a species. Differences in features like this are called **variation**.

Speed and stamina

Animals and plants live together in an **ecosystem**. When conditions are good, most of them survive, and many reproduce. But if conditions get tougher, it becomes a fight for survival.

When there are plenty of prey, most breeding cheetahs will raise at least one cub. But in years when there are few antelopes to catch, the differences between the cheetahs really start to matter.

Some cheetahs have longer legs than others. These cheetahs are faster, so they catch more prey. So the cubs of long-legged mothers are more likely to survive.

Stamina is also important. A mother who can keep running for a few seconds longer than others will also have a better chance of catching prey, and feeding herself and her young.

The fittest survive

The cheetahs with long legs and more stamina are well **adapted**. They are the **fittest**, and they are more likely to survive and reproduce when there is little food.

a Can you think of any other features that might vary from one cheetah to another, and could affect how well it hunts?

Down to the roots

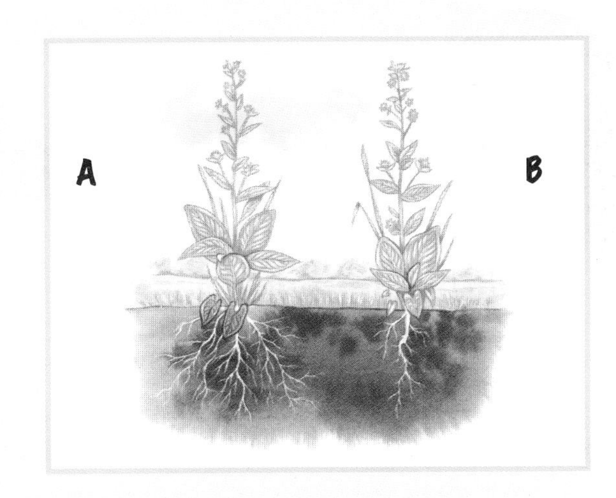

Plants like these thrive and flower when the weather is warm and sunny with showers of rain. But if the summer is long and hot, with weeks without rainfall, only the fittest survive.

Different plants of the same species have small variations between them. Differences in the root system can be the key to survival.

b Which plant is most likely to survive a hot dry summer, and why?

A question of memory

You can't always see and measure variations between organisms. Squirrels store nuts in the autumn to eat through the winter. But, just like people, some squirrels have better memories than others. The squirrels who remember where they hid their nuts are more likely to survive the winter and breed again. In a very hard winter, the food stores are especially important.

Passing it on

Features are often passed on from parents to offspring. Long-legged cheetahs tend to produce long-legged cubs. Plants with big root systems tend to produce more plants with big root systems. From generation to generation, the fittest survive.

What do you know?

1 Why are the cheetahs with long legs most likely to survive when prey are scarce?

2 Why might the following features help the organism to survive and breed?

a a giraffe with a particularly long neck
b a plant with flowers that produce extra scent
c an owl with bigger eyes than usual
d a tree with leaves that last a week or two longer than normal
e a sea urchin with large ovaries which makes several hundred extra eggs

3 A plant that has many flowers in one summer and then dies is more successful than an elephant that lives for 70 years without breeding. Why?

Key ideas

There are **variations** between members of the same species.

Because of these variations, some individuals are more successful than others. In harsh conditions, the **fittest** survive.

All sorts of cells

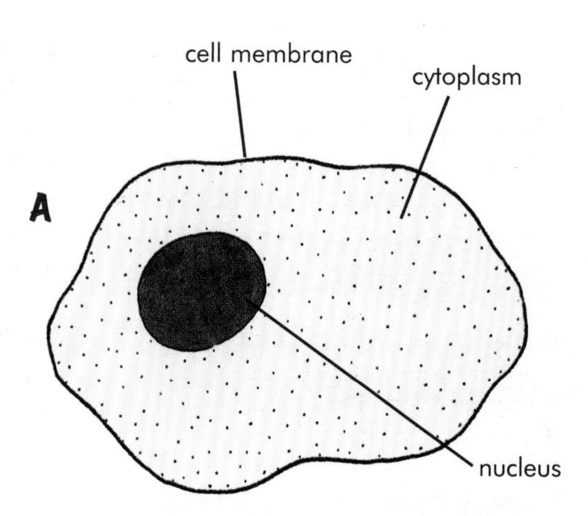

Living organisms are made up of **cells**. There are variations between groups of organisms, and between individual members of a species. There are also variations between the cells that make up those individuals.

Typical cells

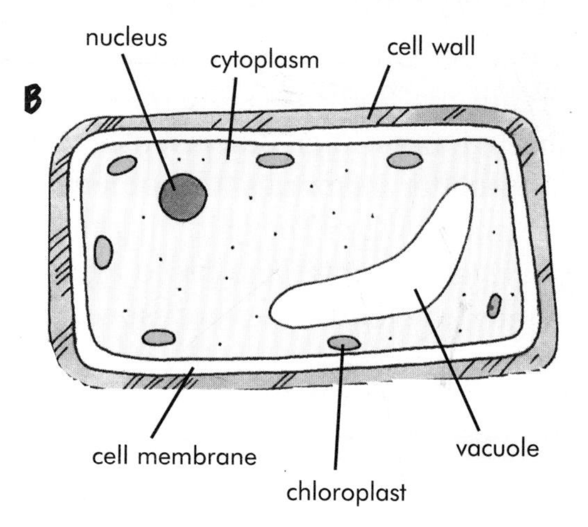

Here you can see simple 'typical' animal and plant cells. Most cells are more complicated than this.

a Which is the animal cell and which is the plant cell? How did you recognise them?

Animals and plants can be grouped into species using the differences between them. In the same way, cells can be grouped into different types. Different cells are **adapted** to do specific jobs or **functions** in an organism. Adapted cells can be very different from 'typical' plant and animal cells.

Cell fact files

Sperm
- produced by most types of animal
- male sex cells which need to swim to the female sex cell and join with it to produce offspring

Adaptations:
- enzymes in the head let the sperm get into the ovum
- nucleus carries information from the male parent to make the new offspring
- mitochondria in the middle provide energy for swimming
- long tail lashes about to move the sperm along

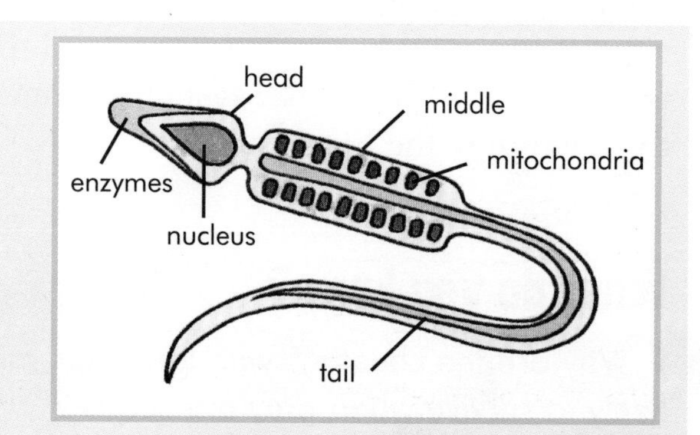

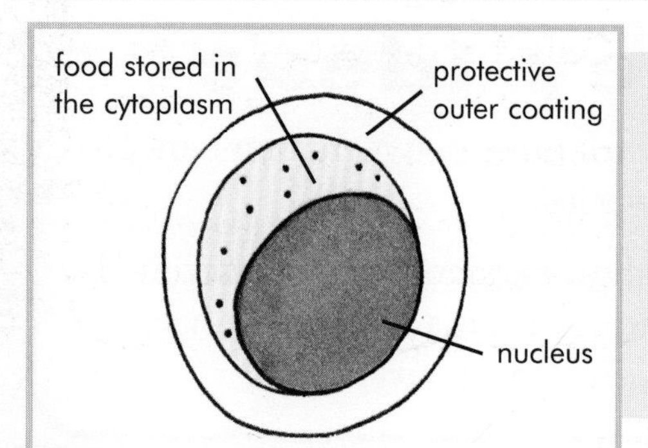

Ovum
- produced by most types of animal

Adaptations:
- nucleus contains information from the female parent to make the new offspring
- protective outer coating makes sure only one sperm gets through
- cytoplasm stores food for the developing embryo

Palisade cells

- found in the upper layers of green leaves, where most photosynthesis happens

Adaptations:

- many closely packed chloroplasts allow lots of photosynthesis to take place in each cell
- the shape of the cell allows lots of these cells to be packed near the surface of the leaf, so again lots of photosynthesis can take place

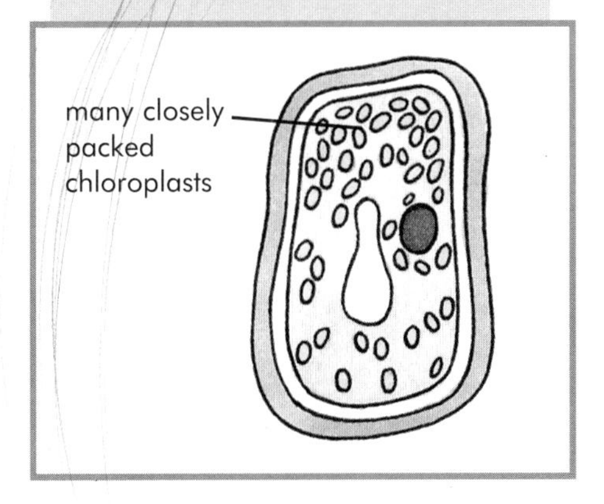

Root hair cells

- found on the outsides of plant roots
- important for water uptake

Adaptations:

- root hairs give a much bigger surface for taking up water
- cytoplasm has no chloroplasts because the roots are underground where there is no light

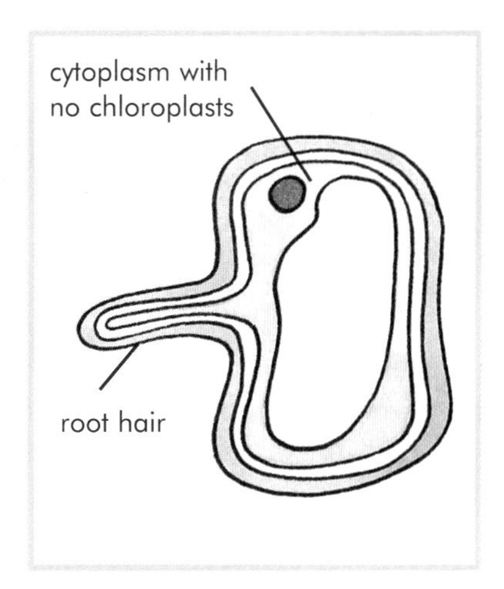

Ciliated epithelial cells

- found on surface of many very small animals, and on parts of larger animals that need to move fluids, such as in the human respiratory tubes

Adaptations:

- cilia beat together to move either an entire small animal, or substances such as mucus inside a larger animal
- many mitochondria supply the energy for the beating of the cilia

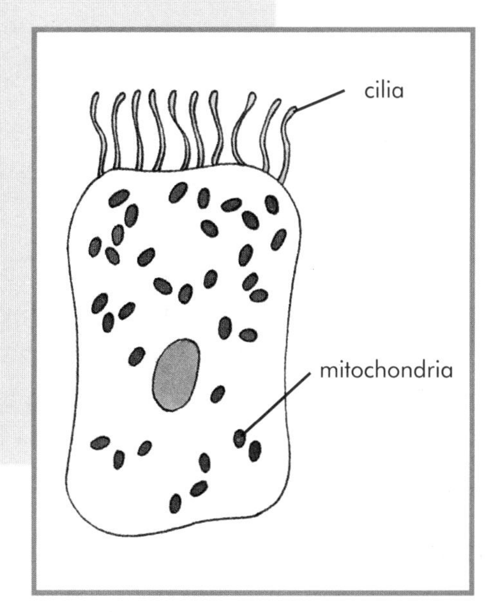

What do you know?

1 Copy the following descriptions with their correct words.

used to move small animals and fluids in larger animals –	ovum
the male sex cell –	root hair cell
the main site of photosynthesis in plants –	ciliated epithelial cell
the female sex cell –	palisade cell
gives an increased surface for the uptake of water by plants –	sperm

2 Copy and complete the table to show the main ways each type of cell is adapted for the job it has to do.

Type of cell	Adaptations

Key ideas

Cells that do particular jobs show variations from 'typical' plant and animal cells.

Cells are **adapted** to their **functions** in an organism.

R

3d Variety packs

In this family group, you can tell which children are brothers and sisters. Features like their hair, their eyebrows and the shapes of their faces are similar to each other, and similar to their parents. However, the brothers and sisters are not exactly the same as each other. Although each was born to the same mother and father, they still look like different people.

a Think about what you know of reproduction. How might this variation in families happen?

The plan for a person

People produce babies by **sexual reproduction**. At the start of every pregnancy, an ovum and a sperm meet. Both these cells contain a nucleus, and these two nuclei join to form a single new nucleus. This contains all the information needed to make a completely new person.

The information in the nucleus provides a plan for all the cells that go to make up a baby. The information is a mixture from the two parents, half from the mother and half from the father.

All different

Brothers and sisters are different from each other because the information is different in every egg and sperm. This means every new person is different. However, for identical twins the information is the same. The egg and sperm join, begin to develop into a baby and then split to form two identical people.

Lots of the things that make you different from everyone else are **inherited** from your parents, such as eye colour, hair colour, the shape of your ears, and the size of your nose.

b Think about your head. How many different visible features can you list that you think are inherited? What features on your head are not inherited?

A plan for every organism

The offspring of all kinds of organisms show variation. Plants pass on their plans in pollen and ovules, which fuse to form seeds. Most animals pass on information in the same way as people, when egg and sperm join together.

What do you know?

1a Why are brothers and sisters in the same family different?
b Why are identical twins so alike?

2 Here are some characteristics of different animals and plants. Which ones do you think are inherited?
a fur colour in mice
b the number of beans in a pod
c the length of a giraffe's neck
d being overweight
e freckles on your skin

3 A spider plant does not usually reproduce sexually, but grows offshoots which turn into new plants with roots. All these new plants are exactly the same as the parent plant. Why?

Key ideas

In **sexual reproduction**, information from two parents is mixed to make a new plan for the offspring. This leads to variation between members of a species.

Half of the information comes from the male sex cell and half from the female sex cell. Each sex cell formed is different from every other one, so no two offspring are exactly the same, except for identical twins.

3e The environment and variation

Identical twins have exactly the same inherited information – but they don't always look exactly the same.

You are what you eat

One thing that can cause differences between people is diet. If twin A eats much more food than twin B, then twin A will be fatter. If twin A eats a diet very much higher in fats than twin B, then twin A will be at higher risk of having a heart attack.

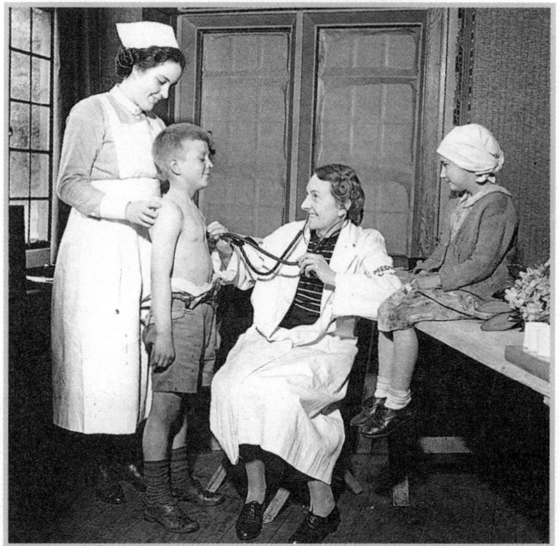

Children given a poor diet will not grow as tall as they would if they had a good balanced diet. Fifty years ago, during the Second World War, food was rationed and there was not as much to eat as there is today.

Over the last 50 years, children have been getting taller as food has become more plentiful. In England, boys are on average 0.5 cm taller now than they were in the 1940s.

So your food affects both your height and your weight, as well as your health. Different diets cause variations between individuals.

The environment and songbirds

The food you eat is part of the **environment** in which you live. The environment affects all living things, and causes variation between them.

Many birds have their own typical song. If baby birds are brought up without hearing the song of their parents, then they do not learn to sing properly. They are born with an inherited plan that lets them recognise their own type of song and learn it easily. But they need to hear the song around them too.

Nettle leaves

Nettles in a shady spot grow bigger leaves than those in a sunny area. They need bigger leaves to trap enough sunlight to make food.

The environment can cause other differences between plants. For example, the appearance of a plant may be affected by the temperature and the amount of minerals and water available.

Mixing and blending

Variation between organisms of the same species is caused partly by the information they inherit from their parents, and partly by their environment. Individuals have different information from their parents, and also different environments with different amounts of food and water available. No wonder no two living things are ever exactly the same!

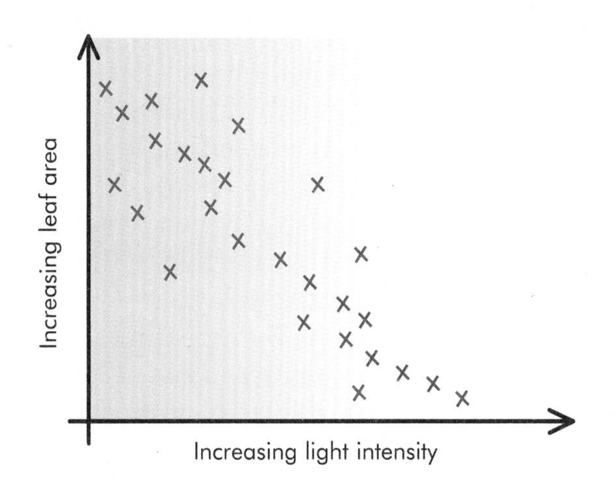

What do you know?

1 Here are descriptions of two organisms. List the features described for both. Say whether you think each feature is affected by the inherited plan, the environment, or both.

a Fluff is a black-and-white cat with long fur. She is very friendly and gentle. She is tall and has long legs, but she is not very good at catching birds as she is very fat.

b The oak tree in the garden is only 35 years old, but it is taller than the holly and hawthorn trees. Last year its leaves went mouldy and it grew very few acorns. This year the leaves have stayed healthy, and there are lots of acorns. The acorns all seem to have a similar unusually round shape.

2 When we look at changes in the height of boys over the last 50 years, we say that **on average** boys are 0.5 cm taller now than in the 1940s. Why do we use the term **on average**?

Key ideas

Variation between organisms of the same species has **environmental** as well as **inherited** causes.

Environmental factors such as diet, light, water and mineral availability, temperature and sound can all cause variation.

3f Selective breeding

We have seen that variety happens as a result of inheritance and the environment. But sometimes people lend a hand to get the plant or animal of their choice.

Fantastic fish

Goldfish are not found in all these amazing forms and colours by accident. People have used **selective breeding** to get the things they want. They choose as parents two animals or plants which have the required feature. The idea is that breeding these two together will give offspring with this feature. By repeating this process again and again, you can eventually end up with an organism that has all sorts of features that you want.

Puppy dog's tails

a What has happened to produce a dog with a big curly tail?

Selective breeding like this has given us all the different breeds of pet dogs and cats. But selective breeding is most useful for producing animals and plants for farming all over the world.

b Can you think of any other examples of selective breeding in animals?

Food for all

In days gone by, people liked their animals big and fat. To please modern tastes, farmers want animals that grow fast but gain little fat. Selective breeding has produced animals which do just that.

Many food crops like wheat grow well in Europe and America, but do not grow so well in the more extreme conditions of the developing world. By selective breeding people have developed crops which can cope well with little water but still produce a lot of grain.

Through selective breeding we can add to natural variation. We can change animals and plants artificially to suit the needs of people.

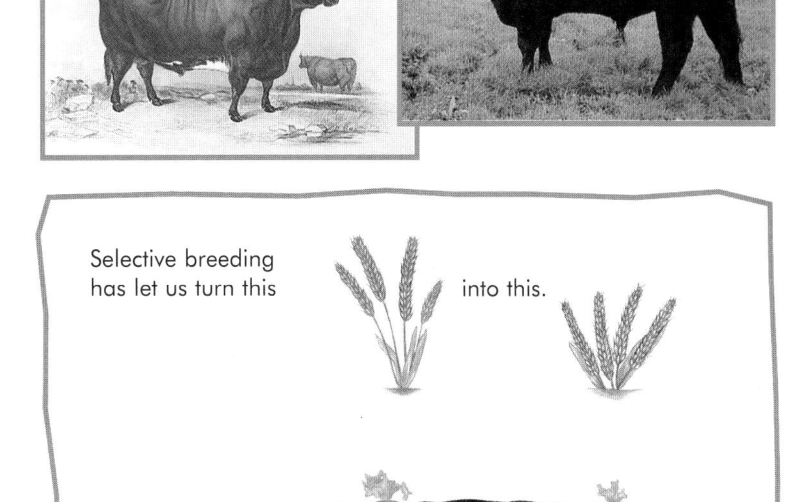

Now we have wheat that doesn't blow over in a storm, and carrots that can grow in stony soil.

What do you know?

1 Copy and complete the following sentences. Use the words below to fill the gaps.

breeds **crops** **selective breeding** **fast** **parents**

The many different varieties of pet cats are an example of ________ ________. People choose ________ for breeding so that their offspring show a particular feature. This method has been used to develop new ________ of farm animals which grow ________, and also new types of plants which give good ________ in difficult conditions.

2 Here are some examples of organisms produced by selective breeding.

a sheep with extra thick and woolly fleece
b turkeys which are so large that their legs cannot support them
c potato plants which produce large, smooth potatoes
d dogs with very squashed-looking noses, which cause breathing problems
e cows with udders which can produce very large volumes of milk

i Why do you think each of these organisms has been produced?
ii Are any of the changes damaging to the animals or plants concerned? Say which you think are damaging, and why.

Key ideas

People can produce animals and plants with the features they want by **selective breeding**.

Selective breeding involves choosing as parents animals and plants which will give the required feature in their offspring.

EXTRAS

3b Where do species come from?

There are 72 different species of antelopes. Why are there so many?

If a great herd of antelopes all eat the same type of grass, there will be competition between them for food. But if some antelopes feed on a different type of grass, they will have less competition. Eventually there will be two herds of antelopes, eating different plants. This is what has happened with the Grant's gazelles and Thomson's gazelles.

Grant's gazelle

Thomson's gazelle

Some antelopes are adapted for special habitats. The sitatunga has long, splayed-out feet which let it walk on marshy ground to feed on swamp plants. This feature has been passed down the generations to give another successful species.

Sitatunga

The greater kudu lives in the areas of Africa where people have settled, and other species are rare. It sleeps hidden in scrub all day and comes out to feed at night. Its behaviour is adapted to avoid being disturbed by people.

Greater kudu

The tiny dik-dik can escape predators and hide in the densest bushes.

Dik-dik

Scientists think all these species of antelope have developed as the animals adapted to their surroundings in different ways. This may be one way the great variety of life has come about.

1 There are other ways in which people think that the variety of life has come about. Some are scientific theories, others are religious beliefs. Describe a religious belief you know about which explains the existence of all the animals and plants. It may be one from your own beliefs and culture, or one you have come across in RE lessons.

2 In the different continents of the world, there are animals which look very similar and have similar lifestyles, even though they are not closely related. There are also animals and plants which are closely related, yet look very different and live very different lives. Can you think of any explanations for these facts?

Evolution and evidence

Evolution is a hypothesis that all the different species developed by adaptation and survival of the fittest. When scientists have a hypothesis, they need to collect evidence which supports that theory. We have evidence for evolution as it slowly goes on today. We also have evidence for evolution from the past.

Evolution today

We know that when a species cannot compete successfully with other species (including us), it can disappear completely and become **extinct**. For example, the dodo was a large, flightless bird which lived on the island of Mauritius. It had never seen people, and so when sailors first landed on the island it showed no fear. It was easy to catch, and made a welcome addition to the menu! The dodo was rapidly hunted to extinction.

Species are becoming extinct all the time. Species do not stay on Earth for ever.

Evolution in the past

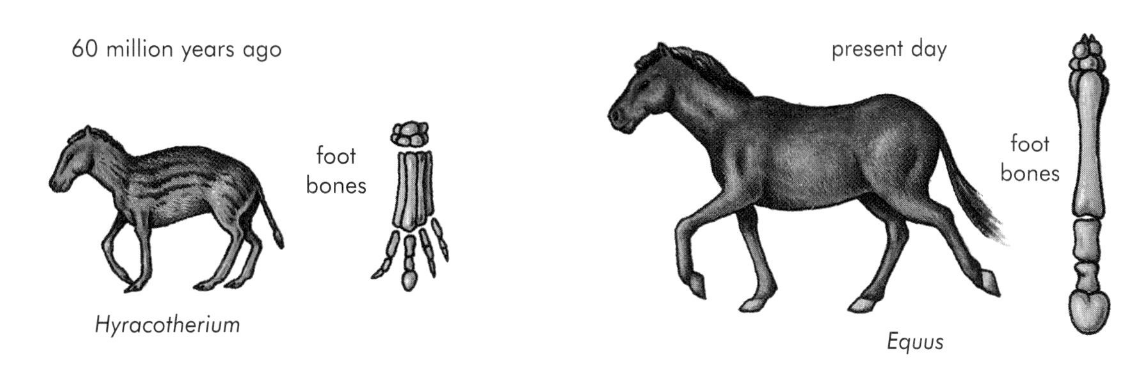

Fossils show how horses evolved. Their forefeet changed from having four toes to a single hoof.

Fossilised remains in rocks show us species which existed millions of years ago. We can tell how they changed and adapted, gradually leading to animals which are alive today.

3 Fossils show us some very strange creatures which lived in the past. In the deep ocean and other isolated environments, there are some equally strange creatures alive today. As the world's environment changes, the most weird and wonderful creatures are often the first to become extinct. Give a scientific explanation for this.

4 You are asked to take part in a debate. The motion is 'Evolution is the only realistic way to explain the species alive today'. Choose whether you want to stand for or against the motion. Prepare your speech, which must last no longer than two minutes.

3f

Cloning – selection without the breeding

Blueberries (as used in blueberry muffins!) grow wild on the mountainsides of North America. There is one thicket of blueberries in West Virginia which is 1 km long, and every blueberry bush carries exactly the same inherited information as the others! How?

Many plants reproduce themselves **asexually**. The offspring inherit exactly the same genetic information as their parents. Blueberries are very good at asexual reproduction, spreading by underground stems from which new plants grow. Blueberries also reproduce sexually to produce berries. The seeds inside are carried to distant areas by birds, but the immediate area is taken over by asexually produced plants.

Asexually produced blueberry plants are **clones**. A clone is a group of cells or organisms which are genetically identical and have all been produced from the same original cell. Blueberries are natural clones, but clones can also be produced artificially. People have produced entire carrots from a single carrot cell, and some animals have also been produced by cloning.

It is also possible to clone bits of human tissue. For example, a single liver cell can be used to produce a whole mass of identical cells. However, cloning whole people is a very long way off.

1 What is the difference between natural cloning and artificial cloning?

2 The use of clones in scientific research makes experiments on plants or animals much more reliable. Why do you think it is so much better to use identical clones rather than members of the same species produced by normal sexual reproduction?

3 Imagine that the technology is being developed to make it possible to clone human beings. Produce a short article for your school magazine discussing what the good and bad effects on human society might be if hundreds or thousands of copies of any one person could be made.

Orchids like these are artificial clones.

Selection for the future?

For generations, people have altered animals and plants by selective breeding. We have made animals tamer, fiercer, smaller or larger as it has suited us.

But now we have a new technology called **genetic engineering**. This gives us the power to change organisms in an even more dramatic way. The inherited information inside a cell is carried by **genes**, found in the nucleus. Scientists have found out how to change this genetic information. This means that they can affect the way cells, and organs, work.

We now have bacteria which have been genetically engineered to produce antibiotics to kill other disease-causing bacteria. The pig with the human heart genes has been engineered to provide organs for human heart transplants. Plants which have been engineered to produce their own pesticides won't need expensive and poisonous sprays. This is a fast-growing and exciting area of biology – and some people would say dangerous too!

Pigs can be genetically engineered to grow a 'human' heart.

Tomatoes can be genetically engineered so that they stay firm as they ripen, instead of going squashy. Foods treated like this do not have to be labelled.

4 Why do you think that changes in animals and plants can be brought about so much more quickly by genetic engineering than they could by selective breeding?

5 Scientists can carry out some genetic engineering on human beings to help cure diseases. However, so far genetic engineering which involves the ova and sperm has not been allowed. What is the significance of genetic engineering involving these sex cells?

6 The advantages of genetic engineering are quite clear, but what do you think might be the disadvantages? Explain any concerns you might have.

REVIEW

3a Variety in use

We use the variation between organisms to classify them into different groups.

Living organisms are divided into animals and plants. Each of these major groups is then divided into smaller and smaller groups.

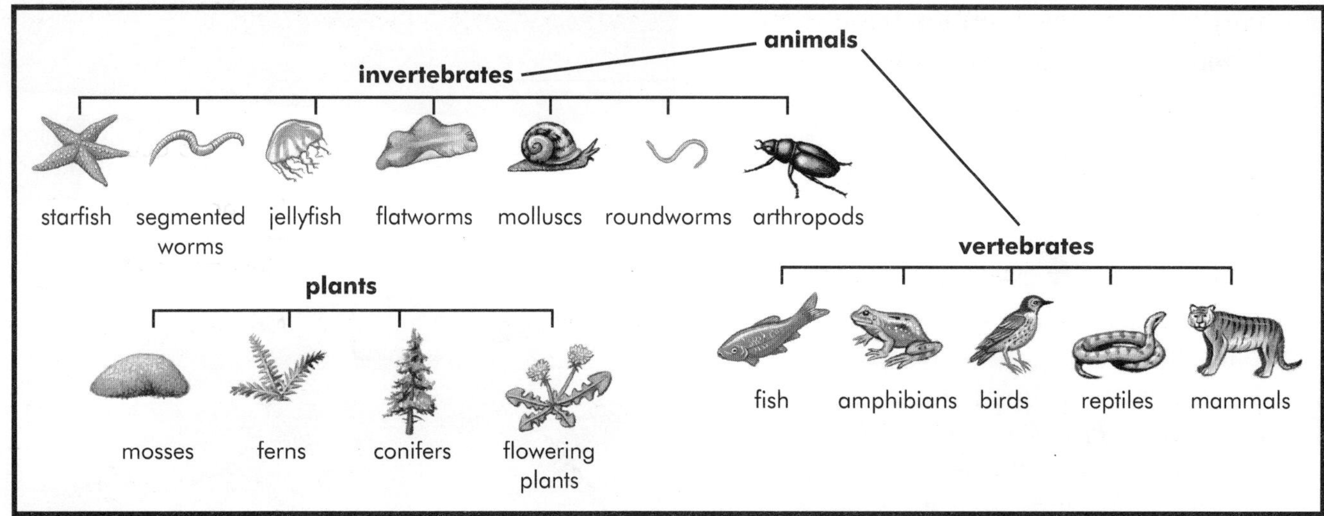

If you lift a large stone or piece of wood up, you will see lots of small creatures. Here is some information about the sorts of creatures you might find.

- arthropods: crustaceans – arthropods with a hard shell and 10 or more legs. They usually live in water but some, like woodlice, live on land.
- arthropods: insects – arthropods with six legs and three parts to their bodies.
- arthropods: centipedes and millipedes – arthropods with many segments to their bodies, and many legs.
- molluscs – have muscular bodies with a shell inside or outside the body.
- segmented worms – have long bodies divided into segments, with no legs.

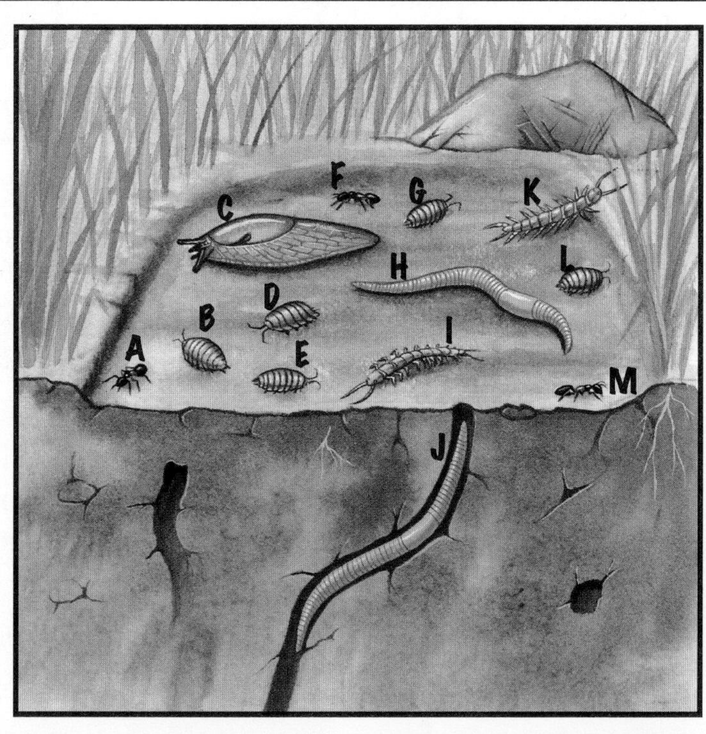

1 Make a table like this one. Look carefully at the picture and identify the organisms under the stone. Write the letter of the animal in the correct column of the table.

Arthropods: crustaceans	Arthropods: insects	Arthropods: centipedes and millipedes	Molluscs	Segmented worms

2 Which of the animals are the most common in the picture?

Variety is the key

You can use the variety between organisms to make a **key**. This can be used to help other people identify them when they are out and about. Here is a key for the animals found under the stone.

1 Has it got legs?	Yes: go to question **2**	No: go to question **4**
2 Has it got six legs?	Yes: ant	No: go to question **3**
3 Is it brown in colour with many legs?	Yes: centipede	No: woodlouse
4 Is its body divided into segments?	Yes: earthworm	No: slug

3 Make a key like this to identify the organisms in the picture. When you have made your key, try it out on a friend!

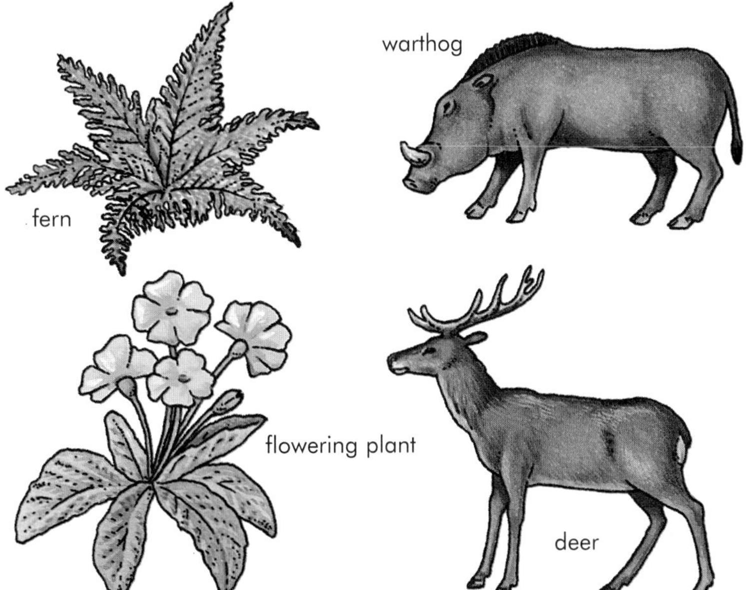

1 Is it green?	Yes: go to question **2**	No: go to question **3**

3c Same plant, different cells

There are plants that can survive in the Arctic Circle, plants in the tropical jungles round the equator, plants in hot, dry deserts and plants in cooler, wetter countries like Britain. They are all adapted to their different ways of life. In each type of plant are cells which are adapted to do different jobs. The cells all work together so the plant can photosynthesise (make its own food).

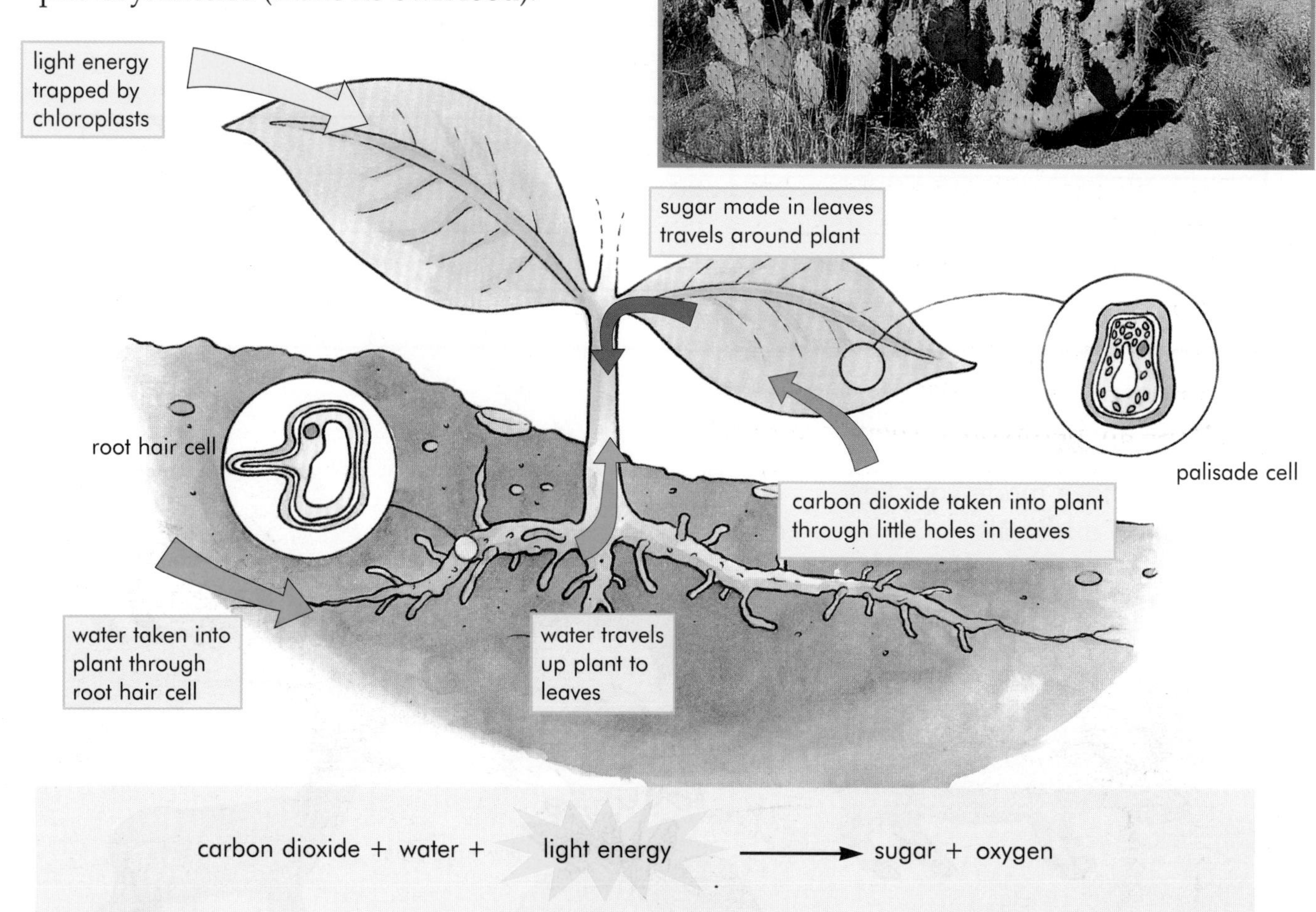

1 Which part of a root cell makes it good at taking in water?

2 Why do all plants need water?

3 Which part of the leaf cell is important for photosynthesis?

4 Why are there as many palisade cells as possible packed into the top layers of a leaf?

5 A palisade cell and a root hair cell are both plant cells, but they look very different. Why are they so different?

6 Why is photosynthesis so important?

3e Moose, wolves and woodlands

Plants can make their own food from materials in their environment – light, air, water and minerals. Animals need to eat food to get the materials they need to survive, grow and reproduce.

Some animals eat plants. Other animals eat animals. At the start of the chain there are always plants, which are eaten by animals.

All the food available for life on Earth comes from plants, so plants are known as **producers**. Because animals eat (or consume) plants, they are known as **consumers**. Producers and consumers are linked in **food chains**.

- Wolves are carnivores. They hunt moose. The wolf pack will kill a moose about once a week. The carcass is shared between them. They pick out a very young, an old or a sick moose to kill.
- The grass and plants of the woodland grow as a result of photosynthesis.
- Moose are herbivores. They need to eat a lot of plants to supply their needs because they are big animals.

1 Draw a food chain for these organisms.

2 Explain how each animal gets its energy supply.

3 Neither moose nor wolves can photosynthesise, but they are very different sorts of animals. Their teeth and their eyesight vary greatly, because they are adapted to different ways of life. What would you expect the teeth and eyes to be like on:
a a wolf **b** a moose? Explain your answer.

Keep them moving

Solid, liquid and gas

You know that all substances are made of **particles**, which are **atoms** or **molecules**. This idea is called the **particle model**. It helps to explain the differences between solids, liquids and gases.

a What are the differences between solids, liquids and gases? How do their particles behave differently?

On the dance floor

Why do things expand when they are heated? The particle model can explain this too.

How much room would your class take up on a dance floor? Not much, if everyone just stands swaying to slow music. But they would soon spread out if you speed up the beat and get them dancing. The more energy everyone puts into their dancing, the more space they take up.

The particles in a solid are like the people dancing slowly. When you heat a solid, you give the particles more energy. This makes them move more – they **vibrate** backwards and forwards. They take up more space because they need more 'elbow room', and the solid **expands**.

When you cool the solid, you take energy out. The particles slow down and move closer together. The solid **contracts**.

The same thing happens in liquids and gases. They expand when you heat them, and contract when you cool them.

Temperature and movement

The **temperature** shows how hot something is. The higher the temperature of a substance, the faster the particles are moving.

b Some thermometers contain mercury. They measure temperatures from 0 °C to 100 °C. At which temperature, 0 °C or 100 °C, are the mercury particles moving faster?

Slowing down and stopping

Even at 0 °C, the particles in liquid mercury are still moving.

At –39 °C, mercury freezes into a solid. The particles have slowed down, but they are still vibrating.

If you could get the temperature low enough, the particles would eventually stop moving. This would only happen at –273 °C. This temperature is called **absolute zero**, because you cannot get any colder!

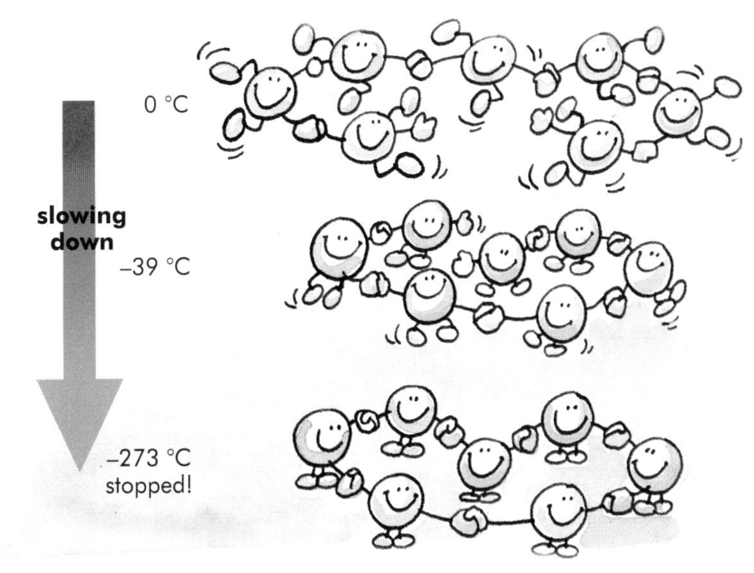

What do you know?

1 Copy and complete the following sentences. Use the words below to fill the gaps.

vibrate particles expand space

When you heat a solid, you give the ________ more energy. This makes the particles ________ more. The more you heat them, the more they vibrate. The more they vibrate, the more ________ they take up. This makes the solid ________.

2 Why do solids contract when they cool down?

3 Sunshine makes your skin feel hot. What is the sunshine doing to the particles in your skin?

4 Jerry said that it is really cold on the planet Pluto. He said it is –500 °C there. Could he be right? Explain your answer.

Key ideas

The **particles** in solids, liquids and gases are always moving.

When you heat a substance, you give it more energy. That makes its particles **vibrate** faster, which makes it **expand**.

As the substance cools, the particles slow down. This makes the substance **contract**.

4b Changing state

In this model solid, the particles are ping-pong balls and the bonds are elastic.

How do the moving particles stay together in solids, liquids and gases?

Think elastic!

In a solid, the particles are held in place by forces called **bonds**. That's why a solid keeps its shape.

But the particles are vibrating, so the bonds must allow them to move a little. The bonds act like elastic bands.

Give it a shake

In this model, the elastic keeps the particles in position, but you can easily make them vibrate.

If you shake the model gently, all the particles vibrate gently. If you put in more energy by shaking harder, the particles vibrate more.

a How could you make the particles in a real solid vibrate more?

Going too far

Now imagine shaking the model really hard. The particles vibrate more and more until the elastic starts to snap. The model starts to break up.

Melting and boiling

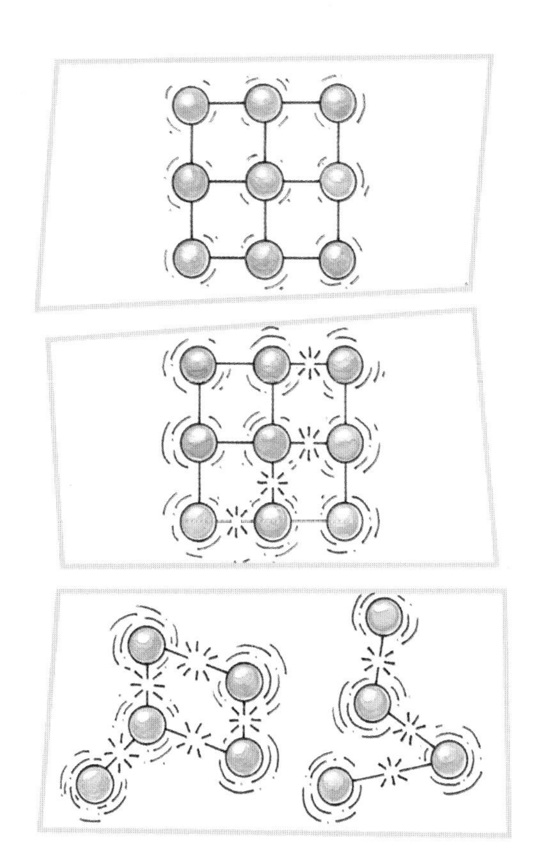

This model can help you understand what happens when a solid melts or a liquid boils.

In a solid, the particles are vibrating, but they are held in place by elastic bonds. As you heat the solid, the particles vibrate faster and faster.

Eventually, some of the bonds snap, and clusters of particles become free to move. The solid **melts** and becomes a liquid.

If you continue to heat the liquid, the particles will eventually all become free. They can whizz around at high speed in all directions. The liquid **boils** and becomes a gas.

The same but different

Melting and boiling are physical changes. In a physical change, the individual particles stay the same. They are just arranged differently.

There are the same number of particles before and after the change, so the mass of the material also stays the same.

What do you know?

1 Copy and complete the following sentences. Use the words below to fill the gaps.

elastic melt vibrate

When you heat a solid, the particles ________ more. If you keep heating, some of the ________ bonds will start to snap. The solid will ________.

2 Draw diagrams to show what happens to the particles when a solid melts and then boils.

3 Copper melts at 1084 °C. Iron melts at 1535 °C. Which metal has the stronger bonds between its particles? Explain your answer.

Key ideas

The particles in a solid vibrate, but are held in place by elastic forces called **bonds**.

If you keep heating a solid, some of the bonds break and the solid **melts**.

If you keep heating a liquid, it will eventually start to **boil**. All the bonds break and it turns into a gas.

The particles in a gas are free and are moving about at high speed.

The total mass stays the same during physical changes.

4c The pressure's on

Have you ever wondered how much air there is above your head? There are about 10 tonnes of air above every square metre of the Earth's surface!

a If you had 10 tonnes of solid on top of you, it would squash you flat. Why doesn't this happen with a gas?

Air pressure

You can feel air pushing against you when the wind is blowing. But the air is pushing you all the time, even when there is no wind. This pushing is known as **air pressure** or **atmospheric pressure**.

The air, like all gases, is made up of billions of tiny particles whizzing about at high speed in all directions. These particles are constantly crashing into each other, and into anything else that gets in their way – including you.

Each collision gives a tiny push. You feel all the collisions together as a constant pressure from the air.

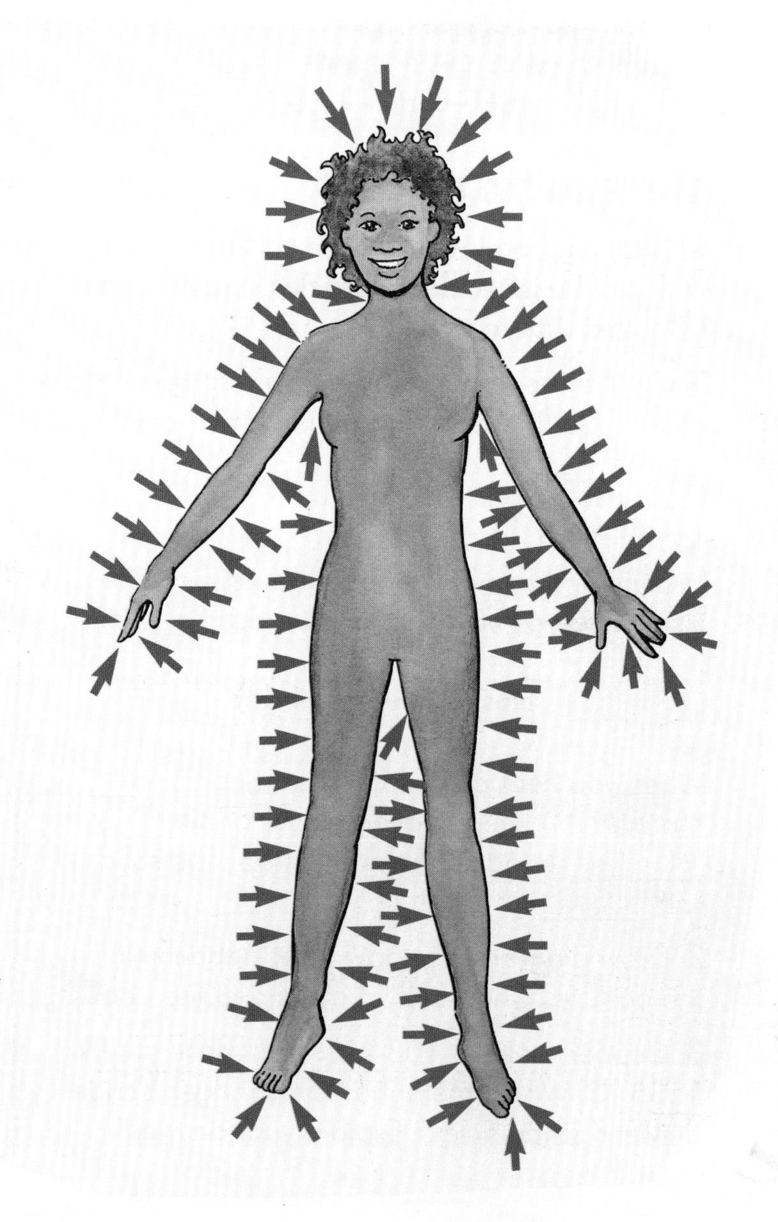

Keeping in balance

All the air particles are moving in different directions. So every surface gets its fair share of collisions from all angles. Because atmospheric pressure acts equally in all directions, you can't usually feel its effect. All the up, down, backwards and forwards pushes cancel out.

Upsetting the balance

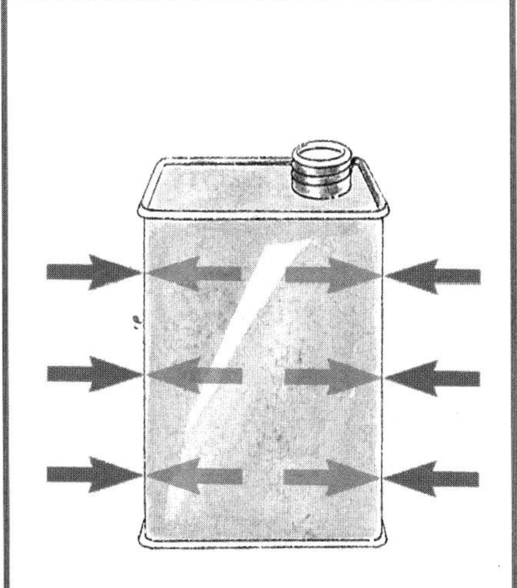

The air pressure inside an 'empty' can is equal to the air pressure outside. The pressure is balanced.

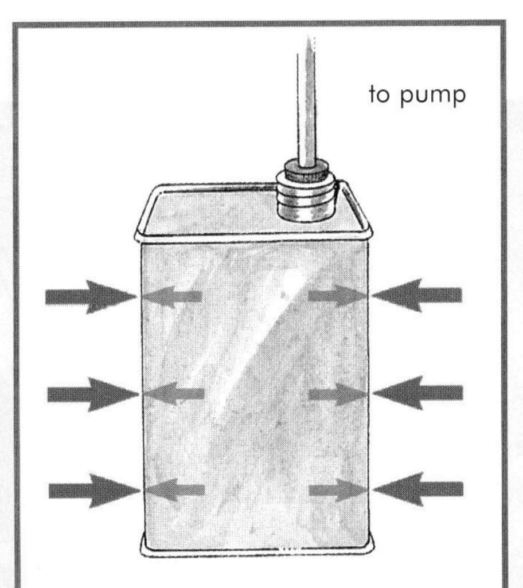

If you suck some of the air out, there are fewer particles to collide with the inside of the can. The air pressure inside the can drops. The pressure outside is now greater than the pressure inside.

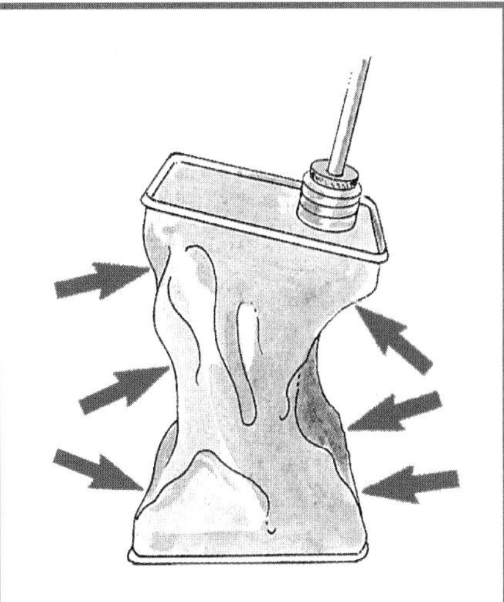

If enough air is pumped out, the atmospheric pressure outside will squash the can.

A pressure trick

Fill a glass to the brim with water and slide a playing card over the top. Now you can turn it upside down without the water falling out.

b Use the idea of atmospheric pressure to explain how this trick works.

What do you know?

1 Copy and complete the following sentences. Use the words below to fill the gaps.

high crash push pressure

Air particles are moving at ________ speed. They ________ into anything that gets in their way. Each collision gives a tiny ________. The effect of all of these pushes is air ________.

2 Explain why atmospheric pressure does not squash you flat.

3 Draw diagrams to explain how air pressure can squash a metal can.

Key ideas

Air particles move at high speed and crash into whatever is in their way.

Each collision gives a tiny push. All the collisions together give a constant pressure, called **atmospheric pressure.**

This pressure acts evenly in all directions.

4d Move and mix

How do you smell?

Smelly chemicals, for example in perfumes or egg sandwiches, evaporate into the air. When you breathe in, the smell particles are detected by special cells in your nose.

a How do you think the particles get from the perfume to your nose?

How smells spread

You might think that the smell particles are blown about by the wind or a draught. But smells will even spread through still air.

This is because the air particles are whizzing around at high speed in all directions. The smell particles get caught up in the movements of the air particles. They are bounced and jostled throughout the room. If you've ever been separated from your friend in a crowd of people, you'll understand how this can happen.

This process of mixing and spreading is called **diffusion**.

b Why is it easy to get separated in a crowd?

Diffusion in action

Smell particles evaporate into the air.

They get caught up with the moving air particles.

In time, they are spread out evenly through the air.

Diffusion in liquids

If you carefully drop some purple crystals into a tube of water and leave it, the bottom of the tube starts to turn purple. If you wait for a few hours, the colour gradually spreads up through the water. Eventually, all the water will be a deep purple colour.

The purple crystals **dissolve** in the water, and then their particles diffuse through the water. But the particles in liquids move much slower than the particles in gases. So diffusion takes much longer in a liquid than in a gas.

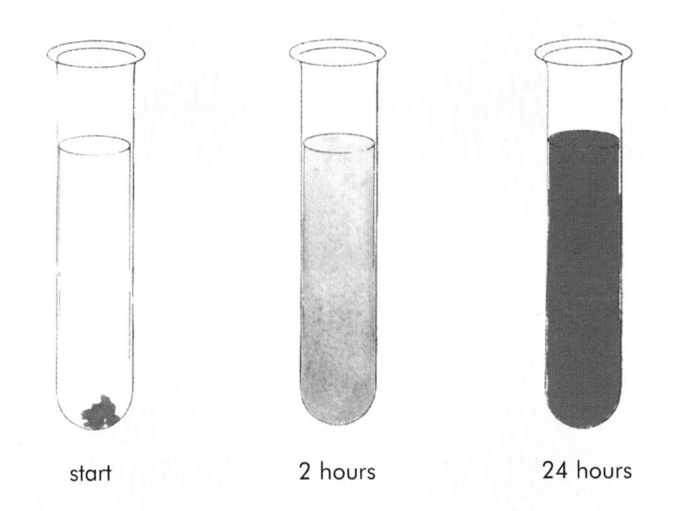

Why do balloons go down?

Balloons always look sad the day after a party. After a few hours they go down, no matter how well you tie them.

The rubber of the balloon is made of particles held together in a solid. Rubber particles are long spaghetti-like molecules which vibrate, just like any other particles. Sometimes the air particles crash through between them and escape.

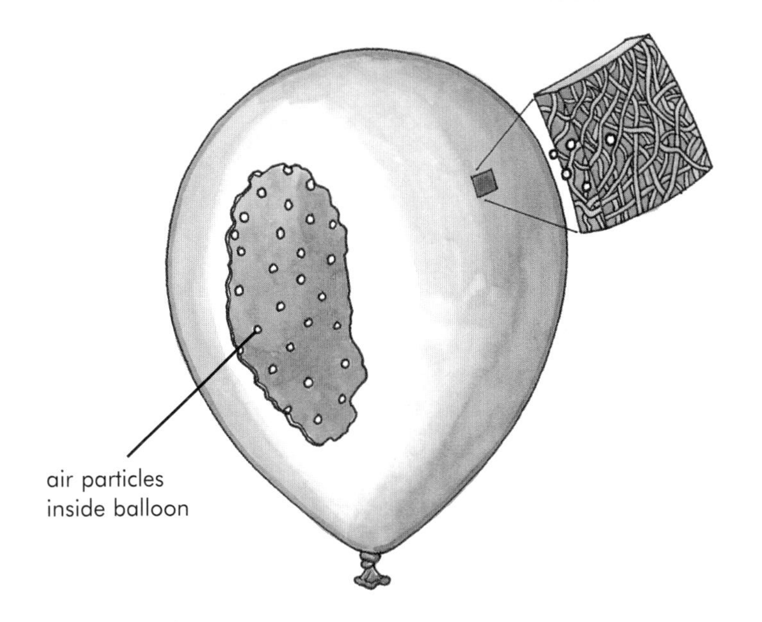

What do you know?

1 Copy and complete the following sentences. Use the words below to fill the gaps.

diffusion **moving** **mixed**

The particles in air are always ________. Any gas particles get caught up in this movement and are ________ in. This mixing and spreading is called ________.

2 Herbie dropped a stink bomb in the corner of the room. Draw diagrams to show how the stink bomb particles spread out through the room.

3 Do you think diffusion would take place faster or slower on a hot day? Give reasons for your answer.

4 Explain why balloons go down.

Key ideas

Gas particles move at high speed, so gases always mix themselves up. This is called **diffusion**.

Diffusion also happens in liquids, but much more slowly.

4e Break it up

Sugar **dissolves** in water. You might like it dissolved in your tea or coffee.

a How can you tell the dissolved sugar is there?

Stirring the coffee makes the sugar dissolve quickly. But given enough time, it would dissolve all on its own. This happens because of moving particles again!

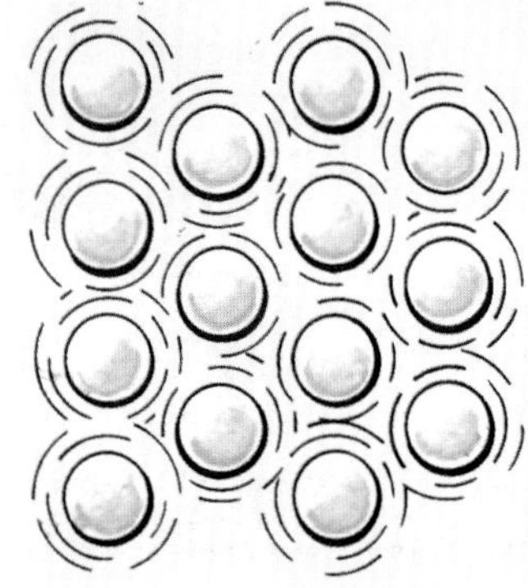

In sugar crystals, the particles are vibrating, but they are held in place by elastic bonds.

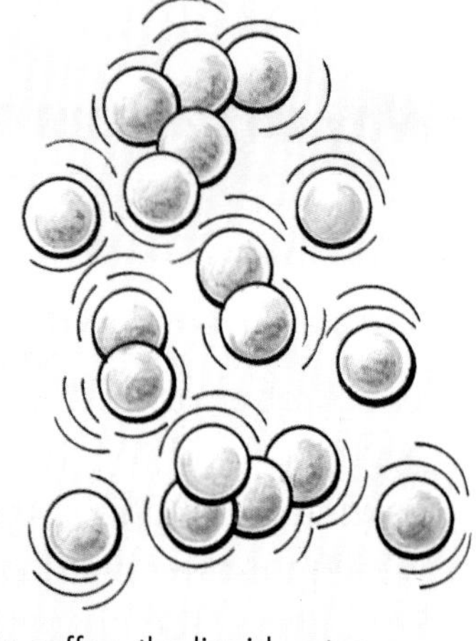

In coffee, the liquid water particles are free to move about.

How sugar dissolves

The picture shows what happens when sugar dissolves. Stirring speeds up the process.

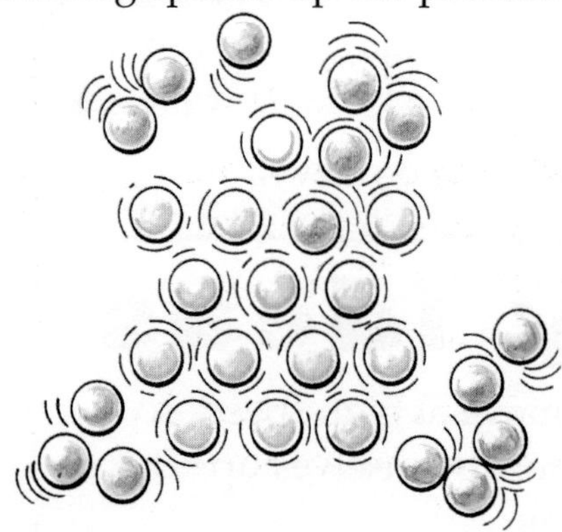

Some of the water particles crash into the sugar particles on the surface of the crystal. They knock some sugar particles loose, snapping the bonds.

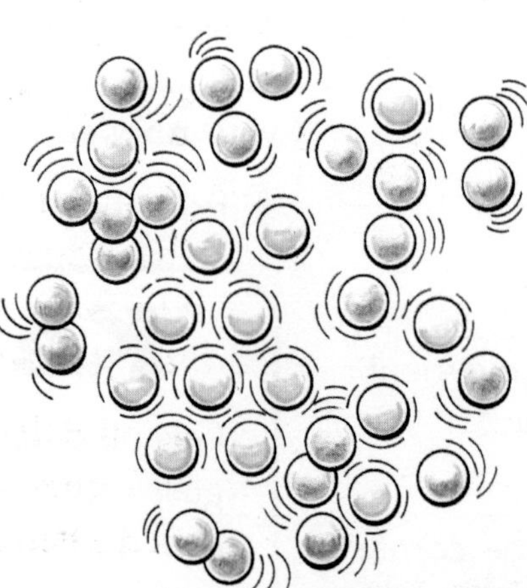

The loosened sugar particles are jostled away by the moving water particles. They diffuse into the water. More sugar particles are knocked loose.

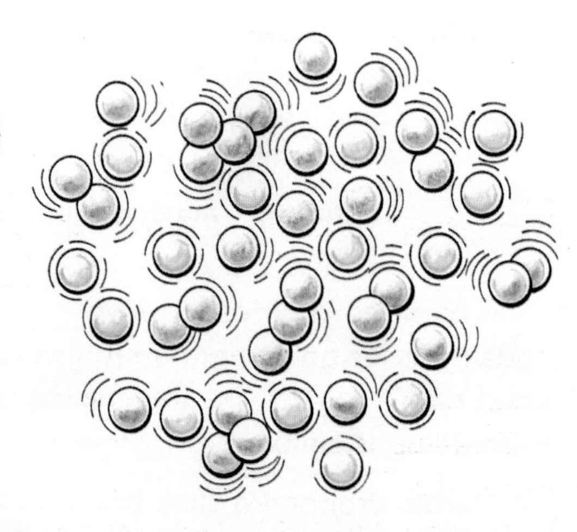

Eventually, all the sugar particles break loose and are carried away by the moving water particles.

Hotter and faster

When you heat water, you make the particles move faster. This means that they hit the sugar particles harder, so they have more chance of loosening them. It also means that the loosened sugar particles diffuse through the liquid faster.

b Does sugar dissolve faster in a hot drink or a cold drink?

The same but different

When sugar dissolves in water, the sugar and water particles get mixed up. But the number of particles stays the same. This means that the mass of the solution is the same as the mass of the water plus the mass of the sugar.

So when something dissolves, the total mass stays the same.

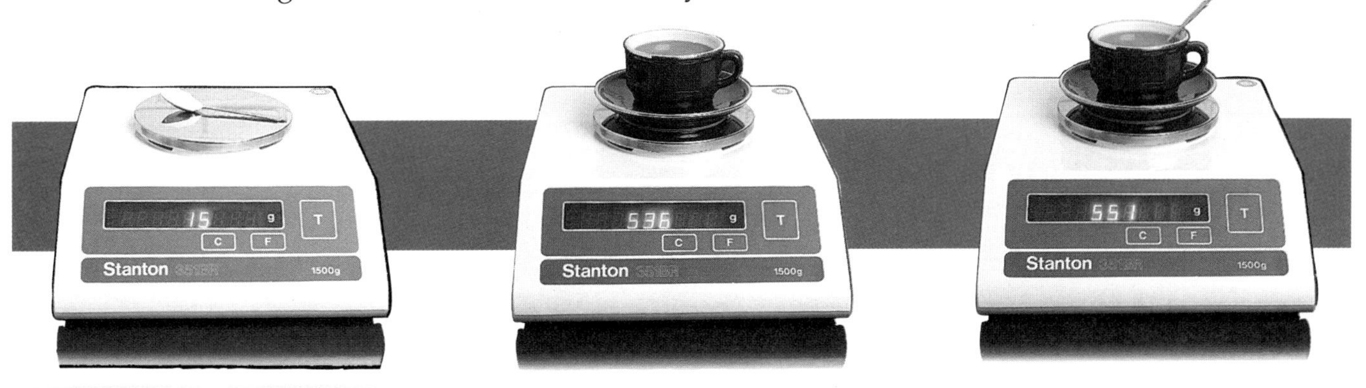

What do you know?

1 Copy and complete the following sentences. Use the words below to fill the gaps.

diffusion moving dissolves loosen

The particles in water are ________. They can ________ the particles in a sugar crystal. The loose sugar particles are mixed in by ________. The solid sugar ________.

2 The tea-leaves inside tea-bags contain water-soluble colours and flavours.

a Describe what happens when you make a pot of tea.

b Zaphrin decided to make some iced tea by putting a tea-bag into a glass of iced water. After waiting 10 minutes, the drink still had no flavour. Explain why.

3 Arthur dissolved 20 g of salt in 200 g of water. What was the mass of the salt solution he made?

Key ideas

When sugar **dissolves** in water, the sugar particles are loosened by the moving water particles. They then diffuse through the water.

Sugar dissolves faster in hot water than in cold water, because the particles are moving faster.

When a solid dissolves in a liquid, the total mass stays the same.

4f More about dissolving

Dissolving in water

Many common chemicals dissolve in water, so water is often used as a **solvent**.

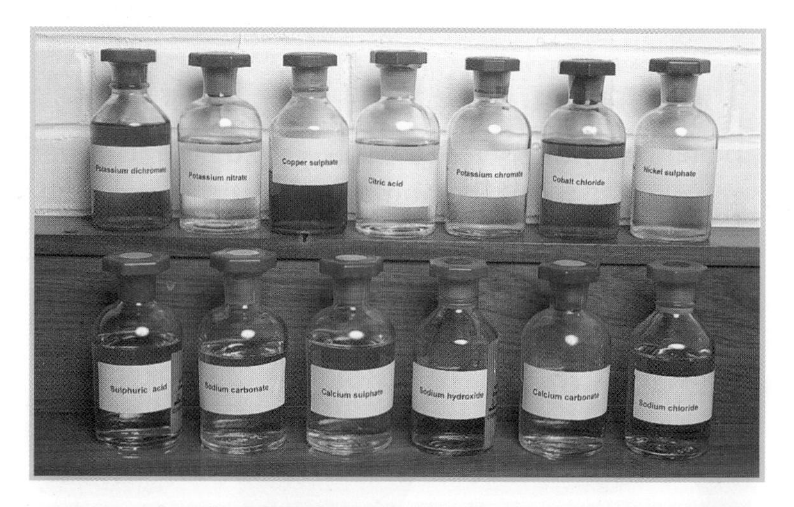

How much?

Common salt is very soluble in water. But if you keep trying to dissolve salt in water, the solution eventually becomes **saturated**, and no more will dissolve. You can dissolve up to 38 g of salt in 100 g of water at room temperature before the solution becomes saturated.

Washing soda (sodium carbonate) is less soluble than common salt. Only about 20 g of washing soda will dissolve in 100 g of water. Plaster (calcium sulphate) is even less soluble. Just 0.2 g of this salt will dissolve in 100 g of water – plaster is almost insoluble.

Only tiny amounts of calcium carbonate will dissolve in water, so people often say calcium carbonate is insoluble. Just over a milligram (0.001 g) of calcium carbonate will dissolve in 100 g of water.

a Corals and shellfish take calcium carbonate from sea water to build their shells. Sea water is almost saturated with calcium carbonate. About how much calcium carbonate is there in every cubic metre of sea water? A cubic metre of sea water has a mass of one tonne (1000 kg).

Hotting up!

If you wanted to make a saturated solution of common salt, you could heat the water to make the salt dissolve faster. But hardly any more salt dissolves in hot water than in cold water.

With many other chemicals, however, increasing the temperature means that more will dissolve. The **solubility** increases.

b Look at the table. Plot a graph to show how the solubility of the chemicals shown changes with temperature.

Temperature (°C)	Sodium chloride	Copper sulphate	Potassium sulphate	Potassium nitrate
10	38	18	8	20
20	38	20	10	30
30	38	24	12	44
40	38.5	28	13	60
50	38.5	34	15	80
60	39	42	16	104
70	39	50	18	152

Solubility of different chemicals (grams per 100 g of water)

Other solvents

Some chemicals, such as fats, waxes and oils, do not dissolve in water at all. That's why you can't clean greasy dishes with just water. Greasy stains are hard to remove from clothes using water.

Fortunately, there are other solvents that can dissolve these chemicals. Dry cleaners use a solvent called tetrachloroethene instead of water to clean clothes.

Waterproof marker pens and paints use different solvents, too. The paints contain coloured solids that are insoluble in water. This is why graffiti does not wash off in the rain. But other solvents will quickly dissolve these coloured solids, so that the graffiti can be removed.

What do you know?

1a Make a list of some chemicals that are soluble in water.
b Make a list of chemicals that are insoluble in water.

2 A stick of blackboard chalk contains 5 g of calcium sulphate. How much water would you need to dissolve it?

3 From the table, you can see that you could dissolve 50 g of copper sulphate in 100 g of hot water. What do you think would happen when the water cooled down?

Key ideas

Many common chemicals dissolve in water.

Some salts are more soluble in water than others.

For many salts, more will dissolve in hot water than in cold water.

Oil and grease do not dissolve in water. They dissolve in other solvents, such as tetrachloroethene.

4b Changing state

Boiling water

When you switch on an electric kettle, energy is transferred to the water. As the particles move faster, the temperature rises.

At 100 °C, the particles can overcome the forces of attraction between them. The water starts to boil – the liquid turns to a gas.

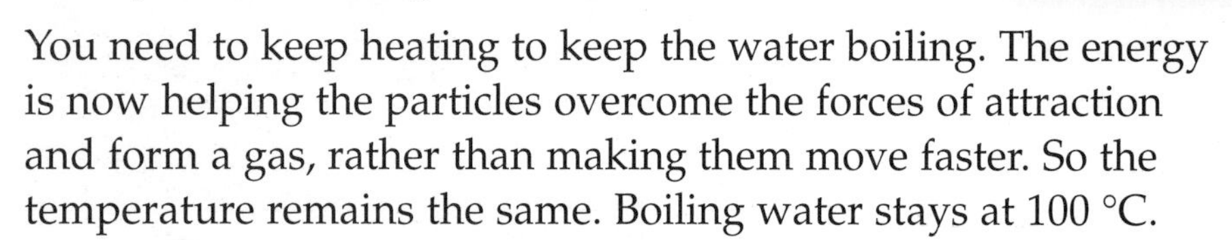

You need to keep heating to keep the water boiling. The energy is now helping the particles overcome the forces of attraction and form a gas, rather than making them move faster. So the temperature remains the same. Boiling water stays at 100 °C.

Condensing

As a gas cools, its particles slow down. When they have slowed down enough, the forces of attraction pull them together and the gas **condenses** to a liquid.

Getting the energy back

You put energy in to make the particles move apart. When they move together again, you get that energy back out. When steam condenses back to water, a lot of heat energy is given out.

1 The table shows the results of an experiment to find the boiling point of ethanol. A temperature probe was put in a tube of ethanol, which was heated in a water bath.

Time (min)	0	1	2	3	4	5	6	7	8
Temperature (°C)	20	36	49	60	68	74	79	79	79

a Plot a graph of these results.
b What is the boiling point of ethanol?
c Why does the temperature stay the same while the ethanol boils?

2 Freezers take energy out of things. If you put a tray of water in a freezer, energy is taken out and the particles slow down. The temperature drops. At 0 °C, the water starts to freeze. The temperature of the water stays constant until it is all frozen. Energy is still being taken out, so why doesn't the temperature drop?

4c OK suckers!

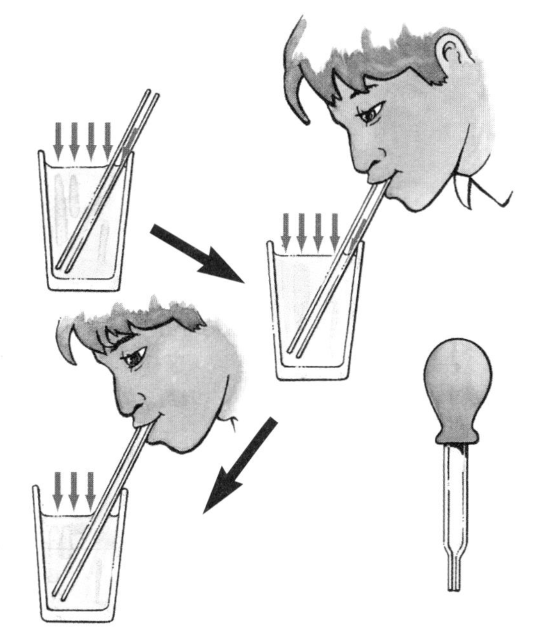

Have you ever had a drink forced into your mouth at high pressure? That's what happens when you drink through a straw.

When you suck a straw, the air pressure inside your mouth gets lower than the air pressure outside. The excess air pressure forces the drink up the straw and into your mouth, to restore the balance.

1 Look at the diagrams showing what happens when you drink through a straw. Dropping pipettes work in a similar way. Draw a series of diagrams to show how you fill a dropping pipette with water.

Suction caps

Suction caps are used for holding a soap tray onto the bathroom mirror, or a towel hook onto the door. They are handy for sticking small things onto smooth surfaces.

But suction caps can be very powerful. They have been used to climb the smooth glass fronts of New York skyscrapers.

2 Look at these diagrams and try to describe in your own words how a rubber suction cap works.

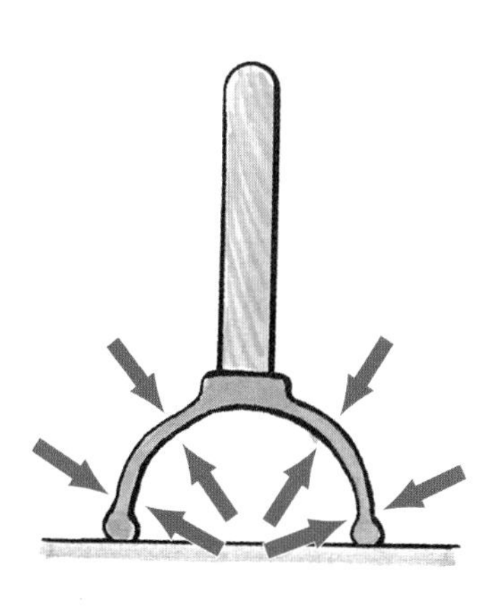

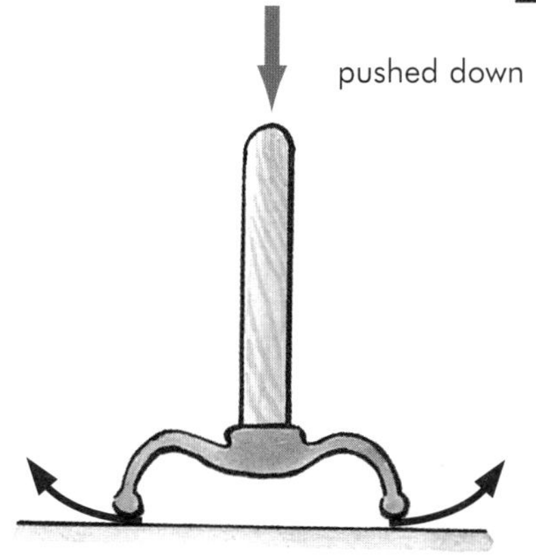

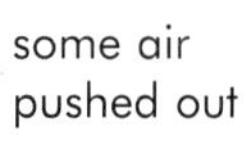

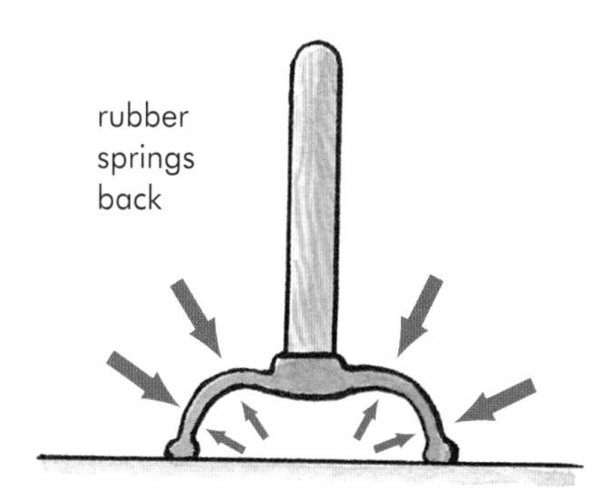

4d Exchanging gases

Diffusion is a very important process in living things. For example, oxygen gets into your blood by diffusion. In your lungs, the oxygen in the air dissolves in the layer of water inside the air sac. The dissolved oxygen then diffuses into your blood through the thin walls of the air sac. This is similar to the way air leaks out of a balloon, though the thin rubber.

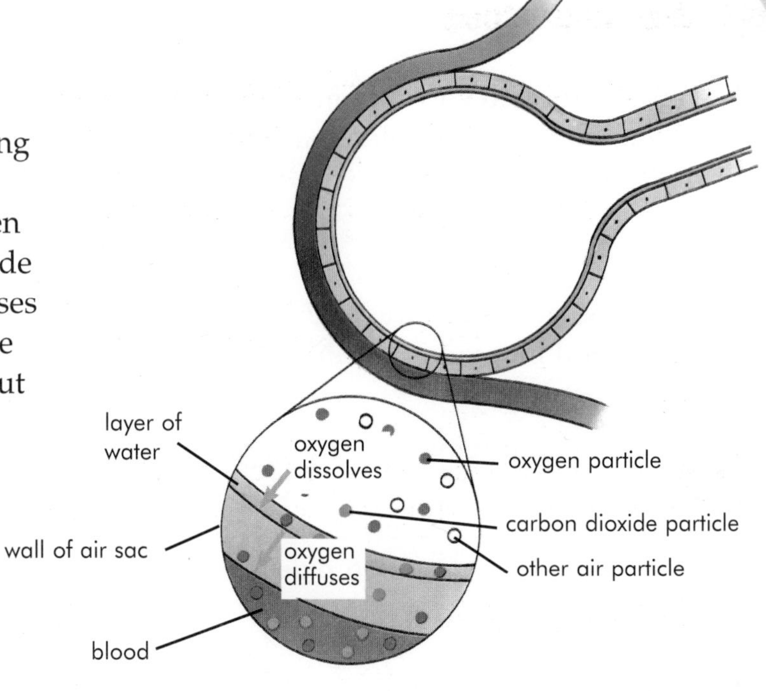

1 How does carbon dioxide get into the air inside your lungs from your blood?

One-way traffic

Diffusion mixes gases or solutions. But diffusion seems to make things move in one direction in living things. How does this work?

If you dissolve the shell off an egg, the egg is still surrounded by a rubbery membrane. Water particles can move through this membrane.

If you put the egg in water, it gets bigger! The inside of the egg is a solution of chemicals in water. The solution inside the egg is more concentrated than the water outside. Water particles move in to try to balance things out. The water makes the egg bigger.

But if you put the egg in concentrated salt solution, the egg gets smaller. The solution outside the egg is more concentrated than the solution inside. Water particles move out to try to balance the concentrations. There is less water inside the egg, so it gets smaller.

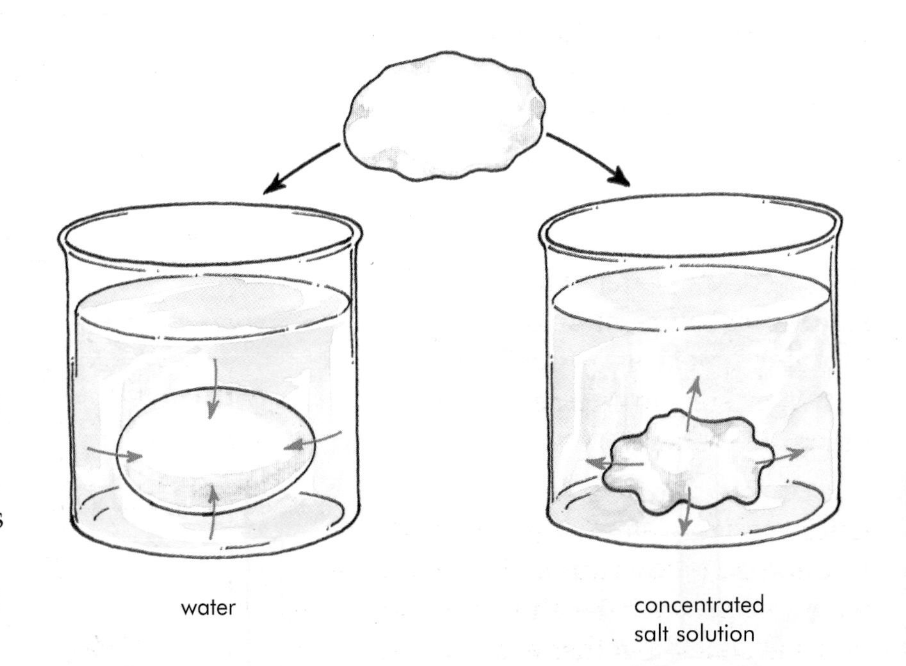

2a If you put a limp lettuce in cold water for a while, it swells and becomes crisp again. What is happening?
b If you put slices of potato into a concentrated salt solution, they go limp. Why is this?

4e Size and speed

A large crystal will dissolve much faster if you crush it first. The water particles can only crash into the particles on the outside of the crystal. When you break up the crystal, you give the water a larger surface area to work on. More particles are exposed, so the crystal dissolves much faster.

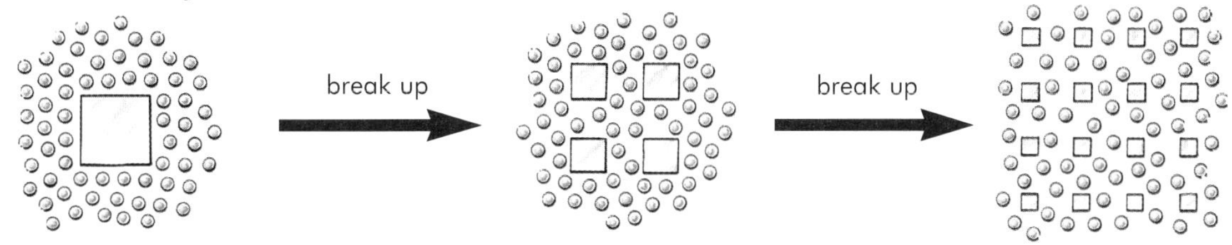

1a What is the surface area of a 2 cm cube?

b This 2 cm cube is broken up into eight 1 cm cubes. What is the total surface area now?

Growing crystals

Growing crystals from solution is like dissolving in reverse. You can grow crystals of alum (potassium aluminium sulphate) by making a saturated solution and then letting the water slowly evaporate away. If you hang a tiny crystal of alum in the solution, it will act as a 'seed'. It grows larger and larger as the water evaporates.

In a dilute solution, the alum particles are spread out in the water. If they crash into each other, they are soon jostled apart by more water particles.

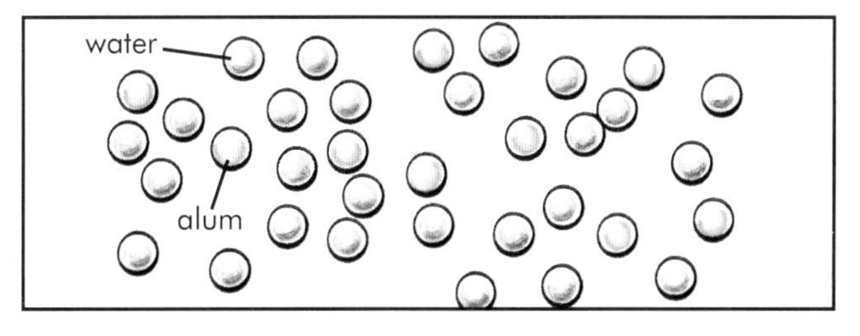

If some of the water evaporates, the solution becomes more concentrated. The alum particles are less spread out. They start to collide with each other more often.

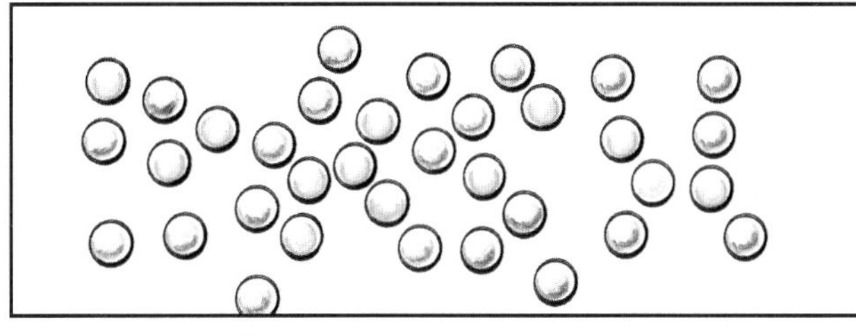

Once enough water has evaporated, the solution becomes saturated. If any more water evaporates, the alum particles will stick back together again when they collide, and crystals will grow.

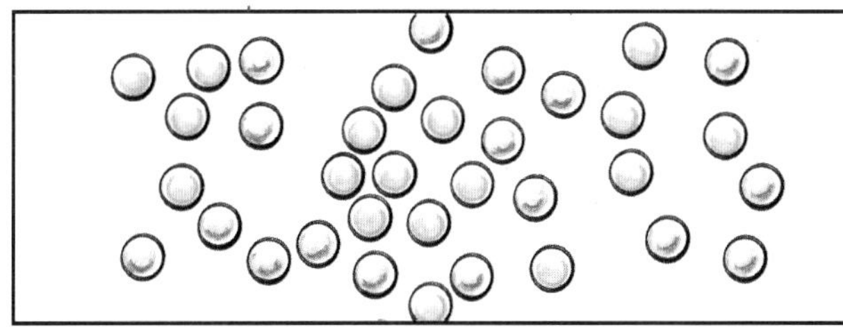

1 For some salts, more will dissolve in hot water than in cold water. If you make a hot saturated solution, crystals will start to grow as the solution cools down. Try to explain why this happens. (Hint: the water particles move faster in hot water.)

REVIEW

4a Solids, liquids and gases

All substances are made up of tiny particles. In solids, the particles are close together and held in place by forces. In liquids, the particles are close together, but they are not all held tightly in place. In gases, all the particles are far apart and free to move about.

1 Copy and complete the table showing the properties of solids, liquids and gases. Draw in the missing picture for the gas.

Solid	Liquid	Gas
fixed shape		no fixed shape
fixed volume	fixed volume	
cannot be squashed		can be squashed

Expanding and contracting

Solids expand when they are heated. You can't stop them expanding, because the forces are much too large. Road slabs and railway lines are laid with gaps between them, to stop them being damaged when they get hot.

Solids contract when they cool. These forces are also very large. Millions of years ago, volcanoes in western Scotland poured lava over the surrounding country. This set to form a massive layer of hot lava rock, that extended all the way to Ireland. As it cooled, it started to contract. But it was stuck to the rocks below, so it couldn't move like a cooling railway line. Instead, it shattered into millions of honeycomb-shaped columns.

2 Terry got fed up weeding his back garden during the summer heatwave, so he had it concreted over. The winter was very cold that year. In the spring, Terry found that the once-smooth concrete was badly cracked, and weeds were poking through! What had happened?

The Giant's Causeway in Northern Ireland

Changing state

A substance is a solid, a liquid or a gas, depending on the temperature. If you heat a solid enough, it will melt. If you keep heating the liquid, it will boil and form a gas.

But different substances melt and boil at different temperatures. At room temperature, a substance is a solid, a liquid or a gas, depending on its melting point and boiling point.

temperature (°C)	
6000	the Sun's surface
4000	
3000	
	white-hot bulb filament
2000	
1500	iron melts
	roaring Bunsen burner flame
1000	rocks melt
700	aluminium melts
400	mercury boils
200	
100	water boils
	alcohol boils
50	wax melts
	your body (37 °C)
25	room temperature
0	water freezes
–50	winter at the poles
	carbon dioxide freezes (–78 °C)
–100	alcohol freezes
	air becomes a liquid
–273	as cold as you can get

1a Copy this temperature line, without the pictures.
b Add: **i** mercury freezes (–39 °C)
ii tungsten melts (3400 °C). (Tungsten is the metal in a bulb filament.)

2 Use the temperature line to answer these questions.
a Mercury is an unusual metal at room temperature. Why?
b Why are mercury-filled thermometers not used at the North Pole?
c Why is tungsten used rather than iron in a light bulb?
d Could you land a space probe on the surface of the Sun?

3 The planet Mars has 'ice-caps' of frozen carbon dioxide at its poles in winter. Is Mars warmer or colder than the Earth?

Dissolving

What liquids do you use at home? As well as water, you might list vinegar, lemon juice, cola, bleach, and so on. In fact, all of these liquids are solutions of other chemicals in water.

In drinks, the dissolved chemicals add flavour and colour to the water. Sometimes water is used to dilute the chemicals, because they are too strong on their own. For example, the acetic acid in vinegar would be strong enough to burn you if it wasn't diluted with water.

1 Copy and complete this table about liquids used in the home.

Liquid	Solute	Used for
vinegar		seasoning
lemon juice	citric acid	cooking
cola	phosphoric acid and flavours	drink
bleach	sodium hypochlorite	
beer	alcohol and flavours	drink
floor cleaner	washing soda	
shampoo	detergents	

Looking at atoms

Elements and compounds

Everything is made up of **atoms**. Sometimes the atoms are found on their own, but often they are joined together in **molecules**.

There are 92 different kinds of atoms on Earth. A substance that has only one kind of atom is called an **element**. Iron, sulphur, carbon, hydrogen and oxygen are elements. In some elements the atoms join together to form molecules. The oxygen in the air has molecules made up of two oxygen atoms joined together.

Different elements often join together to form chemical **compounds**. Water, carbon dioxide and sodium chloride are compounds.

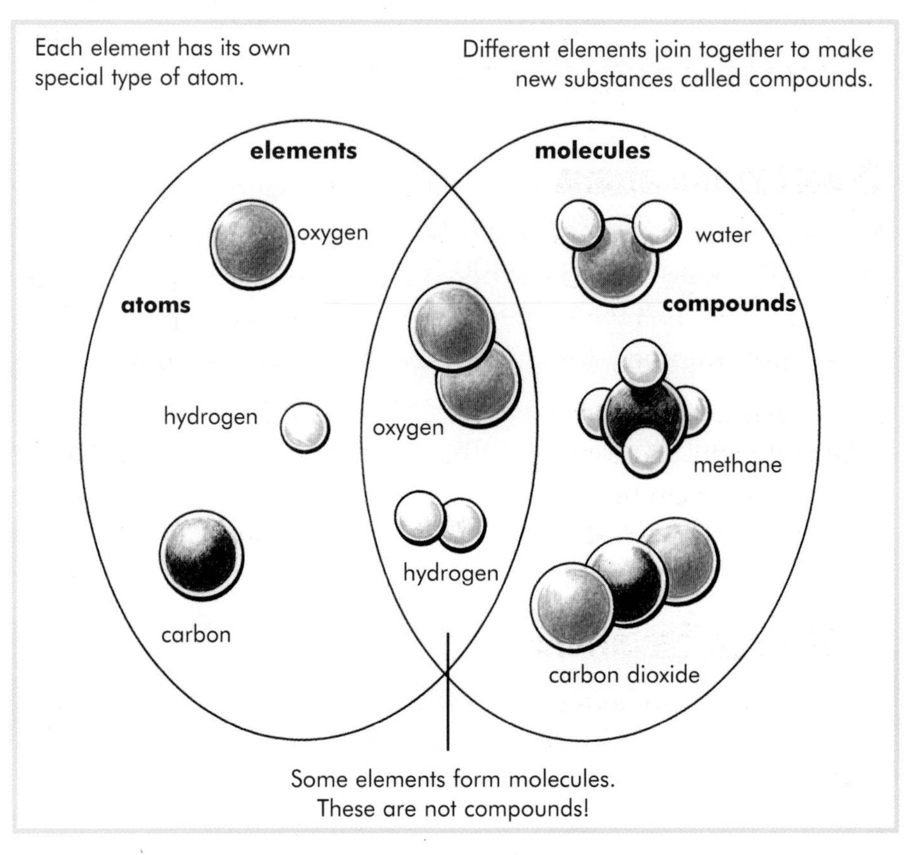

a Explain the difference between atoms and molecules, elements and compounds.

The alphabet model

You use an alphabet of 26 letters. They can be joined together to make a vast number of different words, each with its own special meaning.

The 92 elements are like the alphabet of materials. They can be joined together to make a vast number of different chemical compounds, each with its own special properties.

letters	**words**
D A N	AN AND DAN ADA ADD
elements	**compounds**
oxygen hydrogen carbon	water carbon dioxide methane

Which combinations work?

Just as there are rules for spelling, there are rules for making compounds. The same compound always has the same combination of atoms.

Water is a compound of hydrogen and oxygen. You could call it hydrogen oxide. Every water molecule has two hydrogen atoms joined to one oxygen atom. If you found a different combination of hydrogen and oxygen atoms, it would not be water.

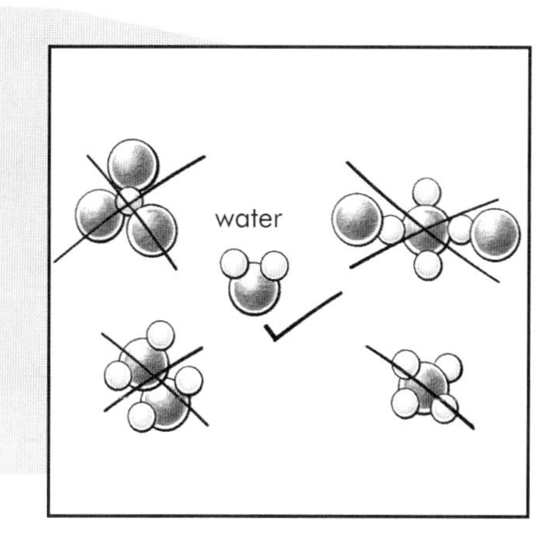

Ordering the atoms

You can put the elements in order according to the mass of their atoms. Hydrogen has the lightest atoms, so hydrogen is number 1. Uranium has the heaviest atoms, so uranium is number 92. This 'order number' for each element is called its **atomic number**.

Atoms contain smaller particles called **protons**. The atoms of different elements contain different numbers of protons. The atomic number tells you how many protons there are in the atoms of that element. Hydrogen atoms have just one proton, carbon atoms have six protons, and so on.

hydrogen 1

carbon 6

iron 26

uranium 92

The atomic numbers of four elements

Shorthand for atoms

Each element can be represented by a one- or two-letter **symbol**. Some symbols are obvious, but others come from older names that are no longer used. You will need to learn some symbols.

H is for hydrogen

...but Fe is for iron!

What do you know?

1 Copy and complete the following sentences. Use the words below to fill the gaps.

compound oxygen element hydrogen

Hydrogen is an ________. Oxygen is an element. Water is a ________ of hydrogen and oxygen. There are always two ________ atoms and one ________ atom in a water molecule.

2 Write down the number and types of atoms in: **a** methane **b** carbon dioxide.

Key ideas

Everything is made up of **atoms**. **Elements** are made up of only one type of atom.

Molecules contain two or more atoms joined together.

Compounds are new substances formed when the atoms of two or more elements join together.

The atoms of the 92 elements are arranged in order of **atomic number**.

5b Spotting the pattern

The elements are put in order according to the mass of their atoms. Does the mass of the atoms affect the way the element behaves? If you look at the elements in order, there is a pattern in their behaviour. Groups of similar elements reappear as you move down the list, like notes on a musical scale.

a Can you spot the repeating pattern from the first 20 elements?

The first 20 elements

Atomic number	Element	Property
1	hydrogen	a very reactive gas
2	helium	an unreactive gas
3	lithium	a very reactive metal
4	beryllium	a metal
5	boron	a non-metal
6	carbon	a non-metal
7	nitrogen	a non-metal
8	oxygen	a non-metal
9	fluorine	a very reactive gas
10	neon	an unreactive gas
11	sodium	a very reactive metal
12	magnesium	a metal
13	aluminium	a metal
14	silicon	a non-metal
15	phosphorus	a non-metal
16	sulphur	
17	chlorine	a very reactive gas
18	argon	an unreactive gas
19	potassium	a very reactive metal
20	calcium	a metal

hydrogen burns in air

helium is unreactive – it does not burn

lithium burns with a red flame

fluorine can dissolve glass

neon is unreactive – it is used in display lights

sodium burns with an orange-yellow flame

chlorine is a poisonous gas

argon is unreactive – it is used to fill light bulbs

potassium burns with a lilac flame

Just count to eight

Sulphur

Did you notice that the pattern repeats after a count of eight?

Helium is completely unreactive. That's why it is safe to use in children's balloons. Helium has atomic number 2. If you count on eight places, you get to neon. This is another unreactive gas. It is used in advertising lights. Count on eight again and you reach argon. This unreactive gas is used to fill light bulbs, so that the metal filament doesn't burn out.

b Is sulphur a metal or a non-metal? Count eight places back and find out!

Put them in a table

This pattern is easier to see if the elements are arranged in a table. Similar elements are put under each other in eight vertical **groups**. These groups are numbered from I to VIII. Hydrogen is kept apart on its own.

Some of these groups have names. Helium, neon and argon are in group VIII, the **noble gases**. These gases are very unreactive.

This table shows the symbols for the elements.

H			groups				
I	II	III	IV	V	VI	VII	VIII
							He
Li	Be	B	C	N	O	F	Ne
Na	Mg	Al	Si	P	S	Cl	Ar
K	Ca						

c Make a list of the first 20 elements. Match the symbols to the correct elements. How can you work out what Na and K are?

What do you know?

1 Copy and complete the following sentences. Use the words below to fill the gaps.

eight elements groups mass

If you arrange the ________ in order of the ________ of their atoms, you get a repeating pattern. The pattern repeats every ________ places. If you arrange the list as a table, similar elements are found in vertical ________.

2 Which other elements are found in the same group as:
a sodium **b** oxygen **c** calcium **d** chlorine?

Key ideas

The elements can be arranged in order of atomic number.

There is a repeating pattern of similar elements every eight places. Similar elements are put into the same **group**.

5c The periodic table

A bigger table

The pattern of similar elements gets more complicated after the first 20 elements. The groups of similar elements continue, but the the simple 'count to eight' rule is lost. A large block of metals wedges in between groups II and III.

The complete table is very useful. Instead of having to remember what all 92 elements are like, you just need to know the family groups. The position of an element in the table tells you a lot about its properties. Because of the way the pattern repeats, the table is called the **periodic table**.

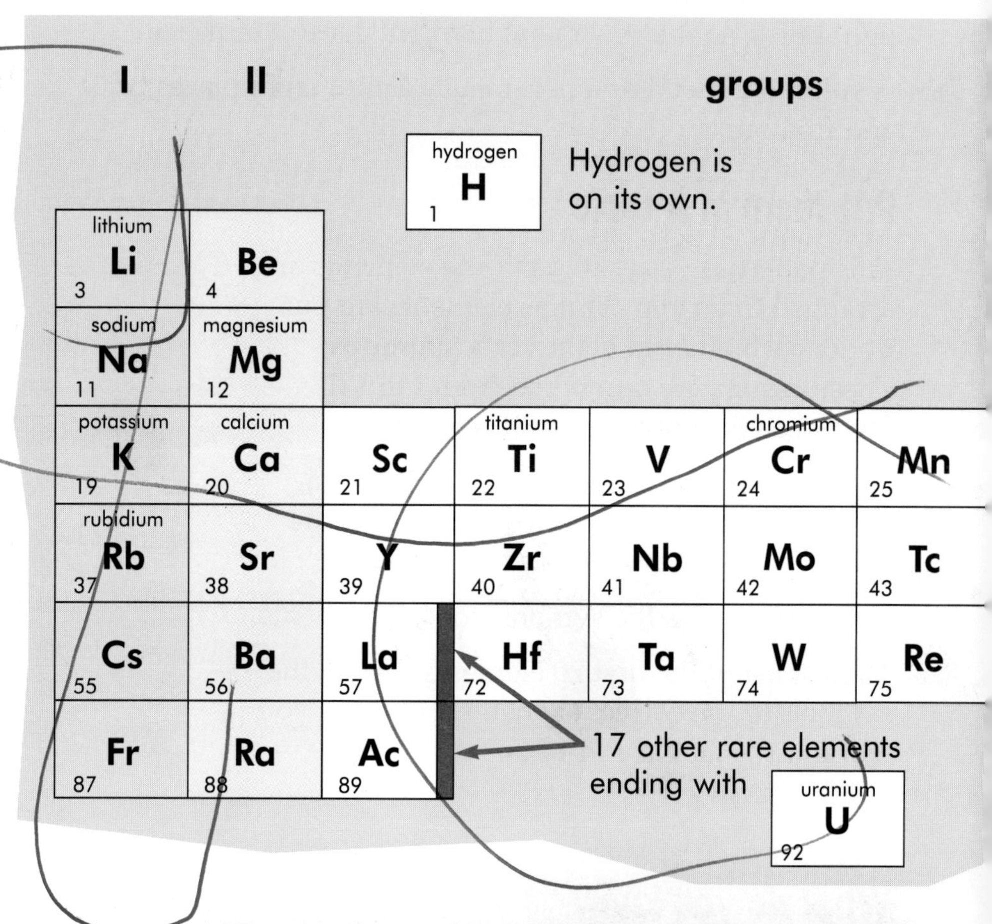

Mainly metals

Group I is a family of soft metals with low densities. They are very reactive. They react with water, giving off hydrogen gas. The solution that is formed is alkaline. Because of this, they are called the **alkali metals**. Sodium (Na) and potassium (K) are in group I.

The block wedged between groups II and III contains more metals. These include the hard, dense and strong metals such as iron (Fe) and copper (Cu).

Sodium

Metals and non-metals

Most elements are metals. The metals are found to the left of the zig-zag line that runs through the table. The non-metals are to the right of this line.

The only gases are found at the top right of the table, and all the way down group VIII (the **noble gases**).

Group VII

Group VII contains a family of very reactive non-metals. They include chlorine (Cl) which is a poisonous, greenish gas.

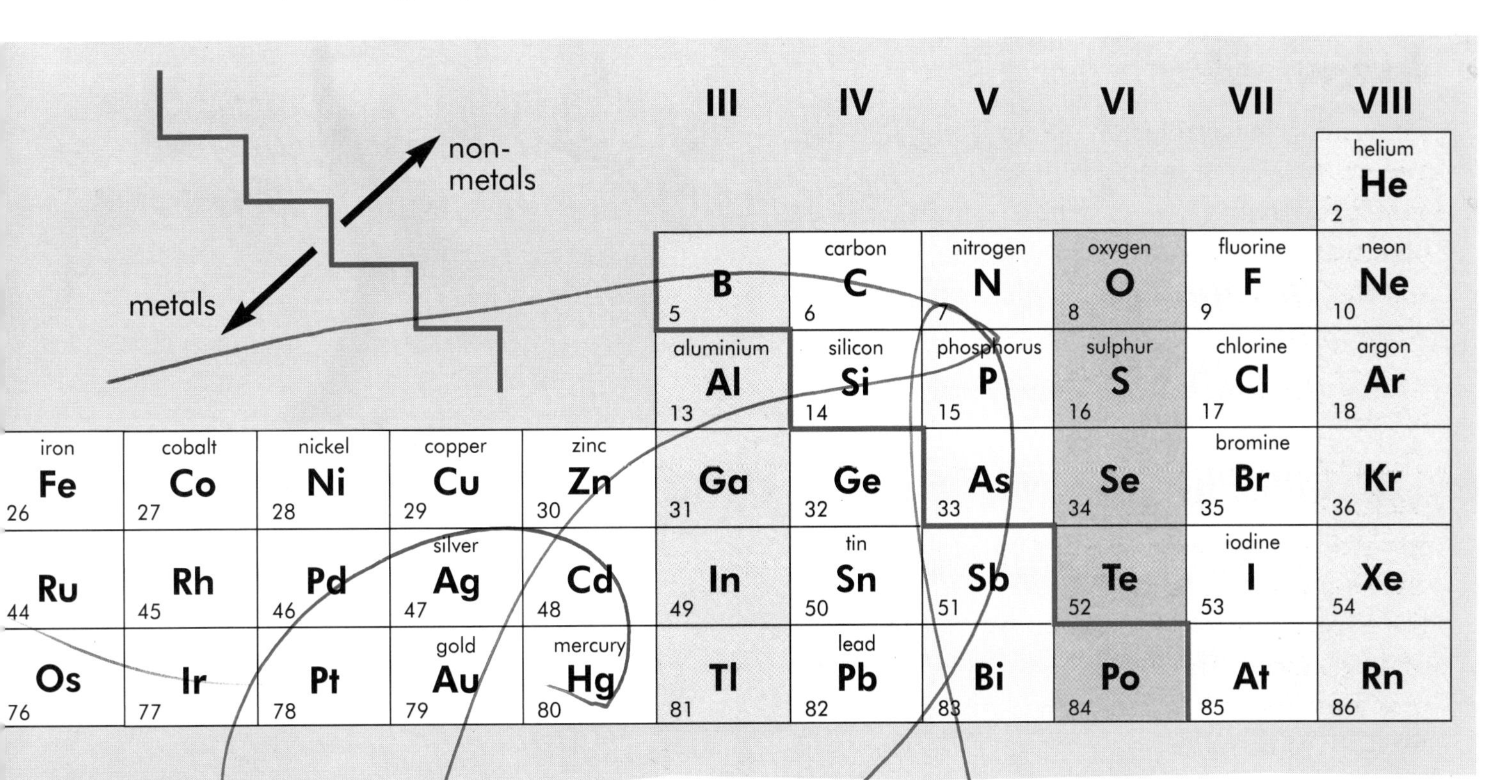

What do you know?

1 Find the following elements in the periodic table. For each, say whether it is a metal or a non-metal.

a vanadium (V)
b caesium (Cs)
c boron (B)
d cadmium (Cd)
e arsenic (As)

2 Which metal do you think would be harder, rubidium (Rb) or molybdenum (Mo)?

3 What kind of element is krypton (Kr)?

4 The family groups are more clear cut at the ends of the periodic table. What is odd about the middle groups? (Hint: compare carbon (C) and lead (Pb) in group IV.)

Key ideas

The **periodic table** shows all the elements in family **groups**.

Metals are to the left of the table and non-metals to the right.

The simple pattern of vertical groups is broken by a block of metallic elements.

Looking at compounds

A shorthand for compounds

You can draw pictures of compounds like the ones on page 66 to show what atoms they contain. This is easy for simple compounds like water. But some compounds are not so easy to draw like this.

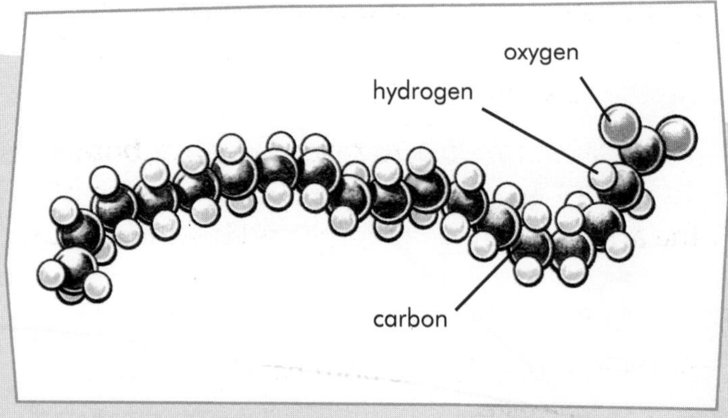

Picture of a soap molecule

a **1** How many carbon, hydrogen and oxygen atoms are there in this soap molecule?

2 Was it easy to count them?

Instead of drawing diagrams, you can use symbols. You show how many atoms there are by writing the number after the symbol below the line, as shown. You do not bother to write the number if it is 1. This shorthand way of writing a compound is called a **chemical formula**.

b Look at these examples. What is the chemical formula for carbon dioxide?

picture	atoms	formula
water	2 hydrogen (H) + 1 oxygen (O)	H_2O
methane	1 carbon (C) + 4 hydrogen (H)	CH_4
carbon dioxide	1 carbon (C) + 2 oxygen (O)	?

Chemical combinations

Each chemical compound has its own formula. This formula tells you which atoms make up the compound. This always stays the same. If you have a different combination of atoms, you have a different compound!

sulphuric acid: H_2SO_4

This means that every sulphuric acid molecule contains two hydrogen atoms, one sulphur atom and four oxygen atoms.

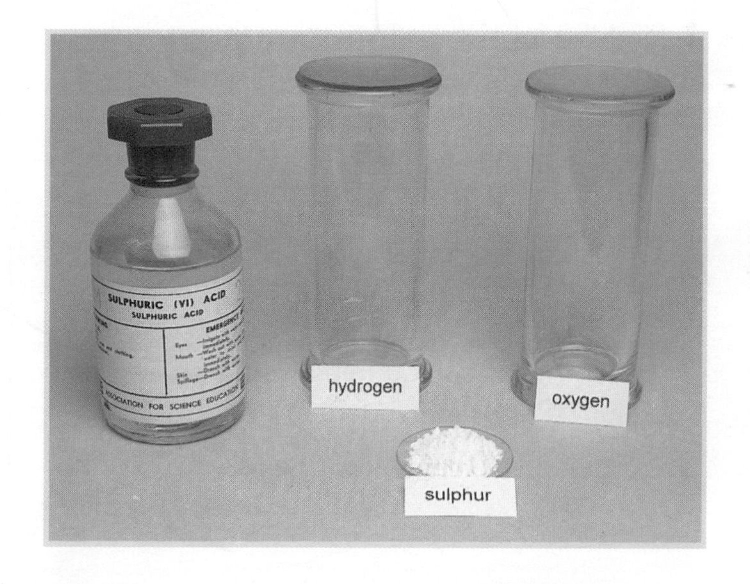

Linking arms

Why do four hydrogens join to carbon in methane, but only two hydrogens join to oxygen in water? You can think of atoms as having different numbers of arms. Some atoms, such as hydrogen, have only one arm. Others, such as oxygen, have two arms, and carbon has four.

These arms can link to form **chemical bonds**. To make a compound, you have to use up all the arms and make the right number of bonds.

water
two hydrogen → H_2O ← one oxygen

methane
one carbon → CH_4 ← four hydrogen

carbon dioxide
one carbon → CO_2 ← two oxygen

Sodium and chlorine both have one arm, so sodium chloride is NaCl.

Calcium has two arms, so each calcium atom can hold onto two chlorine atoms. Calcium chloride is $CaCl_2$.

Oxygen has two arms, so one oxygen atom can hold onto two sodium atoms. Sodium oxide is Na_2O.

In calcium oxide, both partners have two arms. They can do a 'double handshake' and form a double bond. Calcium oxide is CaO.

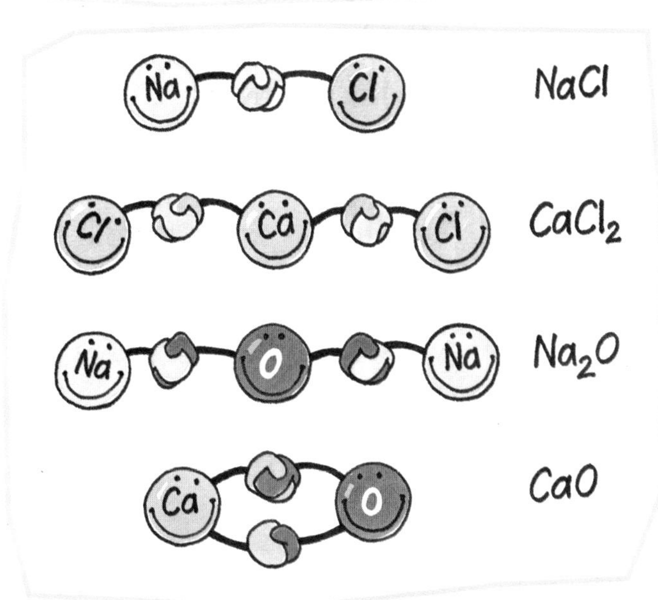

What do you know?

1 What is the chemical formula of:
a methane **b** sulphuric acid **c** salt?

2 How many of each type of atom are there in a molecule of:
a sulphur dioxide (SO_2) **b** ethanol (C_2H_5OH)
c phosphoric acid (H_3PO_4)?

3 Iodine (I) has one arm. What is the formula of:
a sodium iodide **b** calcium iodide?

4 Aluminium (Al) has three arms. What is the formula of:
a aluminium chloride **b** aluminium oxide?
(Hint: you must use up all the arms!)

Key ideas

The **chemical formula** of a compound shows how many of each type of atom are in the compound.

You can work out the formula of some simple compounds if you know the number of arms of the atoms.

5e Reactions in balance

Making a compound

Some compounds can be made directly from their elements. You can make iron sulphide by heating iron filings and sulphur in a test tube.

iron + sulphur ⟶ iron sulphide

a What are the symbols for iron and sulphur?

Joining together

You start with one atom of iron and one of sulphur. You end with one atom of iron and one of sulphur. The only difference is that they have joined together.

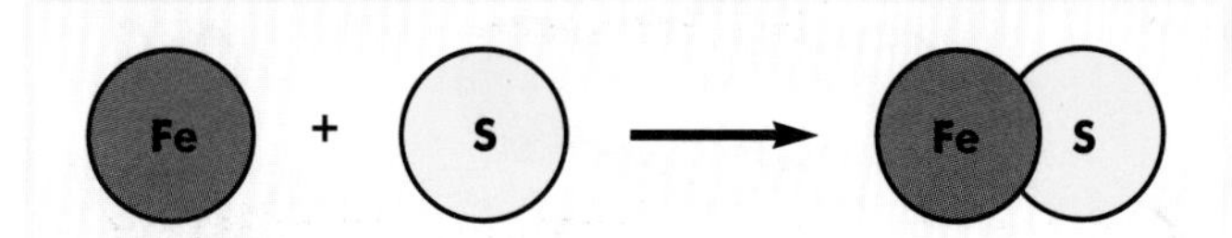

This simple reaction is being repeated billions of times in your test tube, but the total number of particles stays the same.

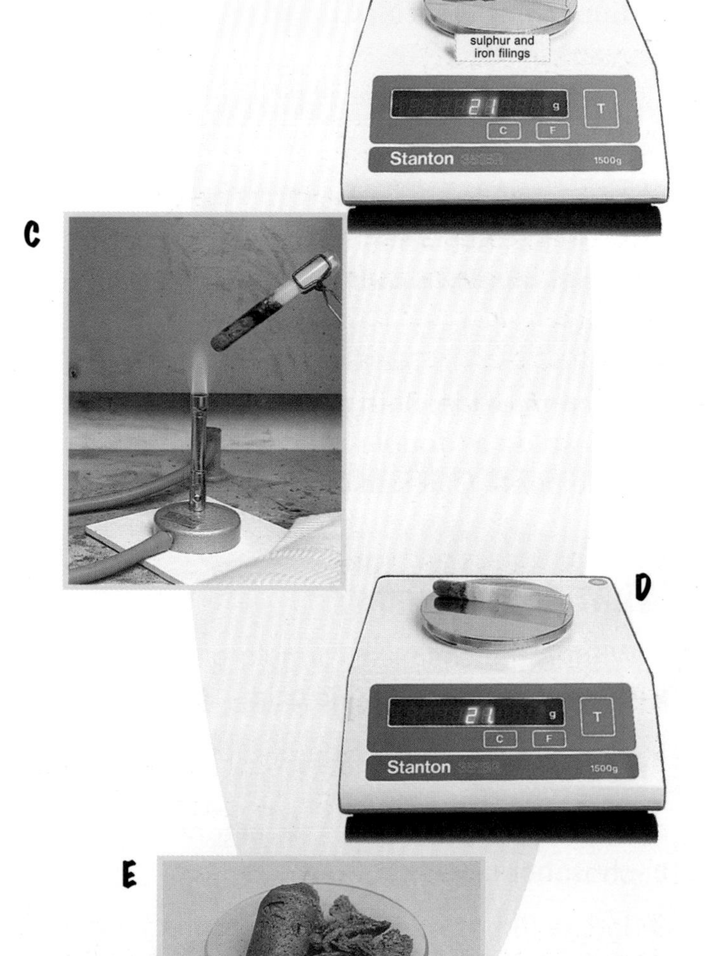

Chemical equations

You can write this reaction using chemical symbols and formulae. You write the **reactants** on the left and the **product** on the right. This is called a **chemical equation**.

$$Fe + S \longrightarrow FeS$$

There are the same number of atoms on the left and on the right. The equation is **balanced**.

The mass stays the same

In any chemical reaction, the number of atoms does not change. They are just rearranged. The total mass stays the same.

Hydrochloric acid and sodium hydroxide react to give sodium chloride and water:

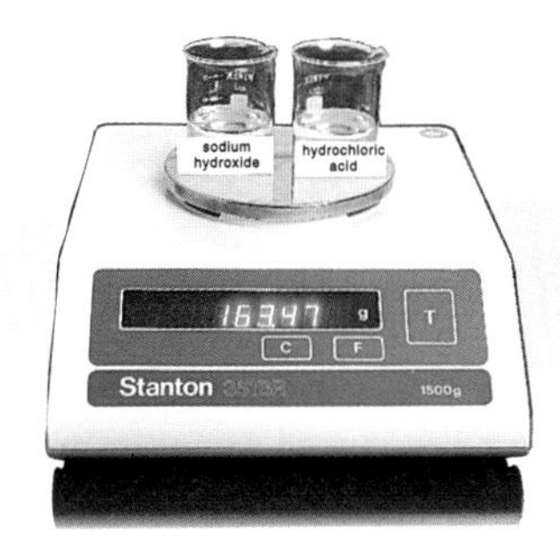

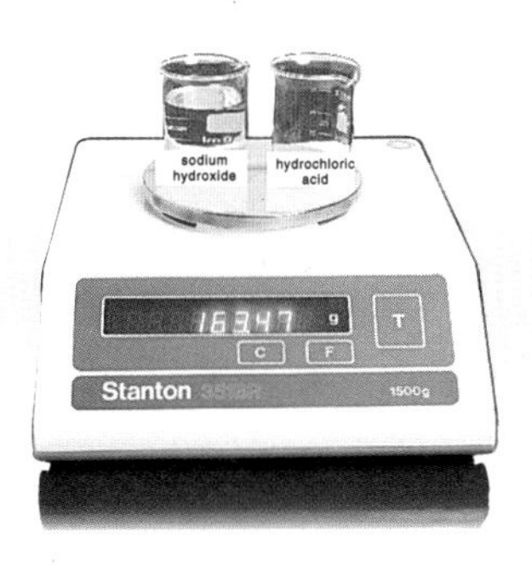

After pouring the acid into the sodium hydroxide solution, we no longer have the same chemicals, but we have the same mass.

hydrochloric acid + sodium hydroxide $\longrightarrow$ sodium chloride + water

b Look at the picture, then write down the formulae for hydrochloric acid, sodium hydroxide, sodium chloride and water.

H Cl Na O H

reactants

Na Cl H H O

products

a balanced equation

Escaping gases

If you burn a piece of coal, it seems to disappear! This is because the carbon dioxide formed in the reaction is a gas, which can escape into the air. If you could measure the mass of oxygen that was taken from the air, and the mass of carbon dioxide formed, the total mass would stay the same.

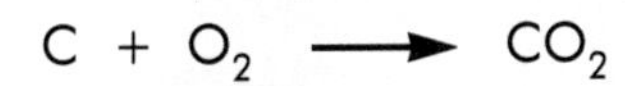

$$C + O_2 \longrightarrow CO_2$$

c Does this equation balance?

What do you know?

1 Copy and complete the following sentences. Use the words below to fill the gaps.

reactants atoms mass

In a chemical reaction, the ________ of the products is equal to the mass of the ________. This is because the total number of ________ stays the same.

2 When you heat magnesium ribbon in air, it burns to give white magnesium oxide. If you burn 2.4 g of magnesium, you get 4 g of magnesium oxide.

a Write this as a word equation.

b Why does the mass seem to go up?

Key ideas

In a chemical reaction, the total number of atoms stays the same. They are just rearranged into new compounds.

The mass of the **products** formed is equal to the mass of the **reactants**.

You can write a chemical reaction as a **balanced equation**.

EXTRAS

What's inside an atom?

Atoms are like miniature solar systems! Most of their mass is in the very centre of the atom, called the **nucleus**.

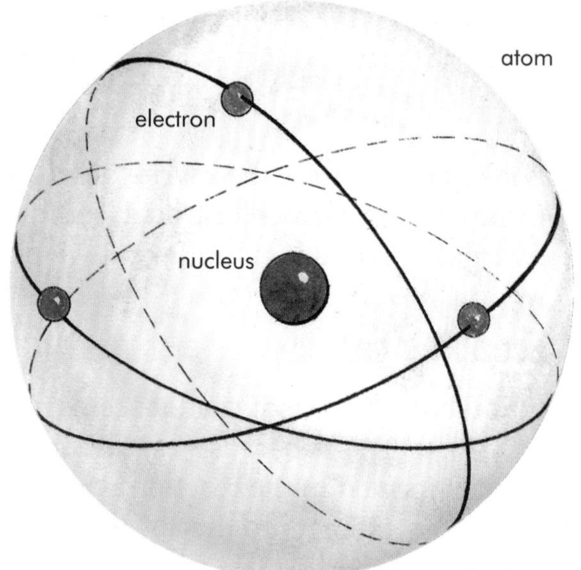

Whizzing around this nucleus are tiny particles that have an electrical charge. They are called **electrons**. These are the charged particles that move when an electric current flows.

The nucleus of the atom has a positive (+) charge. This is balanced out by the negative (–) charge on the electrons.

What's in the nucleus?

The nucleus contains positively charged particles called **protons**. The atoms of different elements have different numbers of protons. Atoms are neutral. There is one electron for every proton in the atom, balancing out the charge.

All the atoms of one element have the same number of protons. All hydrogen atoms have one proton, all helium atoms have two protons, and so on.

The atomic number of an element tells you how many protons it has in each nucleus.

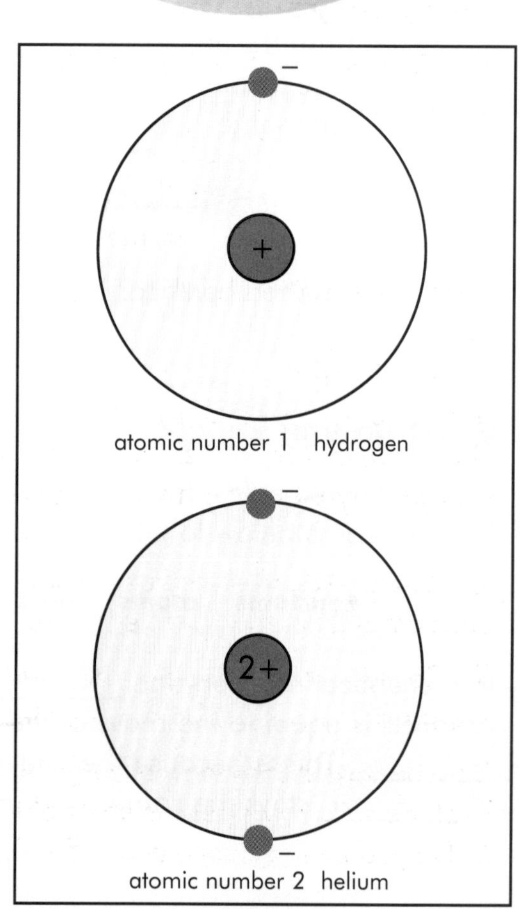

1 How many protons are there in an atom of:
a oxygen **b** argon **c** sodium
d iodine **e** lead **f** uranium?

2 How many electrons are there whizzing round an atom of:
a carbon **b** magnesium **c** iron **d** gold?

3 Sometimes electrons can be knocked off atoms. What would happen to the overall charge on an atom that loses an electron?

The periodic table

In this periodic table, the middle block of metals has been left off. The pattern of metals and non-metals is very clear.

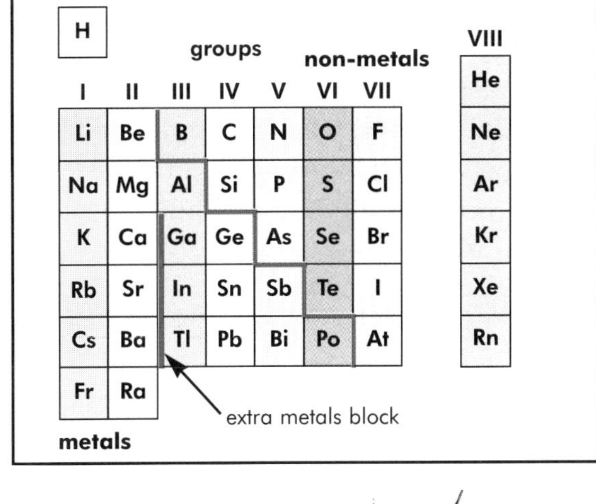

I	II	III	IV	V	VI	VII	VIII
H							He
Li	Be	B	C	N	O	F	Ne
Na	Mg	Al	Si	P	S	Cl	Ar
K	Ca	Ga	Ge	As	Se	Br	Kr
Rb	Sr	In	Sn	Sb	Te	I	Xe
Cs	Ba	Tl	Pb	Bi	Po	At	Rn
Fr	Ra						

Going down group I

All the alkali metals react with water, giving off hydrogen. These metals become more reactive as you go down the table.

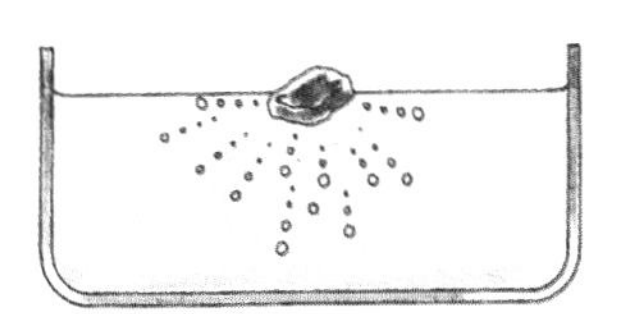

Lithium fizzes rapidly.

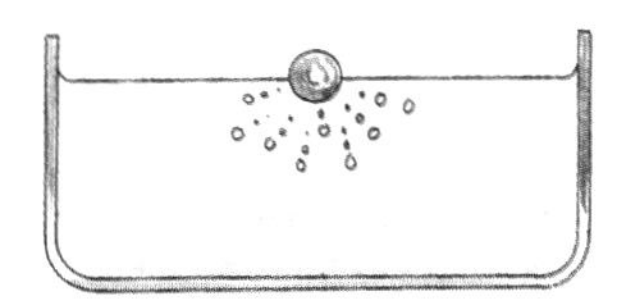

Sodium reacts so fast it melts and forms a silver ball that floats. If you trap it on paper, the hydrogen burns.

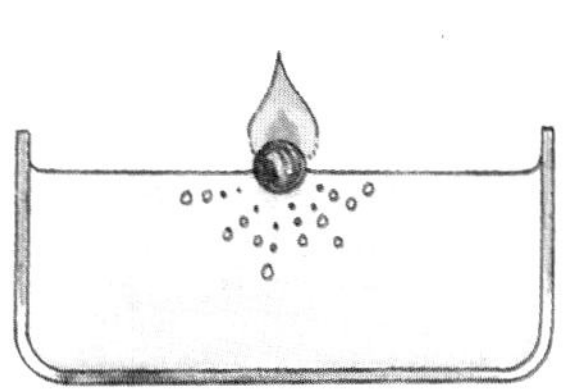

Potassium reacts so violently that the hydrogen catches fire at once.

Rubidium would react explosively. It is too dangerous to use at school.

Going up group VII

- Iodine is a solid. It only reacts with hydrogen if heated strongly.
- Bromine is a brown liquid. Bromine vapour will react with hydrogen.
- Chlorine is a gas. Chlorine and hydrogen do not react in the dark, but will explode in sunlight.
- Fluorine is a gas. Fluorine explodes if you mix it with hydrogen.

These non-metals become more reactive as you go up the table.

In the middle

In the middle groups, the elements gradually change from non-metals to metals down the group. The photograph shows this for group IV.

carbon (C) silicon (Si) germanium (Ge) tin (Sn) lead (Pb)

4 Why do schools not keep a supply of caesium (Cs) in the science laboratory?

5 Calcium reacts steadily with water. Would strontium (Sr) be more or less reactive?

6a Charlotte thinks that astatine (At) would explode with hydrogen. Is she right?

b Do you think astatine is a solid, liquid or gas?

7 Metals become more reactive towards the bottom left of the periodic table. Ignoring group VIII, non-metals become more reactive towards the top right of the periodic table. Which is the most reactive of all the non-metals?

8 Is bismuth (Bi) a metal or a non-metal?

5d Looking at salts

A salt is formed when a metal reacts with an acid. The salt contains the metal and a part that comes from the acid. In some cases, this part is just a single atom. For example, hydrochloric acid gives chloride salts. In these, a one-armed chlorine atom joins to the metal.

With other acids, a group of atoms stay together during the reaction. For example, nitric acid gives salts called nitrates. The nitrate group has one nitrogen atom joined to three oxygen atoms. It can be written as:

$$-NO_3$$

The nitrate group behaves like one atom, with one arm free to make bonds.

In the salt sodium nitrate, both the sodium and the nitrate group have one arm, so the formula is simple:

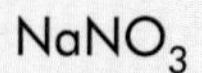

$$NaNO_3$$

In the salt copper nitrate, copper has two arms. So every copper atom can hold two nitrate groups.

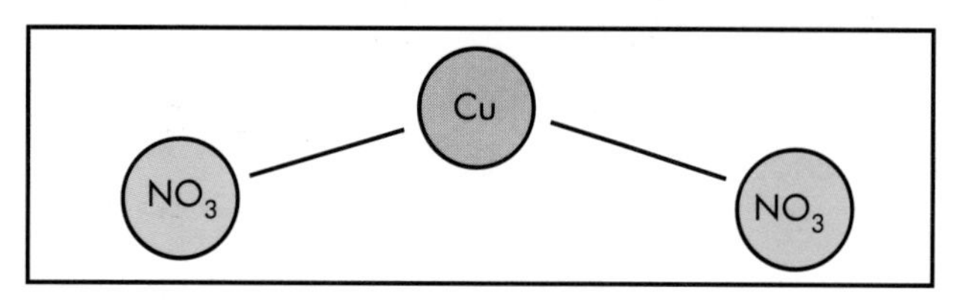

You show this in the formula by putting the nitrate part in brackets:

$$Cu(NO_3)_2$$

The table shows the arm numbers for some metals and some acid groups.

Metals		
1	**2**	**3**
sodium (Na) potassium (K)	calcium (Ca) copper(II) (Cu) magnesium (Mg)	aluminium (Al) iron(III) (Fe)
Acid groups		
1	**2**	**3**
nitrate (NO_3) hydroxide (OH)	sulphate (SO_4) carbonate (CO_3)	phosphate (PO_4)

1a What atoms make up the sulphate group?
b Hydrochloric acid has the formula HCl. Why does sulphuric acid have the formula H_2SO_4 rather than HSO_4?

2 Write the formula for each of these compounds.
a sodium hydroxide **b** potassium nitrate **c** calcium sulphate **d** copper(II) carbonate
e sodium sulphate **f** potassium carbonate **g** calcium nitrate **h** copper(II) hydroxide
i iron(III) nitrate **j** aluminium phosphate **k** aluminium sulphate

5e Balancing equations

A balanced equation has the same number of each type of atom on both sides. Some equations are balanced when you first write them, for example, burning carbon in oxygen:

$$C + O_2 \longrightarrow CO_2$$

Other equations, like the one for burning hydrogen in oxygen to power the Space Shuttle, are trickier. But you can write balanced equations if you follow these simple rules.

1 Write down a word equation for the reaction. For hydrogen burning in oxygen, you would write:

2 Work out the formulae of the reactants and products. Hydrogen and oxygen are both found as molecules with two atoms each:

3 Count up the atoms. Do you have the same number of each type on both sides? In this case, no!

4 You need an extra oxygen on the right. You show this by putting a large 2 in front of the formula for water. This means 'two molecules of'.

5 Does it balance? Again, no! Now you have four hydrogen atoms on the right and only two on the left. You need to start with two molecules of hydrogen.

6 Now the equation is balanced.

Which of these reactions is easier to balance? Read on and find out.

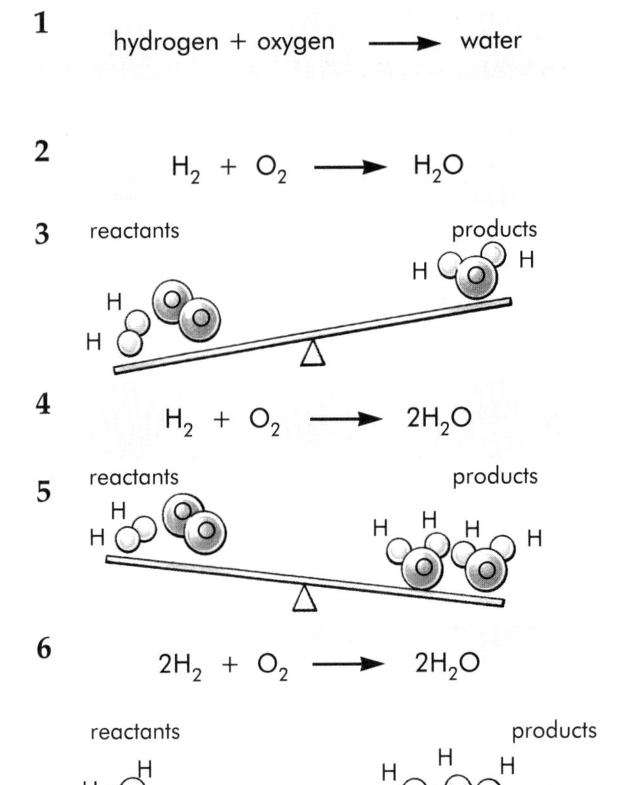

1 Write a balanced equation for the reaction:

magnesium + oxygen ⟶ magnesium oxide

(Hint: start with a single atom of magnesium and a molecule of oxygen. You will have to work out the formula of magnesium oxide.)

2 Write a balanced equation for each of these reactions:

a magnesium reacting with chlorine gas

b sodium reacting with chlorine gas.

REVIEW

5a Looking at molecules

Many compounds are made up of molecules. The molecules are made up of atoms joined together.

The molecules in any one compound are made up of the same number and type of atoms. If you have a different molecule, you have a different compound.

You can draw pictures to represent molecules. Another way of showing molecules is to draw them flattened out on the page. They are easier to draw like this, and you can see clearly which atoms are there.

1 How many of each type of atom are there in a molecule of:
a methane **b** ammonia **c** calcium carbonate?

atoms

hydrogen

carbon

nitrogen

oxygen

calcium

molecules

'realistic' picture | flattened out picture

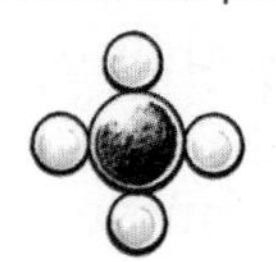
methane

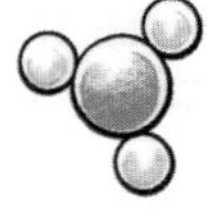
ammonia

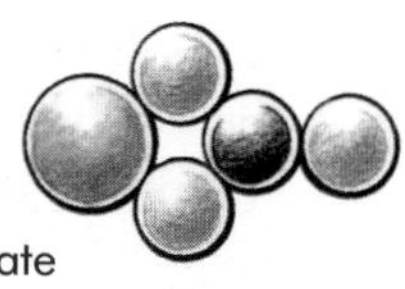
calcium carbonate

5b Using symbols

Each element has its own **symbol** of one or two letters to represent its atoms.

The symbols of some common elements are just the first letter of their name:

C is for carbon O is for oxygen H is for hydrogen

Some use two letters from the name:

Ca is for calcium Mg is for magnesium

The first (or only) letter is always a capital (big) letter. The second letter is always a small letter.

S is for sulphur Zn is for zinc

Some elements have symbols that are nothing like their name. These symbols come from old names that are no longer used.

Pb is for lead Fe is for iron Na is for sodium

1 Why can't the symbol S be used for sodium?

2 Plumbers used to work with pipes made from a metal with the 'old' name plumbum. What name do we use for that metal today?

Mixture or compound?

If you mix cold hydrogen and oxygen gases together, you just get a simple mixture. Both gases keep their properties.

But all it takes is a spark or a flame to set off an explosion in the mixture. A chemical reaction takes place. The hydrogen and oxygen combine chemically to make a new compound, hydrogen oxide – water!

When elements combine, they lose their own properties and form a new compound with a new set of properties.

1 Compare the properties of water with the properties of hydrogen and oxygen.

Writing word equations

To write a word equation, you first need to think about the chemicals you are starting with. These chemicals are the **reactants**. In the reaction shown above, the reactants are hydrogen and oxygen.

reactants: hydrogen and oxygen

You then need to think of what is being formed in the reaction. These are the **products**. In the reaction shown above, there is only one product – water.

products: water only

You then write the names of the reactants on the left and the products on the right, linked by an arrow. This shows the way the reaction is going.

reactants $\longrightarrow$ products

hydrogen + oxygen $\longrightarrow$ water

Over the arrow, you can write any other information about the reaction. For this reaction you could write 'combustion', as this is a combustion reaction.

hydrogen + oxygen $\xrightarrow{\text{combustion}}$ water

1 Write word equations for these reactions:
a the iron filings on a sparkler burn in the oxygen in the air to give iron oxide
b carbon reacts with iron oxide to give carbon dioxide and iron metal
c magnesium dissolves in hydrochloric acid to give hydrogen gas and magnesium chloride

6a Burning metals

Magnesium

If you hold a piece of magnesium ribbon in a flame, it starts to burn with a bright white light. The magnesium is reacting with the oxygen in the air. It is being **oxidised** to magnesium oxide. Many metals react like this:

metal + oxygen ⟶ metal oxide

Sodium

How fast?

Some metals react with oxygen very vigorously, and others react very slowly or not at all.

Sodium metal reacts rapidly with the oxygen in the air, even at low temperatures. It has to be stored under oil to keep it away from the air.

a Write a word equation for sodium burning in oxygen.

Magnesium metal burns well in a Bunsen burner flame, but you can store it open to the air. You have probably seen rolls of magnesium ribbon in the laboratory.

Strips of iron do not burn. But fine iron wool will burn if you hold it in a Bunsen burner flame. The same thing happens to the iron filings in sparklers.

Iron

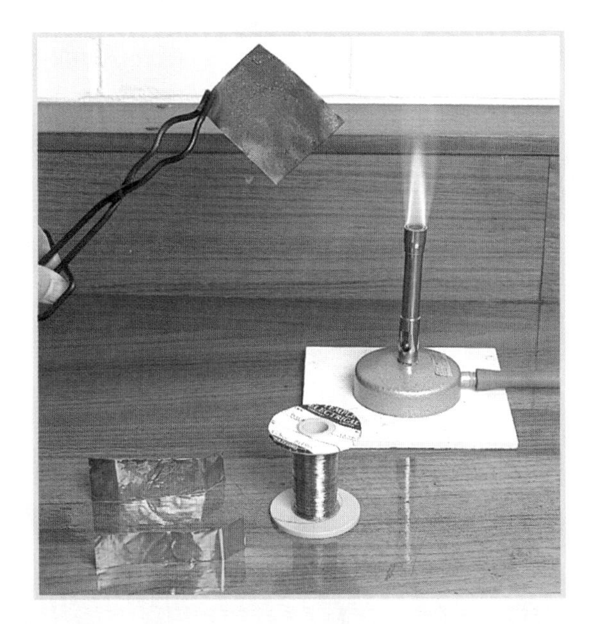

Copper does not seem to burn, but a layer of black copper oxide forms if you heat it. Copper does react, but only very slowly.

Gold does not react with the oxygen in the air at all, even if you heat it. Gold keeps its shine. This is why it is used for jewellery.

Putting them in order

You can put metals in order of **reactivity**, or how easily they react. In the reaction with oxygen, sodium is the most **reactive**, and gold is the least reactive.

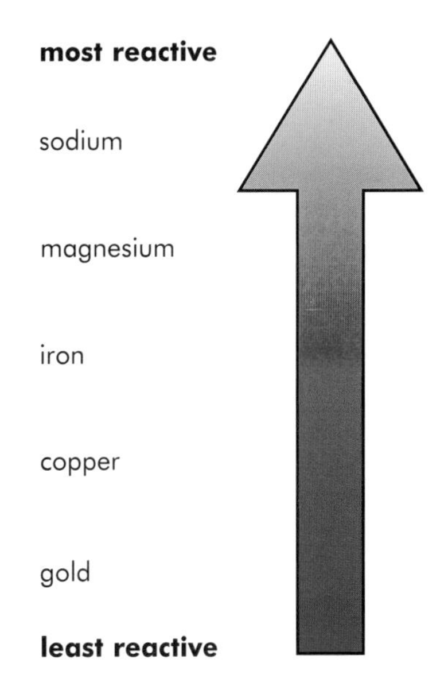

What do you know?

1 Potassium is stored under oil. Which metal is it likely to be closer to in the order of reactivity, sodium or iron?

2 Platinum is used for jewellery as it keeps its shine well. Is it closer to copper or gold in the order of reactivity?

3 Zinc reacts in a similar way to iron. Zinc powder burns well in a Bunsen burner flame. Would it be dangerous to leave large pieces of zinc lying around in the laboratory?

Key ideas

Some metals are more **reactive** than others – they react more easily.

Metals can be arranged in order of reactivity.

6b Fizzing furiously

Reacting with water

Some metals react with water. They take the place of hydrogen in the water. Some metals react with water very vigorously, and others react very slowly or not at all.

- Potassium reacts very violently. The hydrogen catches fire and burns with a lilac flame.
- Sodium also reacts violently, forming a molten ball which whizzes round on the surface of the water. If this ball is trapped on filter paper, the hydrogen will catch fire, but this time the flame is orange.
- Calcium fizzes steadily in cold water.
- Magnesium produces a few bubbles in hot water, and reacts well with steam.
- Iron rusts slowly with water and air.

Potassium is the most reactive metal you are ever likely to meet.

a Write these five metals in order of reactivity for the reaction with water.

Reacting with acid

Metals can also take the place of hydrogen from an acid. With dilute sulphuric acid:

- Sodium reacts explosively.

> ⚠ **Take care**
> Never try this in the Science laboratory.

- Magnesium reacts very rapidly, fizzing furiously.
- Iron reacts steadily, fizzing gently.
- Copper and gold do not react at all.

This is as close as they should ever get!

b **1** Write these four metals in order of reactivity for the reaction with dilute sulphuric acid.

2 How does this list compare with the one from question **a**?

Reactivity series

You probably found that the order of reactivity is the same for the reaction with water and the reaction with acid. It is also the same for burning in oxygen, and for many other reactions. The metals you have looked at and other metals are arranged in order of reactivity to give the **reactivity series** for metals. You can use the reactivity series to predict how a metal will react.

Metal	With oxygen	With water	With dilute acid	Reactivity
potassium	burn very easily – have to be stored under oil	react violently	react very violently – too dangerous to try	most reactive
sodium				
calcium		fizzes steadily	fizz very rapidly	
magnesium	burns well when heated	fizzes slowly		
zinc	burn if in tiny pieces	no visible reaction	fizz steadily	
iron				
lead	form an oxide layer if heated in air		reacts slowly	
copper		no reaction	no reaction	
gold	no reaction			least reactive

What do you know?

1 Mercury comes below copper in the reactivity series. Will mercury react with dilute acid?

2 Lithium fizzes rapidly in cold water, but does not catch fire. Is it above or below sodium in the reactivity series?

3 You can make hydrogen gas in the laboratory by dissolving a metal in dilute sulphuric acid and collecting the gas that forms. Which metal would you use, sodium, zinc or lead? Explain your answer.

Key ideas

The order of reactivity of metals is the same for all reactions. This order is called the **reactivity series** for metals.

6c Who's the bully?

The reactivity series can help you understand some other reactions of metals.

Chemical bullies

If you hang a copper wire in a colourless solution of silver nitrate, the solution gradually turns blue, while beautiful crystals of silver metal grow out from the wire.

The copper has acted as a 'chemical bully', pushing the silver from its salt. It **displaces** the silver. This is called a **displacement reaction**.

copper + silver nitrate ⟶ silver + copper nitrate

This reaction happens because copper is more reactive than silver. Silver is below copper in the reactivity series.

a An iron nail gets coated with copper if you dip it into copper sulphate solution. Why does this happen?

Bullying acids

All acids contain hydrogen. When a metal reacts with an acid, the metal displaces the hydrogen.

You can add hydrogen to the reactivity series. It comes below metals such as zinc and iron.

b Copper can never displace hydrogen from an acid. Is copper above or below hydrogen in the reactivity series?

Getting out the metal

Carbon can be used to displace some metals from their ores. This method is relatively cheap. It works for iron, because carbon is above iron in the reactivity series.

Iron is produced in a blast furnace. The reaction inside takes place in stages, but overall the carbon displaces the iron.

iron oxide + carbon ⟶ iron + carbon dioxide

Sodium and aluminium are above carbon in the reactivity series, so carbon cannot be used to displace them from their ores.

c Find the order of the reactivity series for yourself. This chart shows what happens when different metals are dipped into a variety of metal salt solutions. To find the order, simply count the ticks in each metal's column. The metal with the most ticks is the most reactive.

Solutions	Metals				
	copper	lead	iron	zinc	magnesium
copper sulphate	-	✓	✓	✓	✓
magnesium sulphate	✗	✗	✗	✗	-
lead nitrate	✗	-	✓	✓	✓
sodium sulphate	✗	✗	✗	✗	✗
iron sulphate	✗	✗	-	✓	✓
zinc sulphate	✗	✗	✗	-	✓

What do you know?

1 Copy and complete this simple reactivity series. Put hydrogen and carbon in the correct places.

magnesium _______ **iron** _______ **copper**

2a From the information given on these two pages, arrange carbon, hydrogen and all the metals mentioned in order of reactivity. (Aluminium comes just under magnesium.)
b Compare this order with the one on page 85. Is it the same?

3 None of the metals in the table above can displace sodium from its salt. What does this tell you about the position of sodium in the series?

4 Is it possible to get lead from its ore by carbon displacement? How do you know?

Key ideas

A more reactive element can push a less reactive element from its compounds in a **displacement** reaction. For example:

A more reactive metal can displace a less reactive metal from its salts.

Reactive metals can displace hydrogen from acids.

Carbon can displace some less reactive metals from their ores.

6d Breaking up by heating

Mercury oxide is a red compound of mercury and oxygen. The two elements are only weakly held together. If you heat this compound, it breaks up, giving you the metal mercury.

mercury oxide $\xrightarrow{\text{heat}}$ mercury + oxygen

Mercury oxide

Mercury

Rust is a red compound of iron and oxygen. If you heat this, you just get hot rust! You cannot get the metal iron in this way.

iron oxide $\xrightarrow{\text{heat}}$ iron oxide (no change)

a Why are some compounds easy to split up, while others are not?

Iron oxide

No change

The magnet model

Some magnets are very weak. They are hardly able to pick up anything. If they do pick up a paper clip or pin, it is very easy to shake it off.

Other magnets are very strong. They will pull things towards them from a distance. Once something is stuck to the magnet, it is very difficult to pull it off.

You can use these ideas to understand about metals and their compounds. Mercury is like a weak magnet. It is an unreactive metal. It does not join with other atoms very easily. If it does, the new compounds are weak, and can easily be pulled apart.

Iron is like a strong magnet. It is a more reactive metal. It joins with other atoms very easily. The compounds that are formed are strongly held together. You cannot easily pull them apart.

Reactive metals form unreactive compounds.

Holding on to carbonates

Carbonates have three oxygen atoms bonded to one carbon atom. With a very reactive metal like sodium, they are held very tightly. You cannot break up sodium carbonate by heating it.

Copper is not so reactive, so its carbonate is not held together so strongly. If you heat copper carbonate, it breaks up. Two oxygen atoms and the carbon atom break free as a carbon dioxide molecule. Copper oxide is left behind.

b Where does the carbon dioxide go?

copper carbonate (green solid)	$\xrightarrow{\text{heat}}$	copper oxide (black solid)	+	carbon dioxide (colourless gas)

Calcium carbonate also breaks up if you heat it.

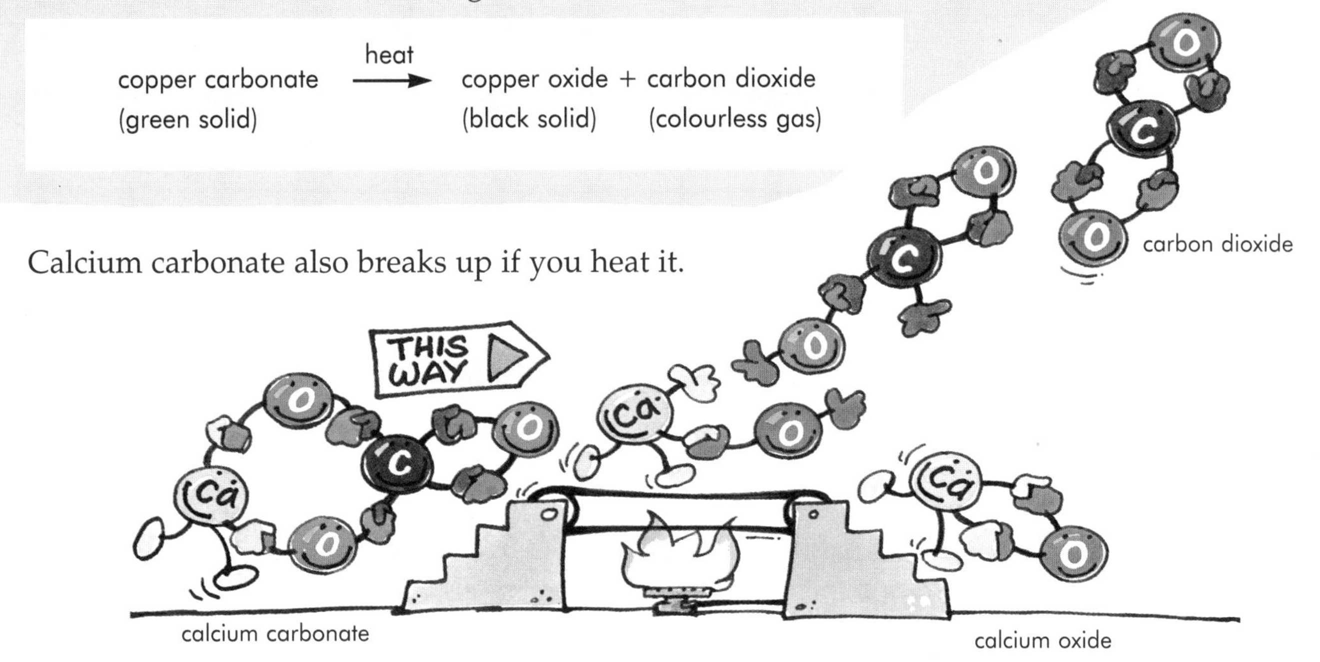

What do you know?

1 Copy and complete the following sentence. Choose the correct word from each pair. There are two correct answers! Can you find them both?

Reactive/unreactive atoms form compounds that are **easy/hard** to break up.

2 Potassium is more reactive than sodium. Lead is less reactive than calcium.

a Which of these compounds would you expect to break up when heated?

i potassium carbonate **ii** lead carbonate

b Write a word equation for this reaction.

Key ideas

Reactive metals make strong compounds which are hard to break up.

Unreactive metals make weak compounds which are easy to break up.

Many metal carbonates break up when you heat them, giving off carbon dioxide gas.

6e Discovering metals

Metal	Percentage of Earth's crust	Date discovered
aluminium	7	170 years ago
iron	4	3000 years ago
sodium	2.5	90 years ago
magnesium	2	130 years ago
zinc	0.007	2000 years ago
copper	0.0045	7000 years ago
lead	0.0015	6500 years ago
tin	0.0002	6000 years ago
gold	0.000 000 5	10 000 years ago

Rare and precious

If you counted all the metal atoms in the Earth's crust, you would find more iron and aluminium atoms than all the other metals put together.

The table shows that many of the metals that you know, such as copper or gold, are really very rare.

The moment of discovery

You might think that the more common metals would have been discovered first, but that is not the case. Gold was discovered thousands of years before aluminium. How could that be?

Aluminium is a very reactive metal. Because of this, the aluminium atoms are tightly locked up in compounds with other atoms such as oxygen and silicon. Mud contains plenty of aluminium, but you cannot easily get it out. You never find aluminium **uncombined** in the Earth's crust.

a There is plenty of aluminium in this mud. But how could you get it out?

Gold is a very unreactive metal. It does not combine with other elements. It may be rare but, if you are very lucky, you could find a nugget of pure gold embedded in the rock!

b Write the metals shown in the table in order of when they were discovered, starting with gold.

Your list of metals should look familiar. It is the reactivity series in reverse!

Gold was well known to the ancient Egyptians.

How were the metals discovered?

Unreactive metals such as gold and silver were discovered easily. This is because they are found uncombined or **native** – pure metal.

This nugget of gold was found in the ground.

The next metals to be discovered were fairly unreactive metals such as copper and tin. They are present in the Earth's crust in weak compounds that are easily broken up. A compound might have been broken up by chance, perhaps in the heat of a cooking fire.

More importantly, wood fires make charcoal, which is mostly carbon. Carbon is more reactive than tin or copper. Carbon can displace these metals from their compounds.

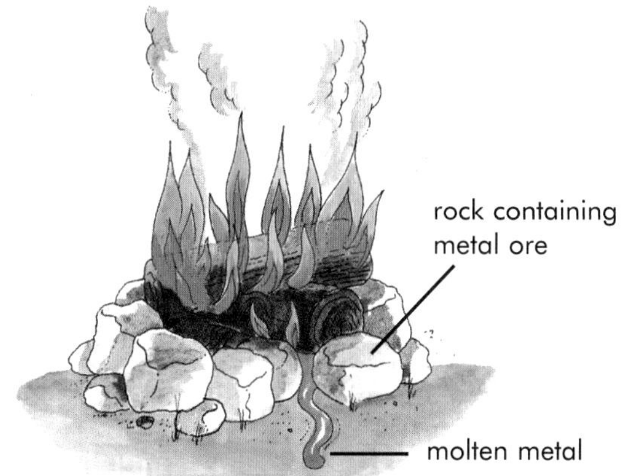

Carbon can also displace iron, but much higher temperatures are needed. Because of this, iron was discovered after copper and tin.

Carbon cannot displace aluminium, as aluminium is more reactive than carbon. Today, electricity is used to remove the metal from its molten oxide ore. The process is called electrolysis.

This Roman gladiator's sword has an iron blade. It is about 2000 years old.

What do you know?

1 Copy and complete this sentence. Choose the correct word from each pair.

Gold/aluminium was the first metal to be discovered because it was so **reactive/unreactive**.

2 Titanium makes up 0.6% of the Earth's crust, but was only discovered in 1791. Do you think it is closer to gold, copper or aluminium in the reactivity series?

3 The heat from a wood fire would help to split copper from its compounds. What else is there in a wood fire that would help this reaction?

Key ideas

Some metals are common in the Earth's crust, while others are rare.

Most metals are found locked up with other elements in compounds.

Only very unreactive metals such as gold are found as the **uncombined** metal in nature.

The unreactive metals were the first to be discovered.

6f Reactivity at work

Iron and steel . . .

Iron is the second most common metal in the Earth's crust. More iron is extracted and used than all the other metals put together.

Iron is usually used in the form of steel. Steel is iron with a little carbon added to make it stronger.

a There is more aluminium than iron in the Earth's crust. Why is iron used more than aluminium?

Steel is very strong. It can be used to make railway lines, bridges and machines. Steel girders support most modern buildings. But when it is hot, steel is quite soft and can be rolled, squashed or bent into shape. It is a very versatile material.

Iron has many uses . . .

. . . but it always ends up the same!

. . . rust away!

There is just one problem. Iron and steel rust. They react with water and the oxygen in the air to form flaky brown iron oxide.

In some metals such as aluminium, the oxide layer protects the metal. But rust blisters off, exposing fresh metal. So rusting can carry on until there is no metal left.

Get galvanised

Today most buckets are made from plastic and most baths from porcelain or fibreglass. In the past they were often made from steel protected by a thin layer of zinc. This **galvanised iron** was cheap to make and lasted well.

Zinc is more reactive than iron, but it quickly reacts with the air to form a tough surface layer. This stays in place and protects the metal. So a galvanised bucket is protected from rust, unless it gets scratched.

If it does get scratched, then water and air can get to the zinc and iron. However, the more reactive zinc starts to corrode, leaving the iron rust-free!

Galvanised bathtubs were cheap and long-lasting.

Protection by sacrifice

This idea is used to protect the steel hulls of ships. Large blocks of zinc are bolted directly onto the outside of the hull, below the water.

Sea water is very corrosive to metals. It can make iron rust very quickly. Again, the more reactive zinc corrodes, but the ship's hull stays rust-free. The zinc is 'sacrificed' to protect the iron.

b These 'sacrificial' zinc blocks often have to be replaced. Why is this?

What do you know?

1a List some of the reasons why iron and steel are used so much.

b Iron is produced by carbon displacement in a blast furnace. Aluminium has to be extracted from its molten ore using electricity. Iron is used more than aluminium. Explain how these facts are connected.

2 Write a simple word equation for the formation of rust (iron oxide).

3 Zinc is more reactive than iron. Why doesn't it corrode away on its own?

4 How is zinc used to protect ships' hulls?

Key ideas

Iron and steel are used more than all other metals put together, because they are so strong and versatile.

Iron and steel rust in air if water is present.

A zinc coating stops iron and steel rusting by keeping the air and water out.

Zinc can be 'sacrificed' to protect the steel of ships' hulls.

6 EXTRAS

6c Reactivity series

The reactivity series can help you to understand the pattern behind many chemical reactions. It can also help you to work out what might happen in reactions that you have not carried out yourself.

Use this 'full' version of the reactivity series to answer the following questions.

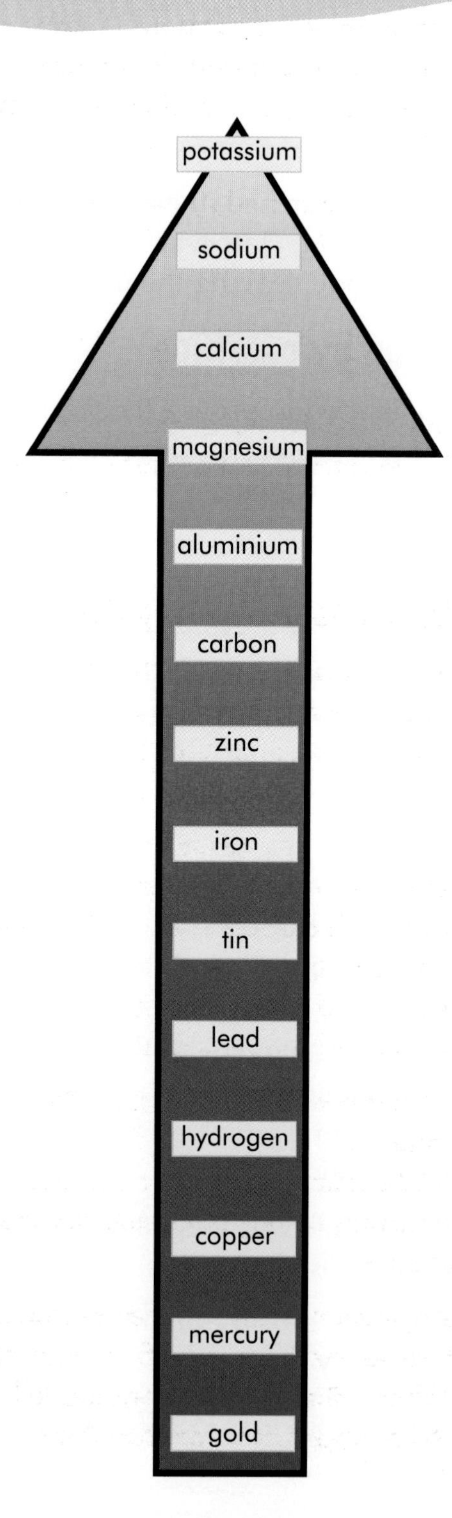

1 If a mixture of iron filings and sulphur are heated together, they react to give iron sulphide and the tube gets red-hot. Would it be safe to try this reaction with magnesium powder and sulphur? Why?

2 Mercury reacts with oxygen if you heat it in air, but gold and silver do not. Silver turns black in polluted air, but gold doesn't change. Where should silver go in the reactivity series?

3 Will mercury react with hydrochloric acid?

4 Metal X reacts slowly with warm hydrochloric acid, giving off hydrogen. If an iron nail is dipped into a solution of one of its salts, crystals of metal X start to form. Can you identify metal X from these reactions? If not, which metals could it be?

5 Aluminium can displace iron from its oxide. Which of the following metals could it also displace?

magnesium copper lead sodium tin

6 You can get iron from its ore by heating the ore very strongly with coal. What happens during this reaction?

7 Carbon displacement is relatively cheap. Why is it not used to get aluminium from its oxide ore?

Breaking up salts

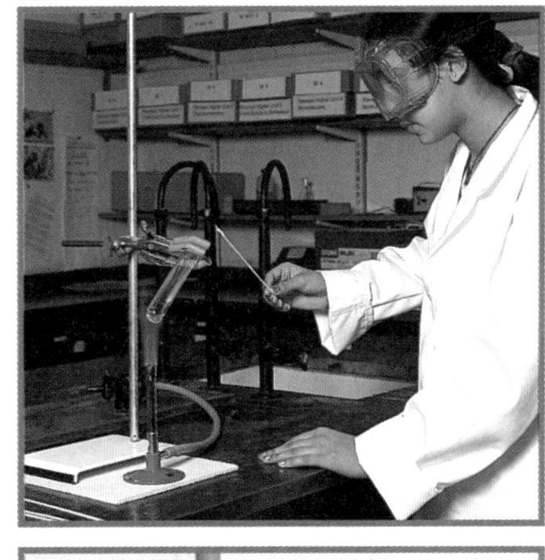

If you heat sodium chloride, it just melts. Sodium is a very reactive metal, so its salts are tightly bonded and cannot easily be split. You would need to use electricity to tear sodium chloride apart, using the process called electrolysis.

Some more complex salts, such as sodium nitrate ($NaNO_3$), do break up a little if you heat them. Nitrates have three oxygen atoms bonded to one nitrogen atom. When you heat sodium nitrate, one of these oxygen atoms breaks free.

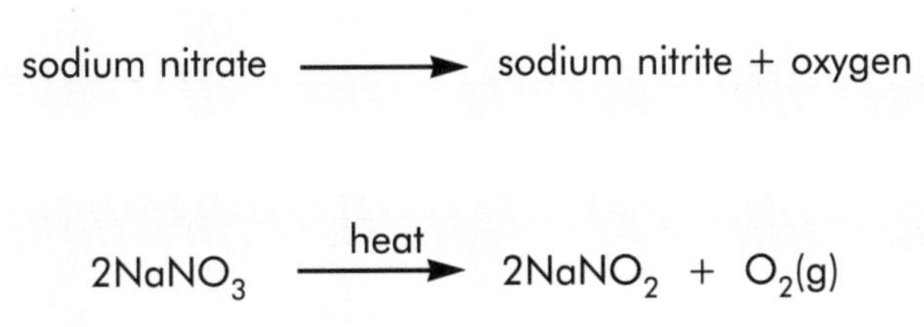

sodium nitrate $\longrightarrow$ sodium nitrite + oxygen

$$2NaNO_3 \xrightarrow{\text{heat}} 2NaNO_2 + O_2(g)$$

1 Why does this balanced chemical equation have to start with two particles of sodium nitrate?

A glowing split will re-light if you put it into a tube where sodium nitrate has been heated. This test shows that oxygen is being produced.

Light the blue touchpaper

The blue touchpaper on fireworks contains potassium nitrate. When it burns, the potassium nitrate breaks down, just like sodium nitrate. This provides extra oxygen to keep the paper burning, even if it is windy or wet!

The gunpowder inside many fireworks uses this same reaction to provide oxygen. Gunpowder contains potassium nitrate with carbon and sulphur. The oxygen from the potassium nitrate reacts with the carbon to give carbon dioxide, and with the sulphur to give sulphur dioxide – plus lots of heat and light!

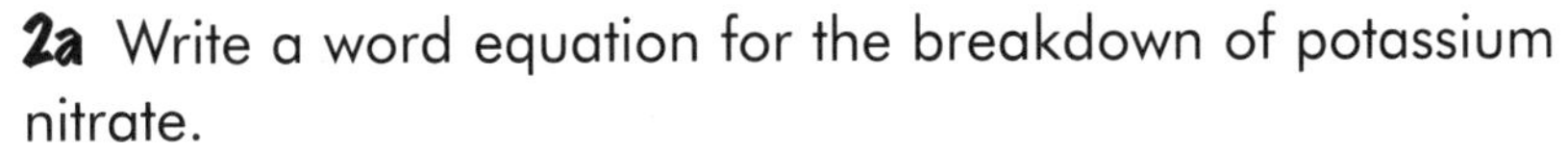

2a Write a word equation for the breakdown of potassium nitrate.
b Write a balanced chemical equation for this reaction. (Potassium, K, has the same number of bond arms as sodium.)

3 Any mist or rain around on bonfire night often has a low pH value, perhaps 4 or 5 instead of the usual 6.5.
a What does the low pH value tell you?
b What might have caused this?

6e Metals and technology

10 000 years ago Your early ancestors had to make tools from wood, bone or natural stone such as flint (a form of silica). Gold was used for decoration but had no real practical use. This period was called the **Stone Age**.

6–7000 years ago Copper and tin were discovered. They were too soft to be useful except as ornaments, but copper objects were good for trading, so people gradually developed metalworking techniques.

4500 years ago Metal workers discovered that by mixing molten copper and tin, they could produce a hard metal which could be used to make sharp knives. Metal mixtures like this are called **alloys**. This alloy is called bronze, and it soon replaced stone for tools. The **Bronze Age** had begun.

3000 years ago Improvements in metal-producing techniques led to the discovery of iron. This metal was difficult to make, but was even harder than bronze. Iron knives and other goods were traded throughout Europe and Asia. The **Iron Age** had begun.

240 years ago New methods of iron production in the blast furnace were developed. This opened up the great industrial age. Vast amounts of molten iron were cast into railway lines, girders and machinery.

60 years ago Aluminium started to be produced by electrolysis on a large scale. Aluminium has a low density, but is very strong for its weight. Aircraft are built from alloys of aluminium and magnesium. Modern air travel would not have been possible without these metals.

30 years ago Plastics started to replace metals for many everyday uses. Modern electronics is based on silicon chips. Could the 'age of metals' be reaching an end?

1 The first people to discover iron tried to keep its production method a secret. Why do you think they did that?

2 Do you think that the 'age of metals' is reaching an end? Make a list of as many different uses of metals that you can think of. For each use, try to find out whether or not the metal could be replaced with a different material.

6f Using reactivity

Titanium the supermetal

When the Americans needed a material to build an ultra-high performance supersonic jet plane, they turned to the metal titanium. Why?

Titanium is tough but very lightweight. Titanium is as strong as steel, but has only half the density. So a plane built from titanium only weighs half as much as an identical one built from steel.

Supersonic planes get hot because of friction with the atmosphere. Titanium has a very high melting point (nearly 2000 °C).

Titanium is very reactive, combining with the oxygen in the air to make a tough oxide layer. This protects the metal from further attack.

Titanium is also quite common, making up 0.6% of the Earth's crust. That is less than aluminium and iron, but it is far more common than copper or zinc.

The catch

The problem is that titanium is more reactive than carbon, so it cannot be produced by displacement. You could melt its ore and use electrolysis, but very high temperatures (nearly 2000 °C) would be needed, making it very expensive.

The solution

Sodium is produced fairly cheaply by the electrolysis of molten sodium chloride. Common salt melts at just 800 °C, so it doesn't need huge amounts of electricity to melt it. Sodium is above titanium in the reactivity series, so it can be used to displace the titanium metal.

Sodium is reacted with titanium chloride:

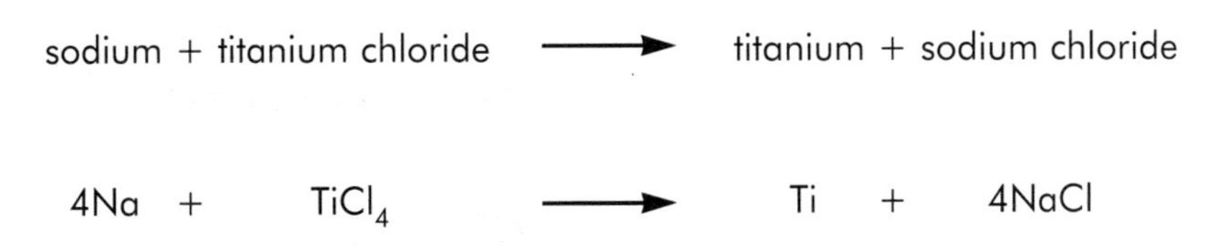

sodium + titanium chloride ⟶ titanium + sodium chloride

$$4Na + TiCl_4 \longrightarrow Ti + 4NaCl$$

1 Why is it important that aircraft materials are lightweight as well as strong?

2 Titanium is also used to make replacement hip joints. A ball of titanium replaces the bone that fits in the socket on the hip. Why is titanium used instead of iron, aluminium or copper, for example?

3 Titanium is as reactive as aluminium. What other metals could be used to displace it from its ore, apart from sodium?

6 REVIEW

6a Burning up

The fuel seems to disappear as it burns.

Many things burn in air if you heat them. They are reacting with the oxygen in the air to make new compounds called oxides.

When fuels burn, the new compounds formed are gases, so the fuel seems to disappear. When oil burns, carbon dioxide and water (vapour) are formed. Water is the common name for hydrogen oxide.

oil + oxygen ⟶ carbon dioxide + water

Some elements burn in air. They are also reacting with oxygen to form oxides. The oxides of non-metals, such as sulphur dioxide, are usually gases. The oxides of metals, such as magnesium oxide, are solids.

1 Gunpowder contains carbon and sulphur. Which two oxide gases are formed when gunpowder burns?

2 Name the solids that form when these elements burn in air:
a aluminium **b** zinc **c** iron **d** sodium.

6b Metals and acids

Many metals react with acids. They fizz as hydrogen gas is given off. The metal pushes the hydrogen from the acid.

1 How could you test this gas, to check that it is hydrogen?

Zinc reacts with sulphuric acid. If you evaporate the solution, you get crystals of the metal salt zinc sulphate.

zinc + sulphuric acid ⟶ zinc sulphate + hydrogen

2 Magnesium reacts with dilute hydrochloric acid, fizzing violently.
a What gas is given off?
b What salt is formed?
c Write a word equation for this reaction.

6c Metal salts

When a metal reacts with an acid, a salt is formed. Zinc sulphate and sodium chloride are two examples of salts.

Many metal salts dissolve in water, but some are insoluble. You can't always tell if a salt will dissolve or not, but there is a pattern. This can help you make a prediction.

- Most nitrates are soluble.
- Chlorides and sulphates tend to be soluble.
- Very few carbonates or hydroxides are soluble.
- All sodium and potassium salts are soluble.
- Calcium, copper and iron have some soluble and some insoluble salts.
- Most lead salts are insoluble.

1 Do you think these salts will be soluble or insoluble in water?

a lead carbonate
b potassium sulphate
c copper nitrate
d sodium hydroxide

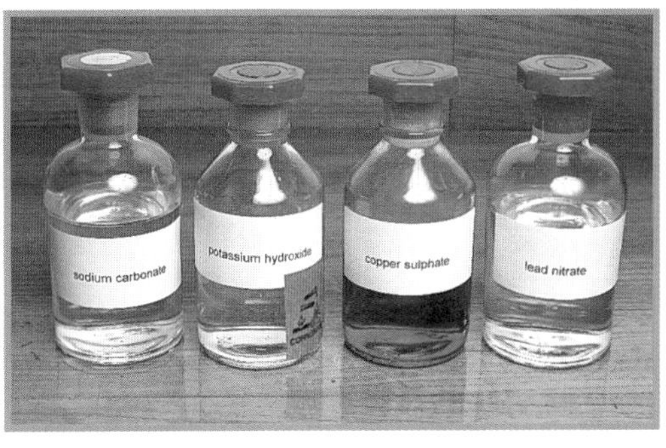

Soluble salts

Insoluble salts

6f Properties of metals

There are lots of different kinds of metals, but they all have some properties in common. Many of them are very useful.

- Metals are shiny. Metals such as gold keep their shine, so they are used for jewellery.
- Metals conduct heat. Aluminium is used for saucepans – it conducts the heat through to the food.
- Metals conduct electricity. Copper is used for electrical wiring.
- Many metals are heavy for their size. Some lamps have heavy metal bases to stop them toppling over.
- Many metals are very strong. Steel is used to build bridges, railways and machinery.
- Metals can be shaped easily. Aluminium cans are pulled out into shape. Car panels are pressed out from sheet steel.

1 How many different uses of metals can you see in the picture? In each case, explain why the metal is being used.

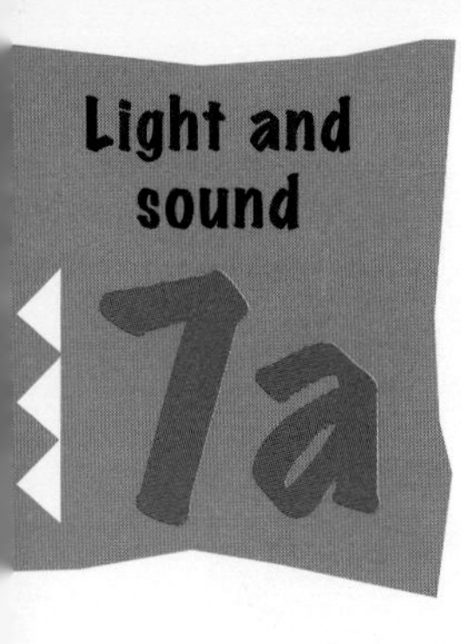

Light direction

Light travels in straight lines. In the photograph, you can see the straight rays of laser light in a spectacular light show.

Light from the stars travels in straight lines through empty space. By the time it reaches your eye, it may have been travelling for millions of years.

Changing direction

You can make a ray of light change direction using a mirror. The mirror **reflects** the light.

A **ray box** produces a single, narrow ray of light. You can use a ray box to investigate how a mirror reflects light. The ray shows up on the white paper.

You can see how the ray of light reflects off the mirror. The mirror must be smooth and flat. Then you can see a clear reflected ray.

The diagram shows a plan view of the ray of light reflecting off the mirror. It hits the mirror and bounces off at the same angle.

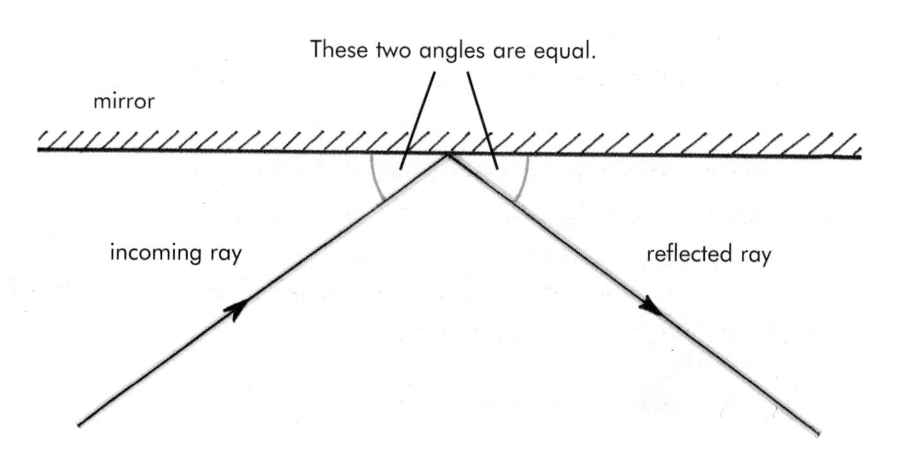

a Make a prediction: What will happen if you shine a ray of light head-on (at 90°) to the mirror? Draw a diagram to support your prediction.

Balls and walls

These children are playing a game. One throws the ball at the wall, and the other catches it when it bounces off. The wall has some smooth, flat areas. Other areas are rough and bumpy.

When the ball hits a smooth area, it is easy to predict where it will go. It bounces off at the same angle as it hit the wall, just like light bouncing off a mirror.

When the ball hits a rough area, it is difficult to predict where it will go. Balls **scatter** off the rough wall. They go in different directions. Light is also scattered off rough surfaces.

b What will happen if you throw a ball straight at a flat wall? What will happen if you throw it straight at a rough wall?

Scattering light

This photograph shows what happens when a ray of light shines on a piece of rough aluminium foil.

c **1** What shape does the light make on the bench, after it has hit the aluminium foil?

2 Try to explain why it makes this shape.

What do you know?

1 Copy and complete the following sentences. Use the words below to fill the gaps.

smooth narrow rough flat straight bumpy

A ray of light is ________ and ________.

To reflect light well, a surface must be ________ and ________.

A surface will scatter light if it is ________ and ________.

2 The diagram shows a ray of light shining on to a flat mirror. Where do you predict the ray will go when it is reflected? Copy and complete the diagram to show your prediction. Mark two angles that are equal.

mirror

3 If you shout near a high, flat cliff, you may hear a clear echo. If you shout near a forest of tall trees, you will probably not hear an echo. Can you explain these observations?

Key ideas

Light travels in straight lines.

When light is **reflected** by a flat, smooth surface, it bounces off at the same angle at which it hit the surface.

When light hits a rough surface, it **scatters** in many directions.

Colours of the rainbow

If the Sun is shining and it is raining at the same time, you may be able to see a rainbow. Light from the Sun shines on drops of water in the air, and the light is split up into all the colours of the rainbow. The colours are (starting at the top): red, orange, yellow, green, blue, indigo, violet.

a People have different ways of remembering the colours of the rainbow. Some people say 'Richard Of York Gave Battle In Vain'. How does this help you to remember the colours?

Splitting light

The Sun is a very hot source of light. It is almost white-hot. We say that light from the Sun is **white light**.

You may have noticed white light getting split up when it shines on certain objects.

A compact disc reflects white light. It splits it up into the colours of the rainbow.

A diamond is clear and colourless. When light shines on it, you can see all the colours of the rainbow.

Photographers have special filters which can split up white light to give interesting effects.

Seeing a spectrum

The colours of the rainbow are called the **spectrum**. Here are two ways you can split up white light to make a spectrum.

White light from a ray box is shining through a diffraction grating (a glass slide with lots of fine slits). The light is split up, and you can see the spectrum of colours on the screen.

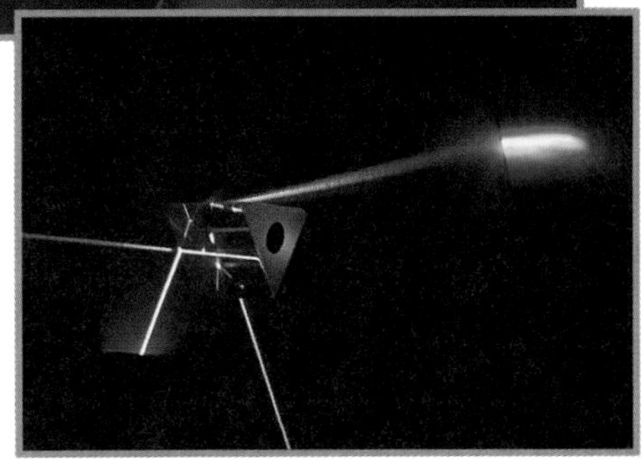

A ray of white light can be split up by a prism (a triangular block of glass). The splitting up of light like this is called **dispersion**. The light has been dispersed.

b A diamond splits up white light. Is it like a glass diffraction grating or a glass prism?

Newton's disc

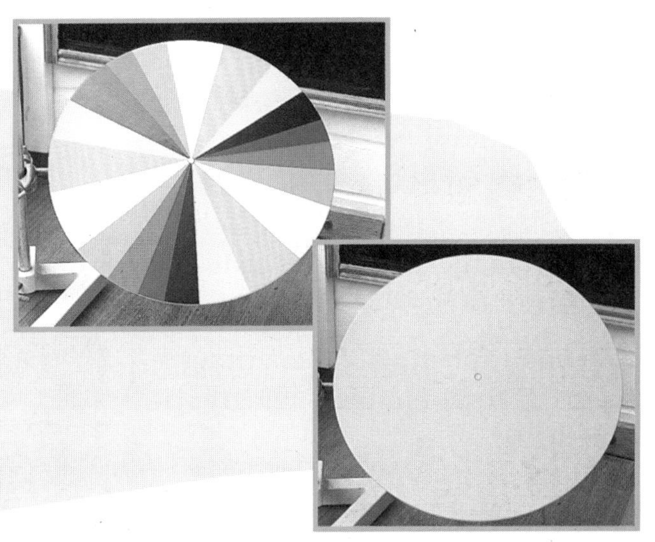

It was Isaac Newton who realised that white light is a mixture of all of the colours of the spectrum. He invented an experiment to show that you could make white light by mixing the colours together again.

Newton's disc is painted with all the colours of the spectrum. When it spins round, all the colours blur together. It looks almost white.

What do you know?

1 Copy and complete the following sentences. Use the words below to fill the gaps.

prism **mixture** **dispersed**
spectrum **diffraction grating**

White light is a ________ of all the colours of the ________. It can be split up (________) using a ________ or a ________ ________.

2 Some people use the name 'Roy G. Biv' to help them remember the colours of the spectrum. Make up your own way of remembering them.

3 A chandelier is made from many cut glass prisms. The light from the lamps is white, but the glass shows many different colours. Why is this?

4 How could you make an artificial rainbow in the garden on a sunny day?

Key ideas

White light is a mixture of all of the colours of the **spectrum**. It can be split up (dispersed) into the different colours using a prism or a diffraction grating. This is called **dispersion**.

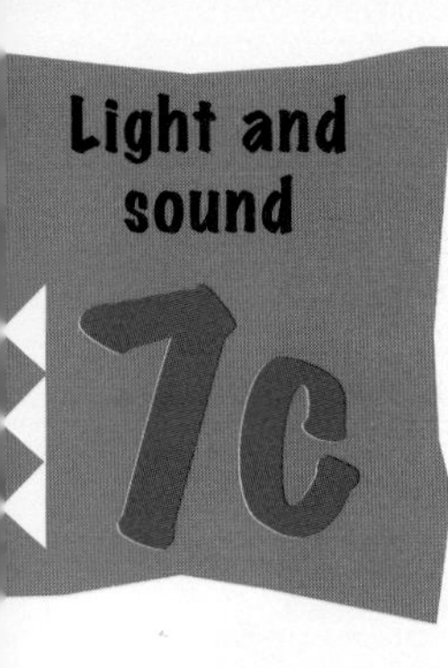

A clear view

In the windows of an old house, the glass may not be very flat. When you look through the window, everything looks distorted. If you open the window, you can see more clearly.

a Where else have you seen bumpy glass which makes things look distorted?

Bending tricks

This stick looks bent. But it isn't the stick that is bent, it's the light! Light from the stick bends as it comes out of the water.

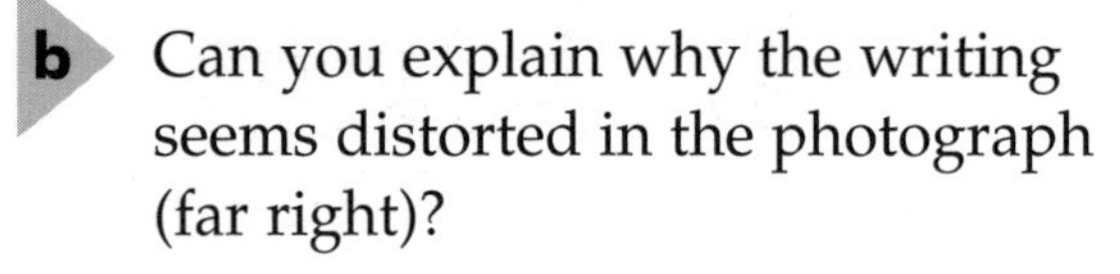

b Can you explain why the writing seems distorted in the photograph (far right)?

Bending in a bucket

Make a coin appear, as if by magic! Put a coin in the bottom of a bucket. Stand so that you can't quite see it because the side of the bucket is blocking your view. Now ask a friend to pour water gradually into the bucket. As the bucket gets fuller and fuller, the coin will come into view.

At first, the light from the coin is blocked by the side of the bucket. With water in the bucket, the light from the coin bends as it comes out of the water, and so it can reach your eye.

Bending in a block

A ray box and a glass block will show you how glass bends a ray of light. When the ray of light goes into the glass block, it bends one way. When it comes out, it bends back the other way.

The bending of light when it goes from one material into another is called **refraction**.

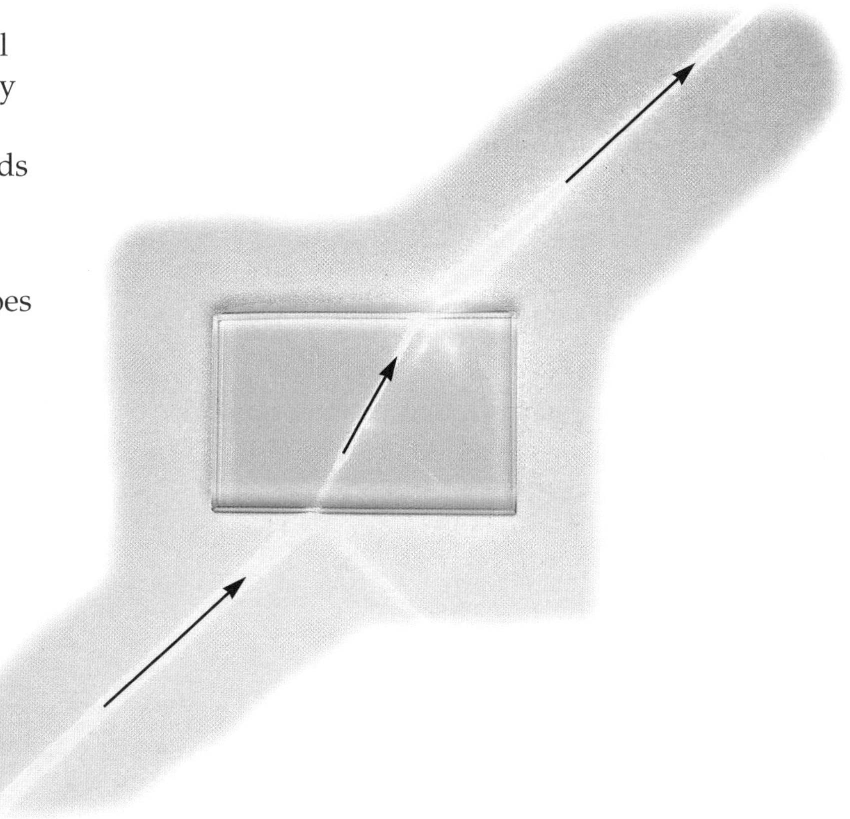

What do you know?

1 Write out these definitions, choosing the correct word from the list below.

refraction **dispersion**

bending of light when it goes from one material to another –

splitting up of white light into different colours –

2 This boy is not very good at catching fish. He sits on the river bank and tries to grab a fish when it swims close to the edge.

a The fish can see the boy. Explain how the drawing shows this.

b Why is the ray of light bent?

c Every time the boy grabs for a fish, he misses. Can you explain why?

Key ideas

Light bends when it goes from one material into another. This is called **refraction**.

Filter effects

Blackpool illuminations

These lights are all the same colour – inside! The filament inside glows brightly. It gives out white light.

When the white light passes through the coloured glass of the bulb, it is no longer white. It becomes red, or blue, or yellow, or whatever the colour of the glass.

On stage

You may have seen coloured **filters** used for stage lighting. The filters are pieces of transparent coloured plastic. The white light from the lamp passes through the filter and comes out coloured.

When the wheel on the lamp is turned, each filter gives the light a different colour.

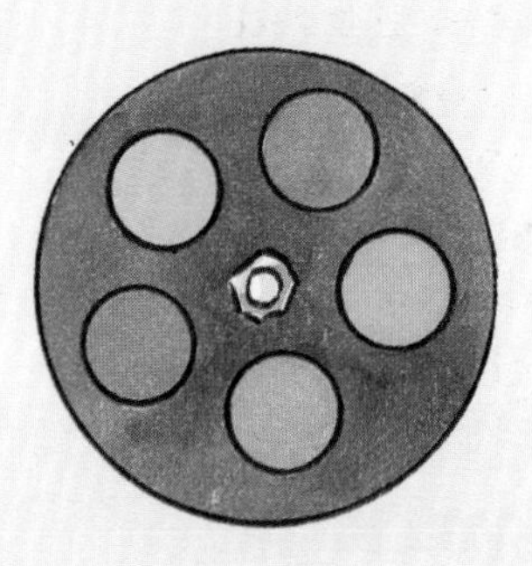
Filter wheel for stage light

What's in a name?

White light is a mixture of all the colours of the spectrum. When it shines on a red filter, only the red light can get through. The other colours cannot pass through the red filter.

Light filters are like the filters that you use for separating mixtures of substances. Only some colours can pass through. The others are stopped by the filter.

a What colour of light can pass through a green filter? What colours cannot pass through?

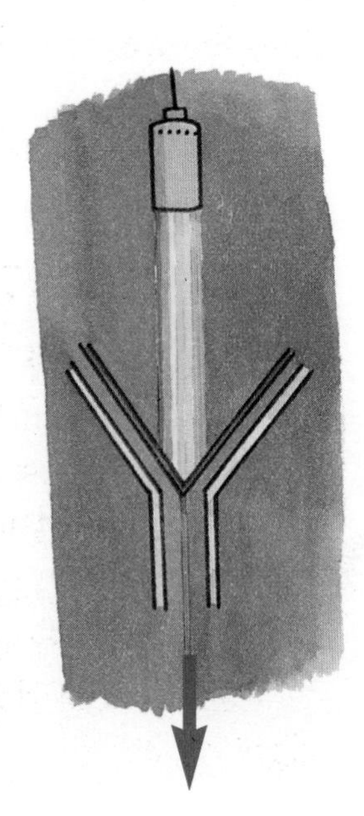

Shine on

You can see the colour of light when it shines on to something white. Red light shining on white paper makes the paper look red. The white paper reflects the red light.

Green light makes white paper look green. White paper reflects all colours of light.

You can see some interesting effects if you shine coloured light on different coloured objects. If you shine red light on a red book, it looks red. A red book reflects red light.

However, if you shine red light on a blue book, it looks black. A blue book reflects blue light, not red light.

You need white light to show up the true colours of things.

b What colour will a red book look if you shine these colours of light on it:

1 red light
2 blue light
3 white light?

What do you know?

1 Copy and complete the following sentences. Use the words below to fill the gaps.

object mixture colours filter

White light is a ________ of different colours of light. When it shines through a ________, it becomes coloured, because only certain ________ can pass through.

The colour of an ________ depends on the colour of the light falling on it.

2a What colour does a blue book look if you shine white light on it?
b What colour does it look if you shine red light on it?

3a Jane puts a red filter in front of a white light. What colour will the light become?
b She now adds a blue filter to the red filter. What will she observe? Explain your answer.

Key ideas

A **filter** can change the colour of white light, because it only lets certain colours pass through.

Coloured objects look different when you shine different colours of light on them. You can see their true colours in white light.

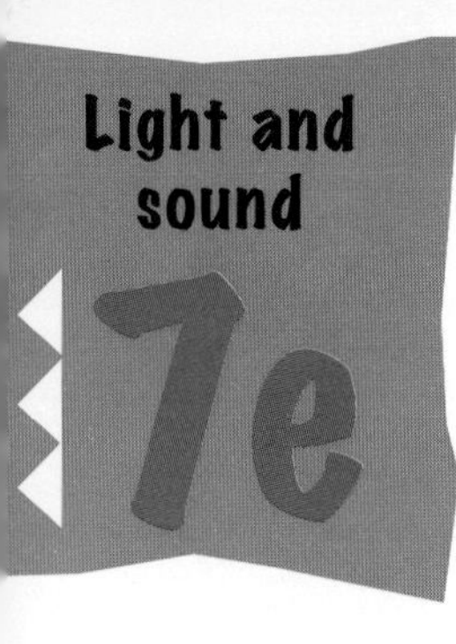

Louder sounds

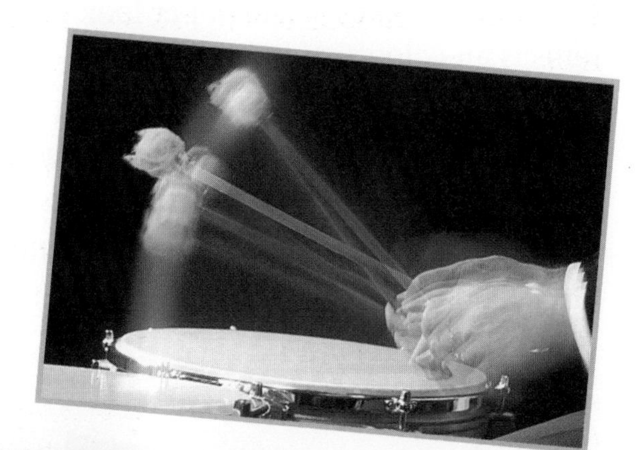

You can make very loud sounds with a drum, by hitting it very hard. When you hit the drum, the skin on top **vibrates** up and down. The harder you hit it, the bigger the vibrations and the louder the sound.

a Name another percussion instrument which sounds louder when you hit it harder.

Louder and softer

Here are some more musical instruments which can make loud and soft sounds.

If you pluck a guitar string gently, it makes a soft note. If you pull it down a long way and let go, its vibrations will be bigger. The note sounds louder.

If you blow into a trumpet gently, it makes a soft note. If you blow harder, the air inside vibrates more and the note sounds louder.

b How can you make a recorder produce:
1 soft notes **2** louder notes?

Twang!

If you hold one end of a ruler on the bench and twang the other end, it vibrates up and down. If you twang it harder, the height of the vibrations is greater. They have a bigger **amplitude**. Then the vibrations get smaller and the sound gets fainter.

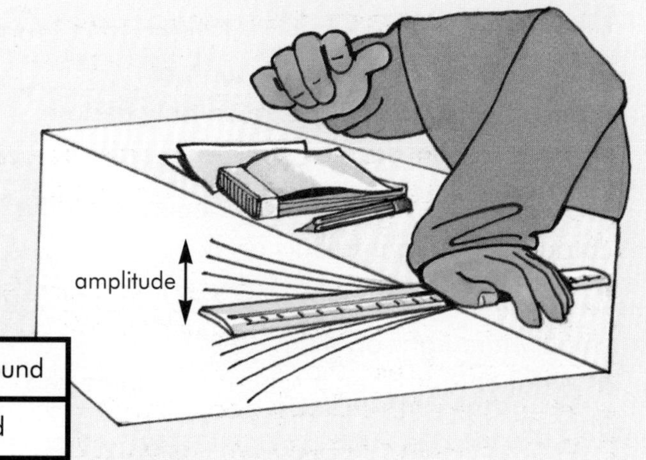

c Copy and complete the table to show how the vibrations change.

large amplitude	big vibrations	________ sound
________ amplitude	________ vibrations	soft sound

Moving vibrations

When a drum skin vibrates, it pushes the air back and forth. It makes the air vibrate. The vibrations travel through the air.

When the vibrations reach your ear, they make your eardrum vibrate. Then you hear the sound.

Vibrations can travel through air. They can also travel through solids and liquids. They cannot pass through a vacuum (such as outer space), because there is nothing there to vibrate.

What do you know?

1 Copy and complete the sentence below. Choose the correct word from each pair. There are two correct answers. Can you find them both?

When the amplitude of a vibration **increases/decreases**, the vibration gets **bigger/smaller** and the sound gets **softer/louder**.

2 The Sun is a giant ball of fire, with huge flames leaping thousands of miles into empty space. We can see the Sun, but we cannot hear it.

a What does this tell you about light?
b What does this tell you about sound?

Key ideas

Sounds are produced when something vibrates. The bigger the **amplitude** of the vibrations, the louder the sound.

The vibrations of a sound can travel through solids, liquids and gases. They cannot travel through a vacuum.

More vibrations

A piccolo is very small. It plays high notes. They have a high **pitch**.

A tuba is much bigger than a piccolo. Its notes have a very low pitch.

a Name a stringed instrument that plays:
1 high notes **2** low notes.

Fast and furious

You can change the note of a ruler when you twang it by sliding it further onto the bench. As the free end gets shorter, the note gets higher.

When a long ruler vibrates, the end goes up and down slowly. It vibrates just a few times each second. It has a low **frequency**, and the note sounds low. The frequency of a sound tells us how many vibrations there are each second.

When a shorter ruler vibrates, the end goes up and down more often – perhaps too fast to see. There are many more vibrations each second. The vibrations have a higher frequency, and the note has a higher pitch.

b Copy and complete the following table. Use the words **high** and **low** to fill the gaps.

many vibrations each second	________ frequency	________ pitch
few vibrations each second	________ frequency	________ pitch

Changing pitch

To play a higher note on a string, you make the string shorter. A guitarist or a violinist does this by pressing on the strings.

When a trombone is extended, it is much longer and it produces lower notes.

You can make a sound by twanging a rubber band. If you blow across the top of a test tube, the air inside it vibrates and makes a musical note.

c How could you make the rubber band produce a note with a higher frequency?

d Which test tube will make the note with the highest frequency? Which will produce the lowest frequency?

What do you know?

1 You can change the frequency of a sound, and you can change the amplitude of its vibrations. Copy and complete the table to show how these changes affect the loudness and the pitch of the sound.

Change	**Observation** (how the sound would change)
more vibrations each second (higher frequency)	
bigger vibrations (greater amplitude)	

2 A loudspeaker vibrates back and forth to make the sounds we hear. It pushes the air, so that vibrations travel through the air to our ears. How would the vibrations of a loudspeaker change:

a when it makes a quieter sound

b when it makes a higher pitched sound?

3 The diagram shows the range of sounds people can hear. Write a paragraph to say what this diagram tells you. Use the word 'frequency' in your answer.

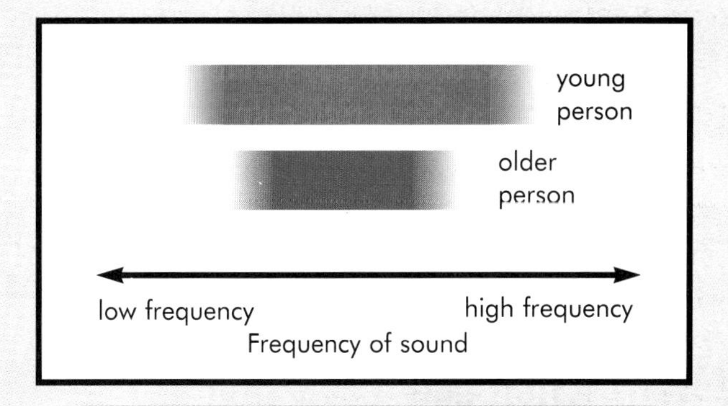

Key ideas

When a sound is made, the more vibrations there are each second, the higher is the **pitch**. The **frequency** of a sound is the number of vibrations each second.

EXTRAS

Behind the mirror

When you look in a mirror, you seem to see a reflection behind the mirror. The picture shows how the reflection is formed.

A ray of light from the lamp reflects off the mirror and into your eye. It seems to be coming from a lamp behind the mirror.

1 Draw a plan view of this drawing (as seen from above). Show the ray of light that travels from the lamp to your eye. Draw a dashed line to show where the light seems to be coming from.

2 On your diagram, mark the angles that are equal to each other.

The law of reflection

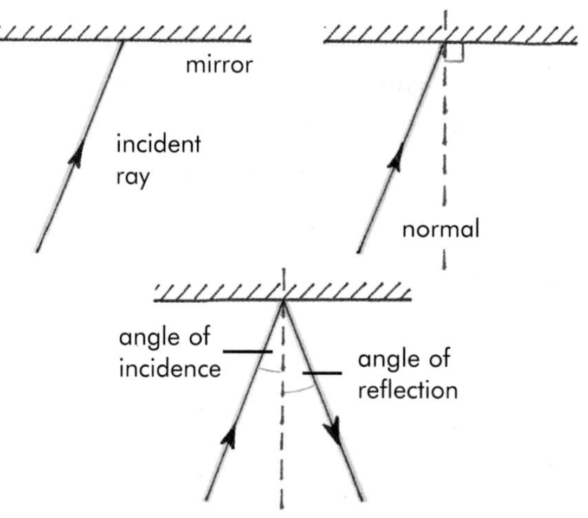
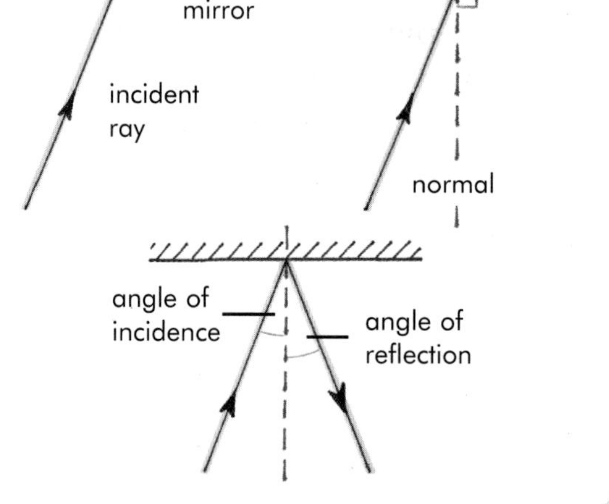

How can you work out where a ray of light will go when it is reflected by a mirror? Here is how:

- Find where the incident ray hits the mirror.
- Draw a line at right angles to the mirror (the normal).
- Using a protractor, measure the angle of incidence.
- Now draw the reflected ray so that the angle of reflection is equal to the angle of incidence.

The **law of reflection** says that the angle of incidence is equal to the angle of reflection.

3 Draw your own diagram to show the law of reflection.

4 Label the incident ray, the reflected ray, the normal line, and the angles of incidence and reflection.

Refraction and dispersion

When a ray of white light hits a prism, two things happen:

- the ray bends (it is refracted)
- the ray splits up into the colours of the spectrum (it is dispersed).

white light

Dispersion happens because some colours are refracted more than others.

1 Which colour is refracted most? Which is refracted least?

2 Draw what you would expect to see if the ray was a mixture of just red light and blue light.

7d Cover colours

A white object reflects all colours of light. A black object reflects no light at all.

Some things reflect more than one colour of light. This green book reflects green light and blue light.

1 What colour would the book appear to be under:

a blue light
b green light
c red light
d white light?

7f Scope for pictures

An oscilloscope lets you 'see' the vibrations of a sound. The trace on the screen shows the pattern of the vibrations.

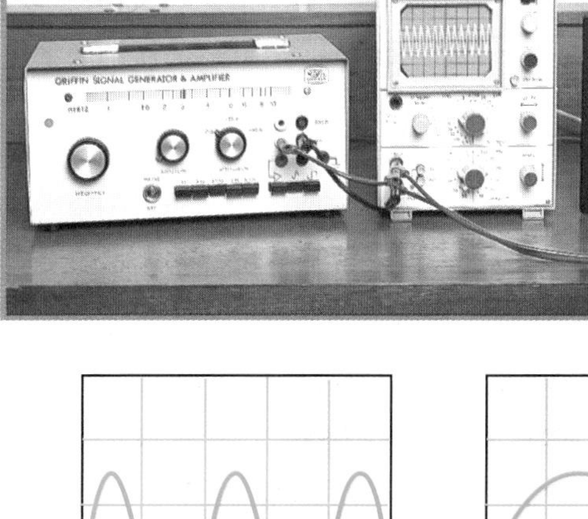

These pictures show how the trace changes when the loudness of the sound changes, and when its pitch changes.

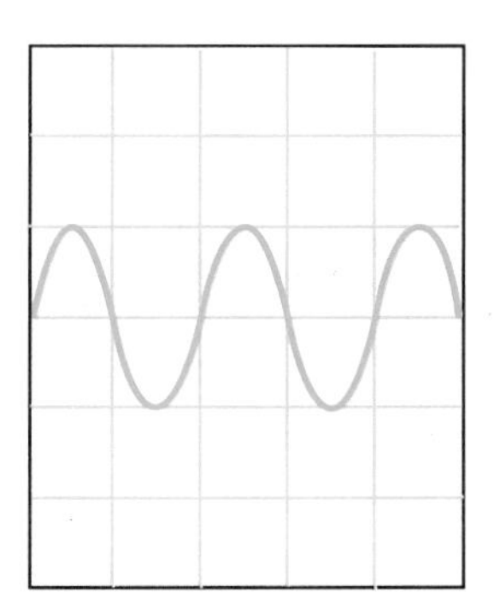

soft …

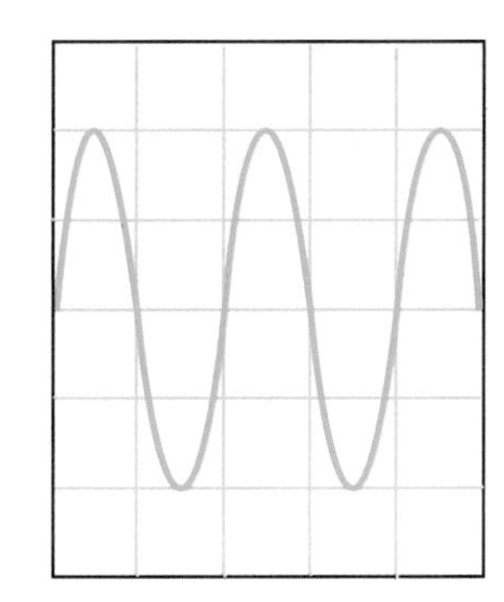

… and loud

high …

… and low

1 Which of these two diagrams, **A** or **B**, shows a sound that is getting higher?

2 What does the other diagram show?

3 Draw a trace to show a sound that is getting quieter.

A

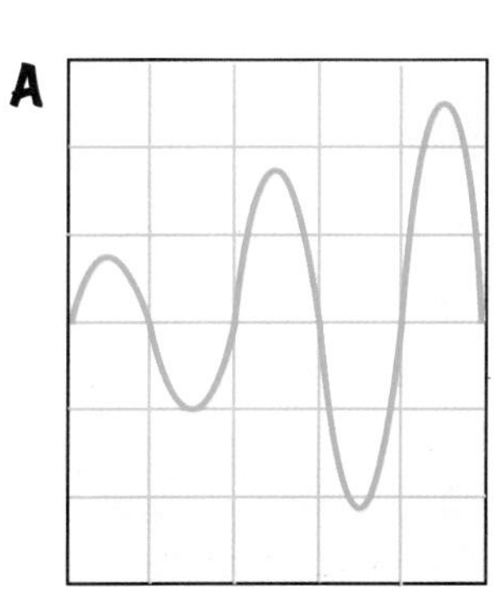

B

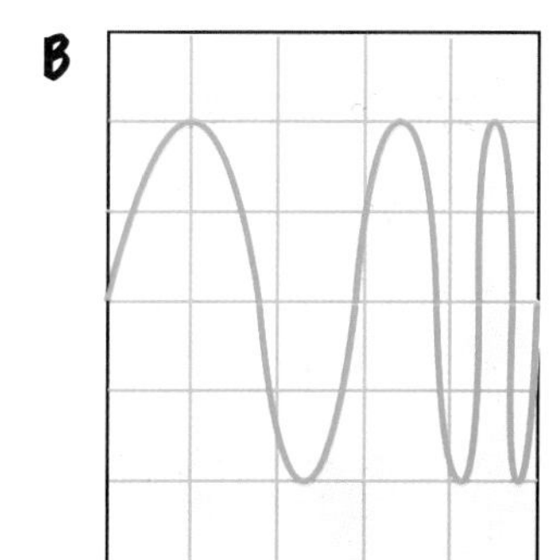

Light and sound 7

REVIEW

7a Making shadows

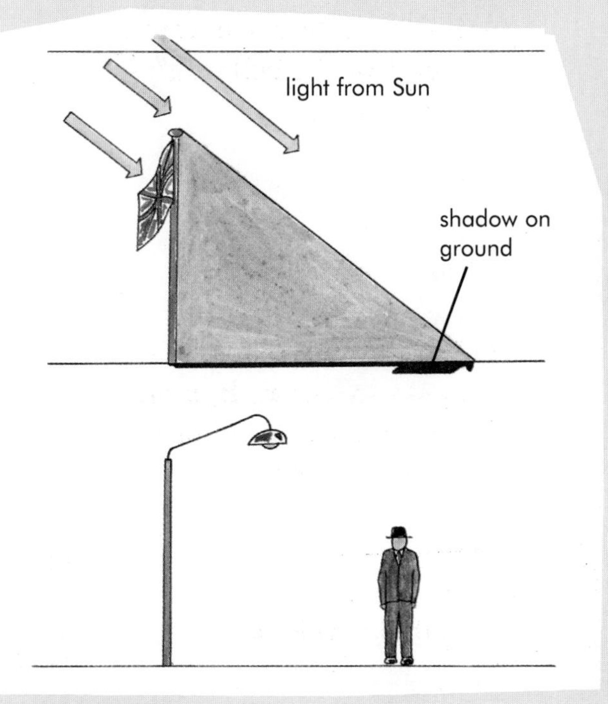

This flagpole makes a shadow on the ground. We can work out where its shadow will be, because we know that light travels in straight lines.

We draw a straight ray of light which just touches the top of the flagpole. The ray continues down to the ground. This shows us where the top of the shadow will be.

1a Copy the drawing of the man standing near the street lamp.
b Draw a ray of light from the street lamp to the top of the man's head, and down to the ground.
c Show where the man's shadow will be.

7b Sources and scatterers

We see some things because they are sources of their own light. We see other things because they scatter light towards our eyes.

1a Is the flame a source or a scatterer of light?
b Is the book a source or a scatterer of light?

2 Here are some more things you might see. Put them in two lists headed 'Sources of light' and 'Scatterers of light'. Add some more examples of your own.

7e Sight and sound

The picture shows an experiment you may have seen. When the air is pumped out of the belljar, you can no longer hear the bell ringing.

1 Copy the table. Complete it by filling in spaces **a**, **b**, **c** and **d** to show what the experiment tells you about sound.

Demonstration	What you observe	What this tells you
The belljar is full of air.	You see and hear the bell as it rings.	Sound can travel through air and glass.
The air is pumped out of the belljar.	You can see the bell vibrating but **a**	**b**
Air is slowly let back into the jar.	**c**	**d**

7f Earache

'Good hearing is very precious. You can damage your hearing by listening to loud sounds whose **vibrations** have a big **amplitude**. If your hearing is damaged, you may not be able to hear high-**frequency** sounds.'

1 Some people may not be able to understand this paragraph, because of the scientific terms printed in **bold**. Rewrite the paragraph in your own words, so that it could be understood by an eight-year-old who has not studied as much Science as you.

How hot?

You soon notice if you touch something that is very hot. You have nerve endings in your skin which detect if something is hotter or colder than you.

a Why are these nerve endings important?

Thermometers at work

In Science, we do not rely on our nerves to tell us how hot or cold something is. We use a **thermometer** to measure its temperature. Usually we measure temperatures in degrees Celsius (°C).

b What is each of these thermometers being used for?

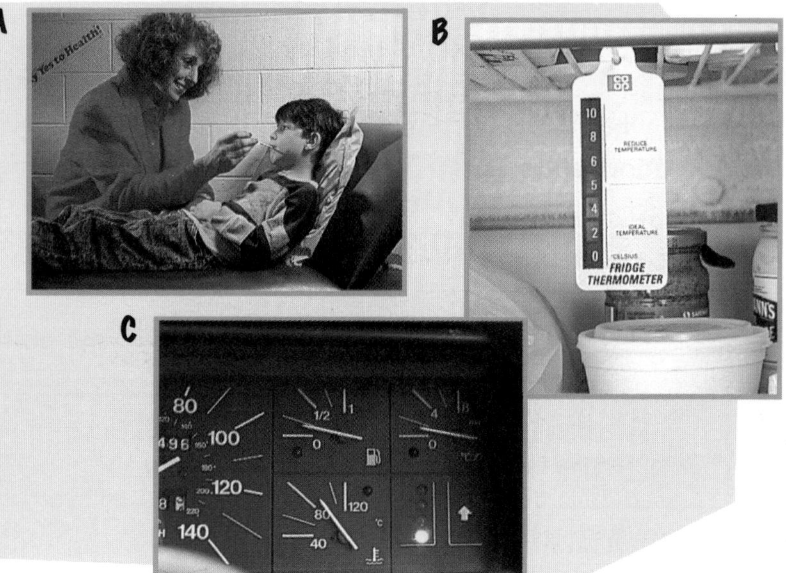

Hotter and colder

Human beings are warm-blooded creatures, and our body temperature is usually about 37 °C. A temperature of about 18 °C is comfortable for working in.

Cooling off

The filament of a light bulb is much hotter than its surroundings. It needs a constant supply of electrical energy to keep it hot. When you switch off the light, the filament cools down rapidly. The heat energy escapes into the surroundings.

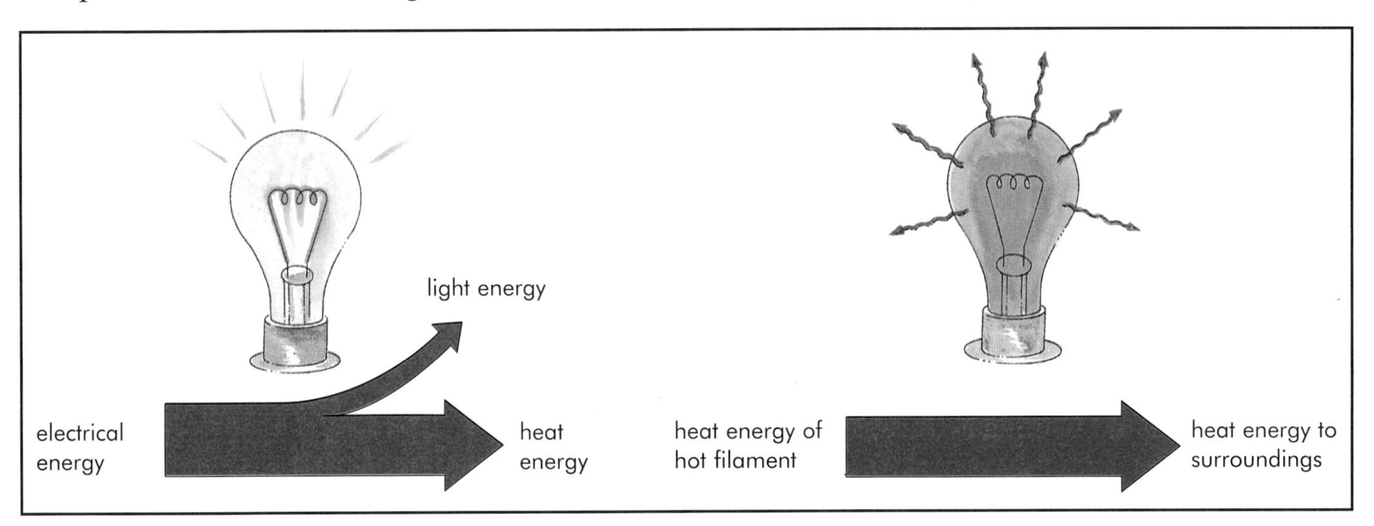

c Humans are usually warmer than their surroundings.
What is our energy supply which we need to keep us warm?

What do you know?

1 Copy this drawing of a thermometer, and add the following labels at the correct points on the scale:

boiling water **melting ice**
average body temperature

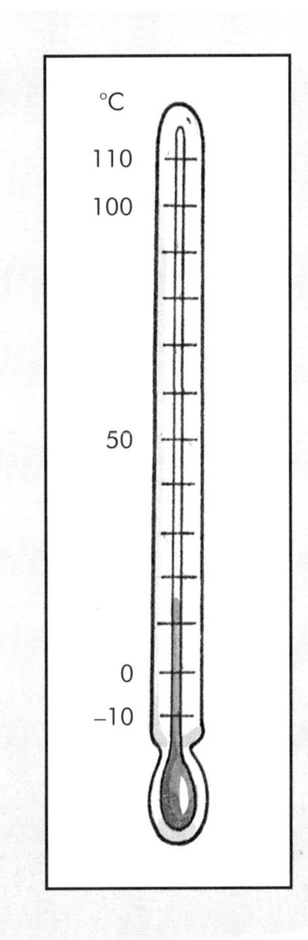

2 Look at the picture on the opposite page.
a What is room temperature?
b Name two things that are colder than their surroundings.
c Name three things that are warmer than their surroundings.
d The radiator stays hot, even though it is transferring energy to the room. What is the energy supply that keeps the radiator hot?

Key ideas

We use a **thermometer** to tell us the temperature of something (how hot it is).

Temperature is usually measured in degrees Celsius (°C).

Energy can be transferred.

How much energy?

This swimming-pool contains a lot of warm water. The water must be warm, or no one would want to stay in for very long. The temperature of the water is 30 °C.

It takes a lot of **energy** to warm up the water in the swimming-pool. The second photograph shows the boiler room where the water is heated using gas burners.

a

1 What kind of energy is stored by the gas?

2 What kind of energy is released when the gas is burned?

Large and small

You need energy to make a hot drink, too. These two drinks are at the same temperature. It takes more energy to make the big drink than the smaller one. So there is more energy in the big drink than in the smaller one.

These two drinks are the same size. One is hotter than the other. There is more energy in the hotter drink than in the cooler one.

b

1 Which is hotter, the swimming-pool full of water at 30 °C or the mug of tea at 60 °C?

2 Which do you think contains more energy?

Even hotter

Sparklers are fun. But are they dangerous? A sparkler glows white-hot. Its temperature is over 1000 °C. But the sparks are very small. If a spark falls on your hands, it probably won't burn you. Although the sparks are very hot, they don't contain much energy.

The lumps of coal on a fire are not as hot as the sparks, but they are much bigger. They contain much more energy and could burn you badly.

So a small object at a high temperature may contain less energy than a larger object at a lower temperature.

c Look at the pictures on these two pages and find things that answer the following descriptions:

1 a large, cool object which contains a lot of energy

2 a small, hot object which contains a small amount of energy.

What do you know?

1 Copy and complete the following sentences. Choose the correct word from each pair.

We must supply **force/energy** to increase the temperature of something.
A small object at a low temperature has **more/less** energy than a **large/small** object at a **high/low** temperature.

2 Look at the things in this list:

a cup of hot tea
a cup of cold tea
a lump of ice
a swimming-pool
a spark from a sparkler

a Put them in order, from coldest to hottest.
b Put them in order again, starting with the one that contains the least energy and finishing with the one that contains the most. (You may have to make some guesses.)

3 These two electric kettles look the same, but **B** contains twice as much water as **A**. They are switched on at the same time.
a Which kettle will boil first?
b What can you say about the temperatures of the water in the two kettles when they are both boiling?
c Which will contain more energy when they are both boiling?

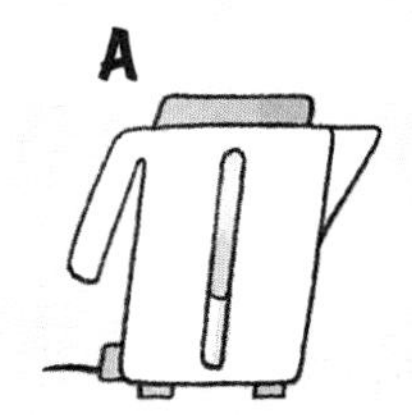

Key ideas

To raise the temperature of something, we must supply it with energy.

When something is hotter, it contains more heat energy.

A large object at a low temperature may contain more energy than a small object at a high temperature.

8c Making the most of energy

Energy costs money, so we don't want to waste it. We also don't want to use up the Earth's non-renewable energy supplies, such as coal, oil and gas.

a What do we mean when we say that coal, oil and gas are non-renewable?

Better bulbs

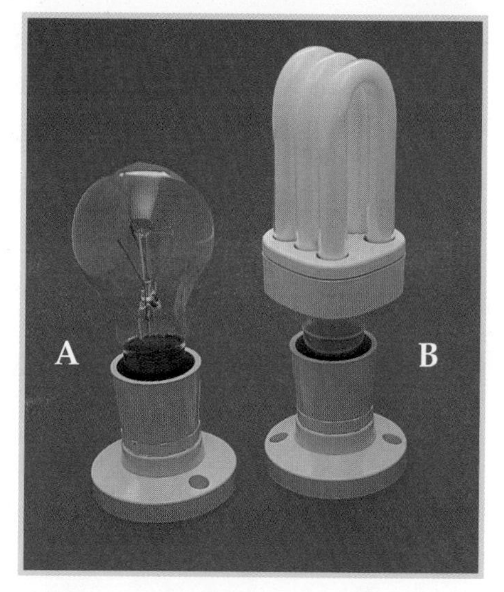

These two light bulbs give the same amount of light, but one is much cheaper to run than the other.

Bulb **A** gives 3 J of light energy every second, but it takes 100 J of electrical energy each second to make it work. It produces 97 J of heat energy each second. The bulb gets very hot.

Bulb **B** also gives 3 J of light energy every second, but it only takes 12 J of electrical energy each second to make it work.

b
1. How much heat energy does bulb **B** produce each second?
2. Which bulb gets hotter?
3. Which bulb wastes more energy? Which wastes more money?

Energy accounts

This stereo system changes electrical energy into sound energy. It needs 50 J of electrical energy every second, but it only produces 1 J of sound energy. Where does the rest of the energy go?

The answer is that the stereo system gets warm, and so do the loudspeakers. The stereo system produces heat energy.

Energy can't just disappear. It may change from one form to another, but the total amount always stays the same. We can use this idea to work out how much heat energy is produced by the stereo system each second:

electrical energy in = 50 J
sound energy out = 1 J
heat energy out = 50 J – 1 J = 49 J

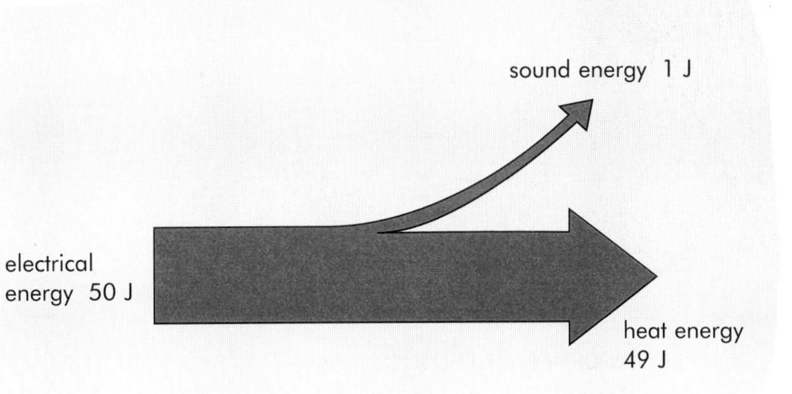

Energy spreading out

We want our light bulbs to produce light and our stereos to produce sound. We don't want them to produce heat energy. Engineers try to design electrical appliances that waste less energy as heat.

Heat energy is often produced when we don't want it. Heat energy is a problem because it tends to escape and spread out. Then it is less useful.

This mountaineer worked out that she would need about 1000 kJ of energy to climb to the top of Ben Nevis. In fact, she has used 8000 kJ.

c She needed 1000 kJ to increase her gravitational energy. Where did the rest of the energy go?

What do you know?

1 Copy and complete the following sentences. Use the words below to fill the gaps.

surroundings form heat amount

Energy can change from one ________ to another. The total ________ always stays the same. Often ________ energy is produced when we don't want it. It becomes less useful when it escapes to the ________.

2 This gas heater burns enough gas to produce 1500 J of heat energy every second. It supplies 1000 J of heat energy to the room.

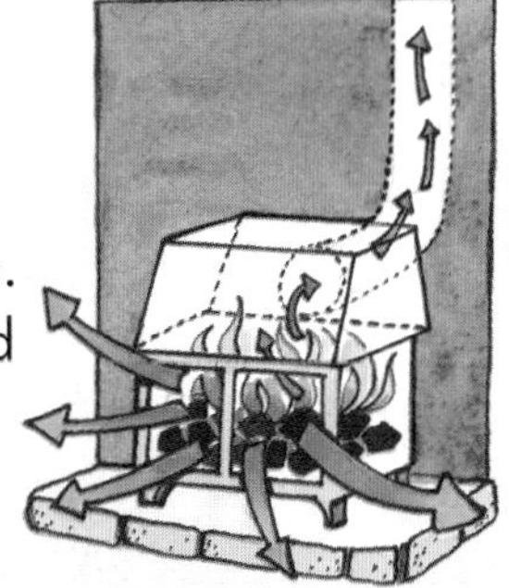

a How much heat energy is wasted each second?

b Where does the wasted heat energy go?

Key ideas

When energy changes from one form to another, the total amount stays the same.

Heat energy is often produced when we don't want it. Heat energy tends to spread out and escape to the surroundings. Then it is less useful.

EXTRAS

8a Deceptive feelings

We can use the nerve endings in our skin to judge how hot or cold something is. At times, our senses can deceive us.

This lab stool has a wooden seat and metal legs. The seat feels warm to the touch but the legs feel cold. In fact, the metal and the wood are both at the same temperature.

The stool is colder than you – it is at room temperature. When you touch the wood, you make it warmer. Heat from your finger goes into the wood. The heat cannot be conducted away through the wood, and so it feels warm.

When you touch the metal, the heat from your finger is conducted away. The metal doesn't get warm, and so it feels cold.

1 Use these ideas to explain the following. You are walking down the street on a cold and frosty morning. You find a pencil and a coin lying on the pavement. Why does the coin feel much colder than the pencil?

8b Brewing up

1 Can you work out how long it will take for this kettle to boil?

mass of water in kettle = 1 kg
temperature of water from tap = 10 °C
boiling point of water = 100 °C
electrical energy supplied = 3000 J each second

It takes 4200 J of energy to raise the temperature of 1 kg of water by 1 °C.

8c Making use of waste heat

Electricity is generated in power stations. Unfortunately, a lot of the energy from the fuel burned there goes to waste. A conventional power station produces a lot of waste heat energy which escapes into the surroundings.

A Combined Heat and Power (CHP) station makes use of some of the waste heat. It supplies hot water to homes and offices nearby.

The diagrams show how the energy from the fuel is used in both types of power station.

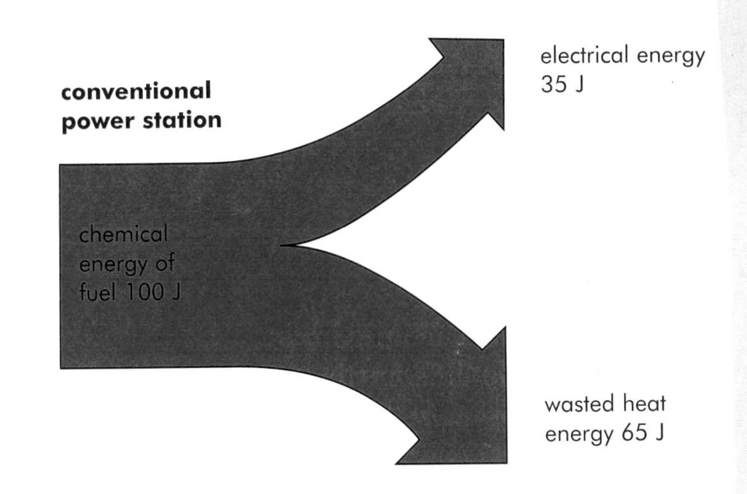

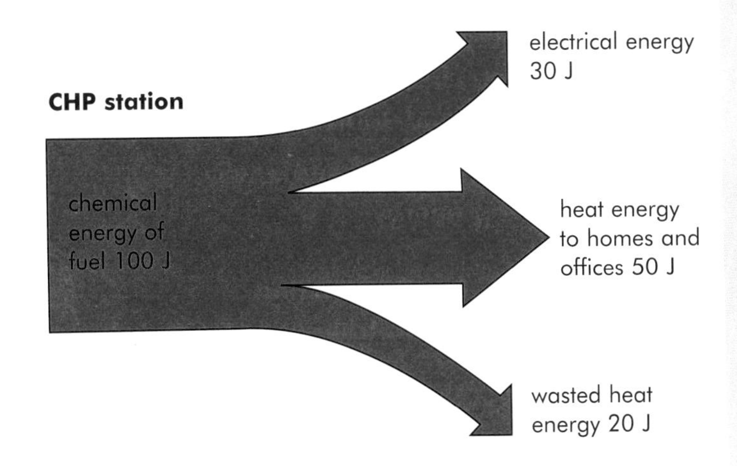

1 In what way is the conventional power station better than the CHP station?

2 In what way is the CHP station better than the conventional power station?

Energy can't just disappear, or appear out of nowhere. This idea is known as the **principle of conservation of energy**.

3 How is this idea shown by the diagrams for the two types of power station?

Cooling tea

A hot cup of tea cools down rapidly at first, then more and more slowly.

4 Which of these graphs shows correctly how the temperature of a cup of tea changes as it cools down?

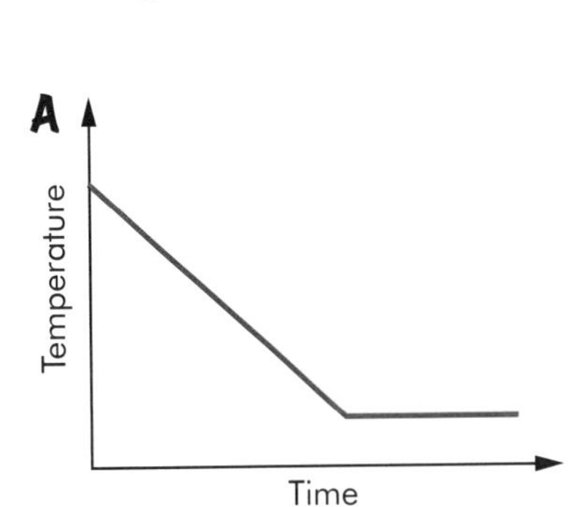

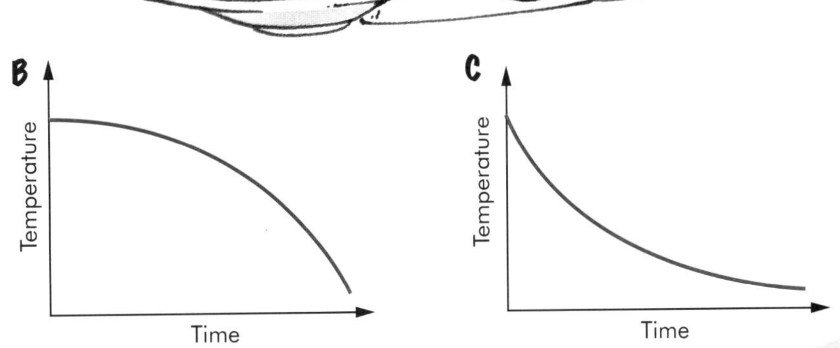

8a Energy transfers

Energy transfers are important. Whenever you lift something up, you transfer energy to it. You give it gravitational energy.

When you switch on the television, electrical energy is transferred to it. The television changes the energy to light energy and sound energy.

1 These words describe some ways of transferring energy:

kicking heating lifting pulling stretching

Copy and complete the table of energy transfers below. Use the words above to fill the boxes.

transferring energy to a book so that it stores gravitational energy	
transferring energy to a rubber band so that it stores elastic energy	
transferring energy to a ball so that it has kinetic energy	
transferring energy to a kettle of water so that it gets hotter	
transferring energy to a stiff drawer so that it opens	

8b Raising the temperature

To make something hotter, we need to give it more heat energy. We can do this by burning a fuel such as coal or gas. Fuels are stores of chemical energy, and when they burn, this is changed to heat energy.

Another way to make something hotter is to use electricity. In an electric heater, electrical energy is changed to heat energy.

1 Look at the following list. Which one thing in the list is not a fuel?

coal wood charcoal electricity oil gas

2a What fuel does the Bunsen burner use?
b What other substance is needed to burn the fuel?

3 Copy and complete the energy transfer diagram for the Bunsen burner.

4 Draw an energy transfer diagram for an electric heater.

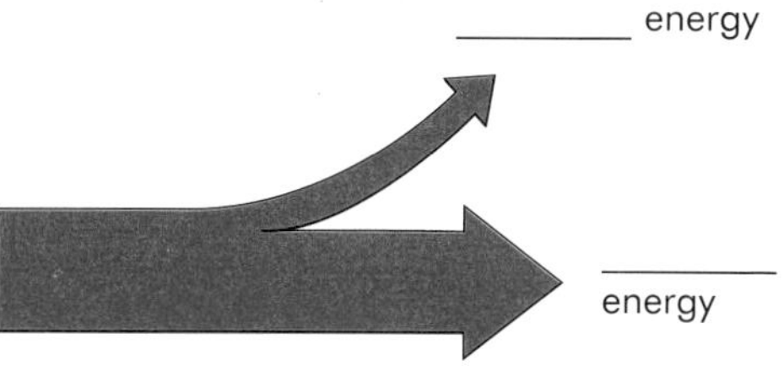

8c Heat energy escaping

It can be difficult to keep things hot, because heat energy is always escaping from hot things. It escapes to the surroundings, which are cooler. We use **insulating materials** so that the heat energy escapes very slowly.

Sometimes we want hot things to cool down. You can't drink a hot cup of tea until it has cooled down to about 50 °C.

1 How can you make a cup of tea cool down more quickly? Explain how your method takes the heat energy away from the tea.

2 If you are going for a long hike in the winter, you might want to take a hot drink with you. A thermos flask is good for this. How does the flask help to keep the drink hot?

9a Charging up

Your hair might stand on end if you thought you saw a ghost. But there is another way to make your hair stand up: comb it vigorously. Then hold the comb just above your hair. Your hair is pulled upwards. It is being attracted by the comb.

When you comb your hair like this, you produce **static electricity**. You may even hear tiny electrical sparks jumping between your hair and the comb.

Charging by friction

Here are two more examples of static electricity which you may already know about.

If you rub a balloon on your jumper, it becomes charged up by the force of friction. Then it will stick to the wall. It will also stick well to your jumper.

If you rub a plastic ruler on a cloth, it becomes charged up. It will attract a stream of water running from the tap.

a A balloon that has been blown up for a few days becomes covered in dust. Why does this happen?

Investigating charge

When you rub something plastic, you give it an **electric charge**. Plastic is an **insulating material**. The charge cannot easily run away through it.

This polythene rod has been rubbed with a cloth. This gives it a negative electric charge. The rod can move easily. When another charged polythene rod is held close to it, it moves away – it is **repelled**.

Each of the polythene rods has been given a negative electrical charge. The two negative charges repel one another.

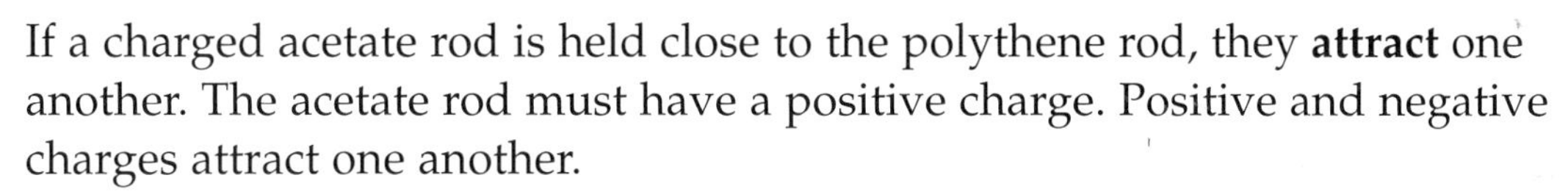

If a charged acetate rod is held close to the polythene rod, they **attract** one another. The acetate rod must have a positive charge. Positive and negative charges attract one another.

b Make a prediction: What would you expect to observe if two acetate rods were used? Give a reason to support your prediction.

Two kinds of charge

There are two opposite kinds of electrical charge, **positive** and **negative**. The table shows how they affect each other. Opposite charges attract. Like charges repel.

c This is similar to the rule for magnets. What is the magnet rule?

positive and positive	← (+) (+) →	repel
negative and negative	← (−) (−) →	repel
positive and negative	(+) → ← (−)	attract

What do you know?

1 Copy out these definitions, choosing the correct word from the list below.

attraction **friction** **repulsion**

the force that makes static electricity when something is rubbed –

the force between two like charges –

the force between two opposite charges –

2a If you rub a polythene rod with a cloth, what kind of charge does the rod have?
b The rod will now attract the cloth. What kind of charge does the cloth have?

3 You can charge a glass rod by rubbing it with a cloth. How could you find out if it has a positive charge or a negative charge?

4 Static electricity is a bit like magnetism. What experiments would you do to show someone that they are **not** the same?

Key ideas

You can make **static electricity** by rubbing an **insulating material**. The force of friction gives it an **electric charge**.

There are two types of charge, **positive** and **negative**. Opposite charges attract, like charges repel.

9b Sparks

You can make a small amount of static electricity by rubbing a balloon. You can make a lot more using a **van de Graaff generator**. This girl's hair has so much charge it is standing on end.

a

1 Are her hairs attracting or repelling each other?

2 Do they all have the same charge, or opposite charges?

Thunder and lightning

A flash of lightning is a giant display of natural electricity. A **spark** jumps from a cloud down to the ground. We see the spark, and then we hear the roll of thunder.

b Why do we usually see the lightning before we hear the thunder?

The van de Graaff generator can make sparks. The metal dome has a lot of charge. If another metal ball is placed nearby, a spark jumps between them. You hear a 'crack!' and you see the spark. Charge has jumped through the air, like a miniature flash of lightning.

Sparks – useful and dangerous

Have you ever had a shock when you touch the door getting out of a car? Your clothes have been rubbing on the seat, and this makes static electricity. A spark jumps from your hand to the metal door.

Here are some other places where you might see sparks:

- Some gas cookers use a spark to light the gas.
- When you switch on a fluorescent light, it may flicker at first. Sparks are travelling along inside the tube.
- Sometimes there are sparks if electrical wiring is faulty.

Current and charge

A flash of lightning is a natural electric current. If we could measure it, we would find that many thousands of amperes are flowing.

Many tall buildings have a **lightning conductor**. A copper rod sticks up from the highest point of the roof. The electric charge from the lightning flows safely down the rod and into the ground.

That is what we mean by an **electric current** – it is a flow of electric charge.

c Why are lightning conductors often made of copper?

What do you know?

1 Copy and complete the following sentence. Choose the correct word from each pair.
An electric **charge/current** is a flow of electric **charge/current**.

2 On these two pages are examples of electric sparks. Make two lists headed 'Useful sparks' and 'Dangerous sparks'. Include some examples of your own.

3 Explain the following:
a If you pull off your jumper in the dark, you may see tiny flashes of light.
b It is dangerous to walk around with an umbrella up in a thunderstorm.
c Oil tankers have to be made of special materials so that people do not generate static electricity when they walk around.

Key ideas

A **spark** may jump between two charged objects. Charge is moving between them. This is a kind of **electric current**.

9c A flow of charge

These wires are carrying a large electric current from a power station. The current goes to houses, factories and shops.

The wires must be very thick so that it is easy for the electric charge to flow through them. They must have low **resistance**.

The wires must be high up in the air, so that dangerous sparks do not jump down to the ground.

a If the wires were thinner, would they have more or less resistance? How would this affect the flow of charge?

Flowing along

You can think of an electric current as being a bit like a flow of water.

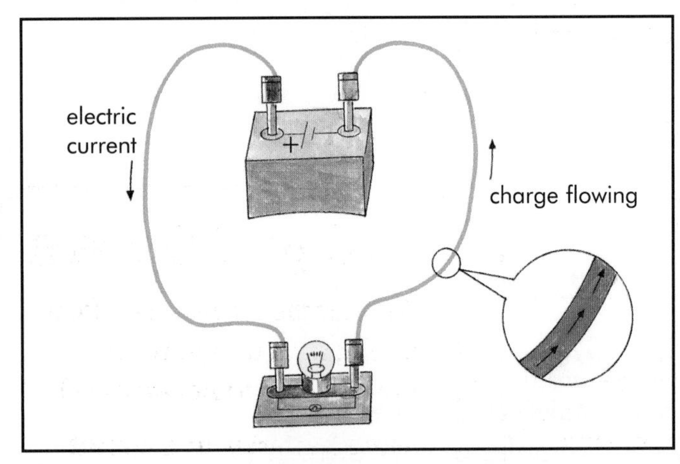

In this circuit, the battery pushes an electric current around to light the lamp. Inside the wire, electric charge is flowing.

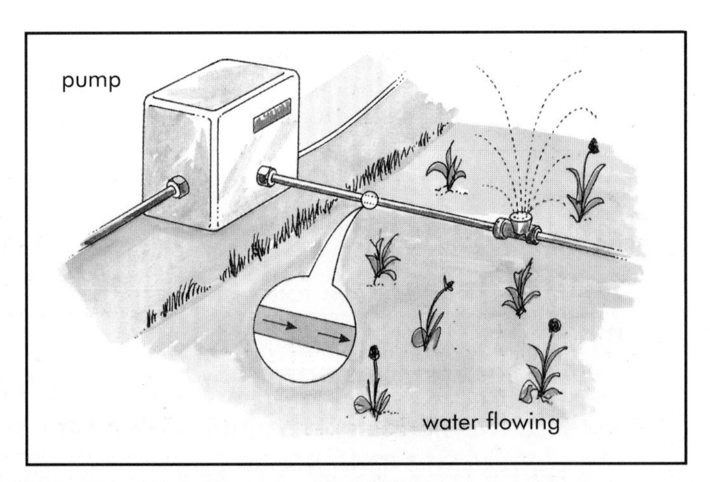

The pump pushes water along the pipe to irrigate the fields. Inside the pipe, water is flowing.

Electric charge is like the water in the pipes. When the charge flows, we have an electric current. Current is like the flow of water in the pipes.

Electric current flows from positive (+) to negative (–). The positive charge flows around the circuit because it is attracted to the negative terminal of the battery.

Go slow

If there is more resistance in a circuit, the current will be smaller. It is harder for the electric charge to flow around the circuit.

If there are three bulbs in **series** in the circuit, there will be three times as much resistance. The current will be one-third as big.

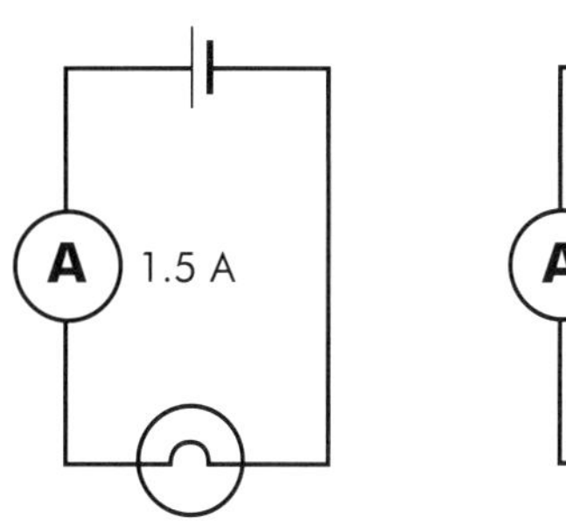

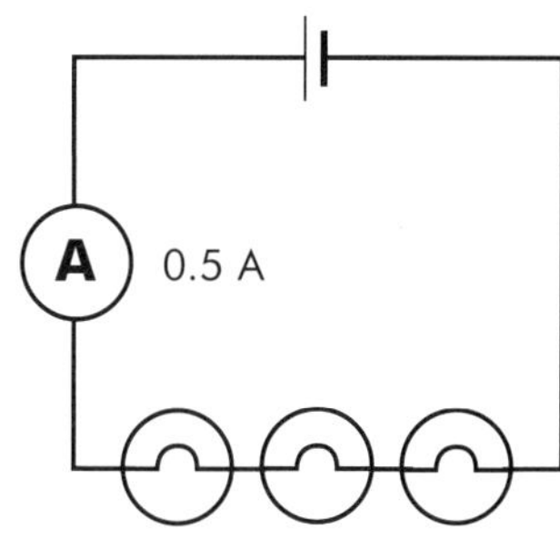

b What current would flow in this circuit if there were two bulbs?

More flow

You can make the current bigger again by using more batteries. Two batteries connected in series give twice the push, so the current is twice as big.

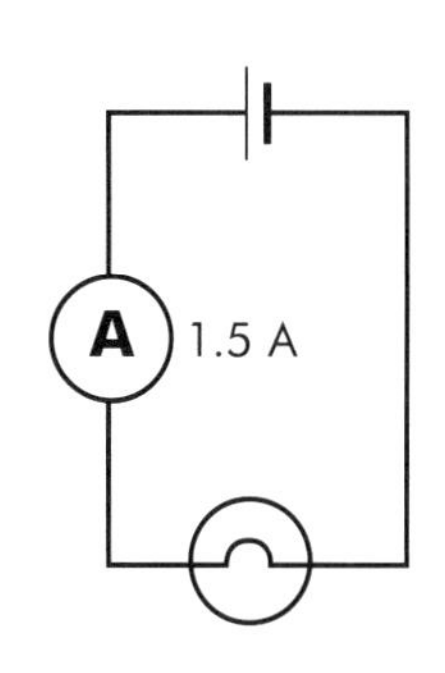

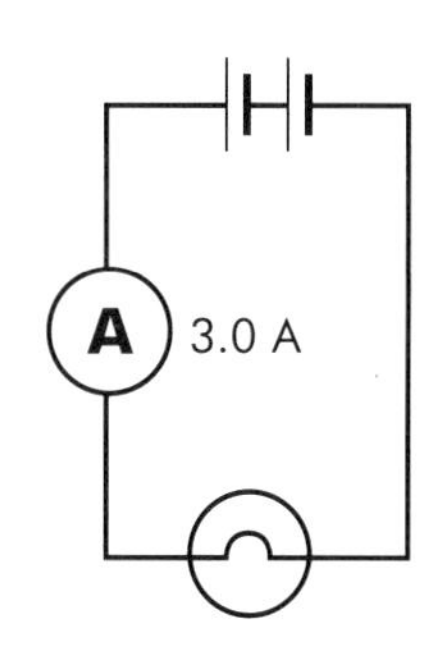

c **1** Draw a circuit diagram to show three batteries pushing current through a bulb. Include an ammeter.

2 How much current will flow through the bulb?

What do you know?

1 Copy and complete the table. Choose the correct word from each pair to show how the current can be changed in a circuit.

How the circuit is changed	How the current changes	How the flow of charge changes
more resistance	**bigger/smaller** current	**bigger/smaller** flow of charge
more batteries	**bigger/smaller** current	**bigger/smaller** flow of charge

2 Janet has two lights in her room.

Light	Brightness	Used for
ceiling light	very bright	getting dressed, practising guitar, homework
bedside light	much dimmer	reading in bed

a Which light has the bigger current flowing through it when it is switched on? Give a reason for your answer.
b Which light has the greater resistance? Give a reason for your answer.

Key ideas

An electric current is a flow of electric charge, from positive (+) to negative (–).

More batteries in a circuit give more push, so a bigger current flows.

If there is less **resistance** in a circuit, it is easier for a current to flow.

9d Bringing energy

Electric current is a useful way of carrying energy from one place to another. Current flows along wires, bringing energy to our homes from the power station. Current flows from a car's battery to make its headlights work.

a Copy and complete the energy transfer diagram which shows the energy changes that make a car's lights work.

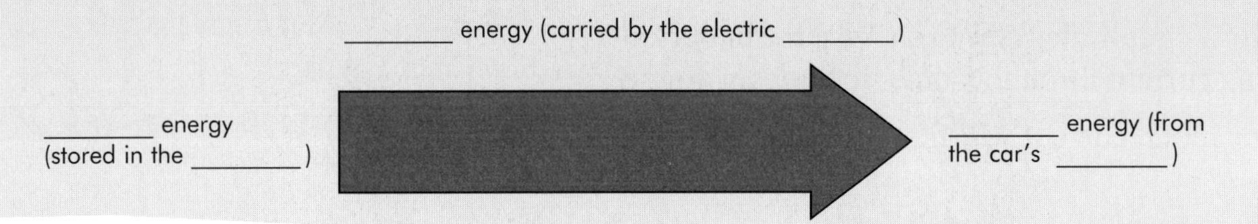

Round and round

An electric current needs a complete circuit to flow around. It won't flow if there is a break in the circuit.

In this circuit, the current is bringing energy from the power supply to the lamp. Electric charge flows in the wires. It gives its energy to the lamp. Then it flows back to the power supply to collect more energy.

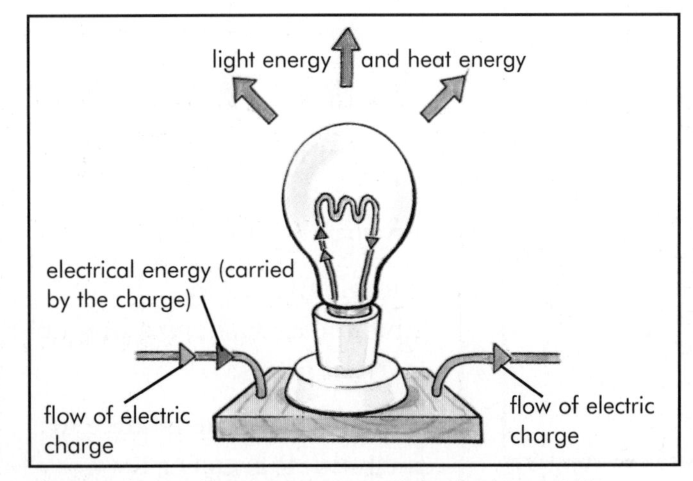

Electric charge brings energy to light the lamp. When the charge comes out, it has given up its energy. But the charge passes right through the lamp – it doesn't get used up.

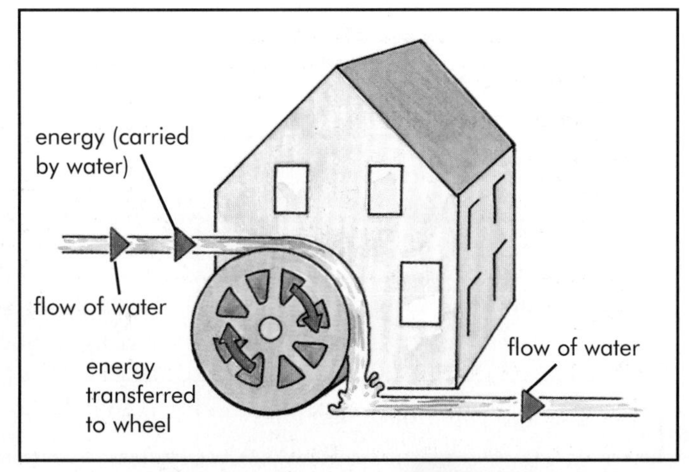

Water brings energy to turn the mill. When the water comes out, it has given up its energy. But the water passes right through the mill – it doesn't get used up.

Ammeter connections

We use an **ammeter** to measure electric current. The current flows through the ammeter, and we can see how many amperes are flowing.

An ammeter must be connected in series, so that the current will flow through it.

b Who is right? Explain your answer.

What do you know?

1 This circuit diagram shows how a battery can be used to make a buzzer sound.

a Copy the diagram. Add arrows to show how current flows around the circuit.

b Add another arrow to show the movement of electrical energy.

2a The second ammeter in this circuit reads 0.8 A. What will the first ammeter read?

b A second battery is added, in series with the first. How will the ammeter readings change?

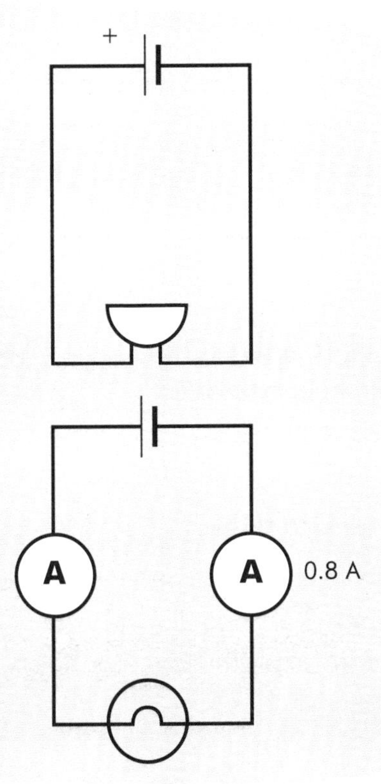

Key ideas

When a current flows around a circuit, it brings energy from the battery or power supply to the components in the circuit.

The charge flows all the way round the circuit – it doesn't disappear.

EXTRAS

9a Positive, negative and neutral

This is how we picture what happens when a polythene rod is rubbed by a cloth.

- At first, the rod has equal amounts of positive and negative charge. We say that it is **neutral**.
- When the rod is rubbed by the cloth, the force of friction rubs negative charge off the cloth onto the rod.
- Now the rod has more negative charges than positive ones.

1 At first, is the cloth positive, negative or neutral?

2 When the rod has been rubbed, is the cloth positive, negative or neutral?

3 Explain why the rod and the cloth now attract each other.

4 When an acetate rod is rubbed, it becomes positively charged. Draw a series of diagrams to show how the charges change. (Remember, it is negative charges that move.) Add a sentence to say what happens.

On the wall

When you rub a balloon on your jumper, you give the balloon a negative charge.

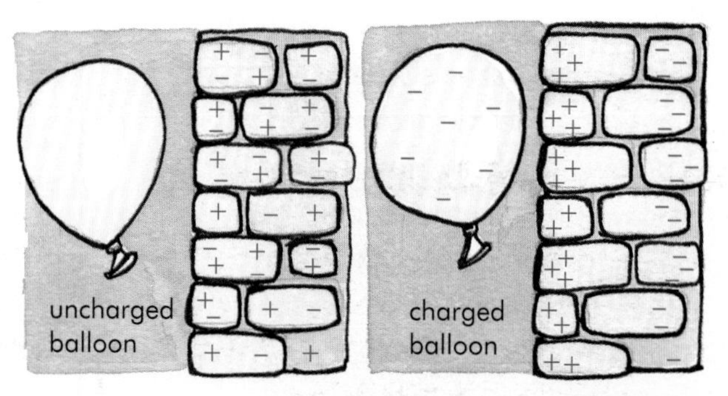

5 Why will it now stick to your jumper?

The balloon will also stick to the wall, although the wall is neutral. The balloon attracts positive charges in the wall. It repels negative charges.

Now there are positive charges next to the negative charges of the balloon, and they stick together.

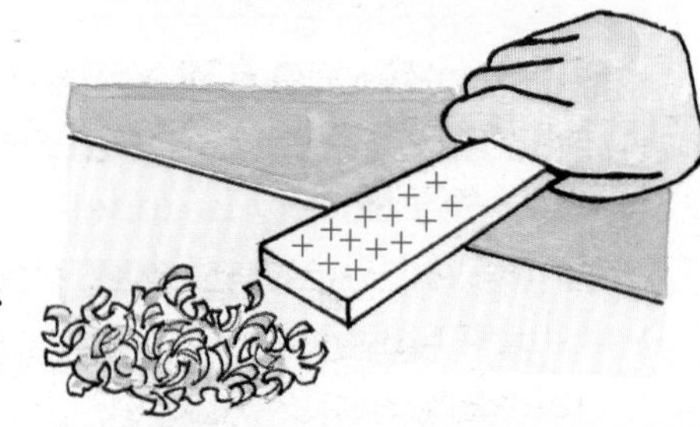

6 A positively charged acetate rod is held near to some small pieces of paper. The pieces of paper are neutral. The rod attracts them. Use the ideas above to explain how this happens.

9c Current changes

There are two ways to change the current flowing around a circuit:

- change the resistance in the circuit
- change the number of batteries in the circuit.

1 For each of the circuits shown, decide whether the reading on the ammeter will increase, decrease, or stay the same when the extra component is added to the circuit. Give a reason for each answer.

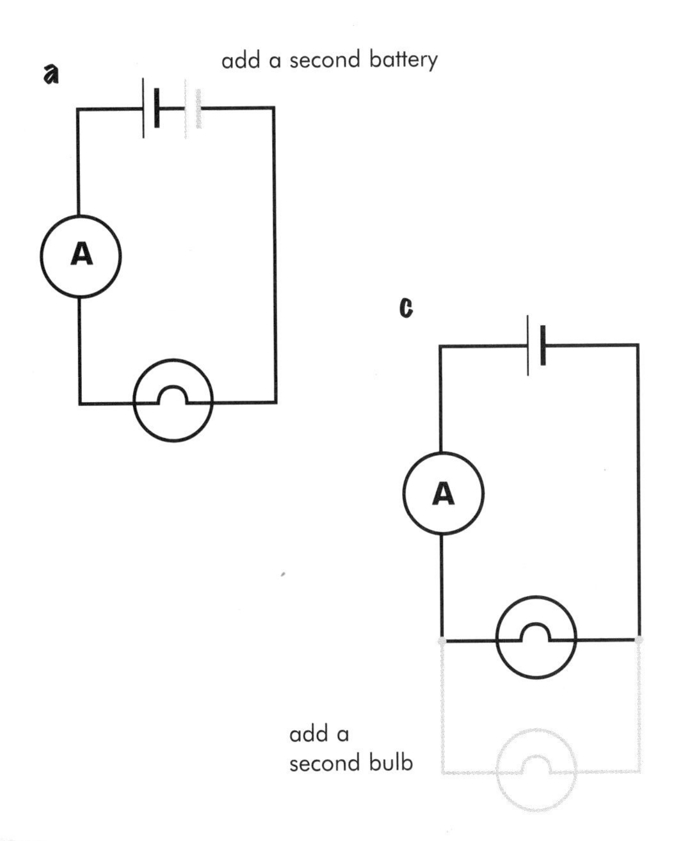

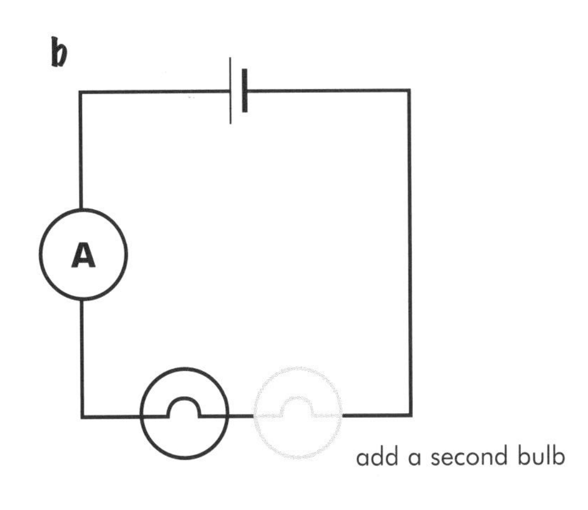

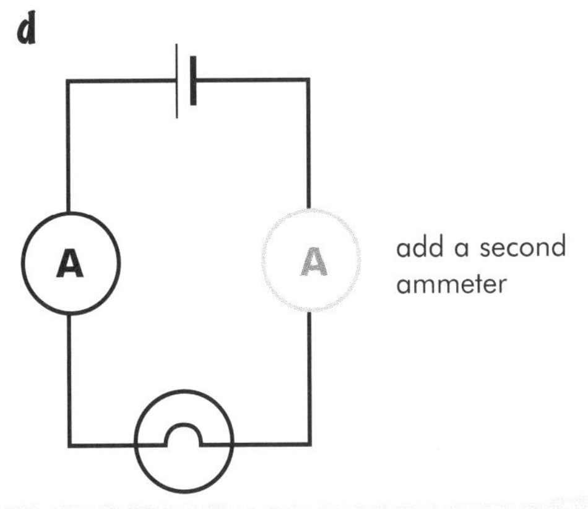

Current is conserved

The current flowing in a circuit is the same all the way round. Current cannot disappear, because charge cannot disappear. We say that current is **conserved**.

1 Use the idea that current is conserved to work out the readings on the ammeters in this circuit.

2 If the circuit had two batteries instead of one, what would the readings be on each of the four ammeters?

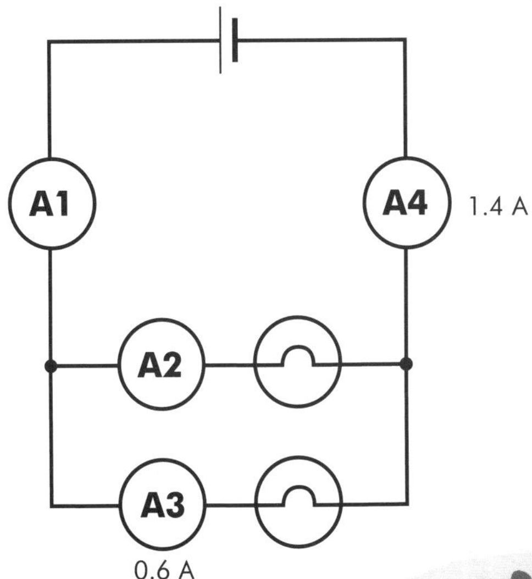

9 REVIEW

9a Attractions

When a plastic ruler has been charged up with static electricity, it can attract things to itself. A magnet can attract things too, but it works by magnetism, not static electricity.

Magnets attract magnetic materials, such as iron or steel. Many metals, such as copper and aluminium, are not magnetic.

Look at the things in this picture.

1 Which of these things can be attracted by a charged plastic ruler?

2 Which of these things can be attracted by a magnet?

3 It is the two ends of a bar magnet that do the attracting. What do we call these?

9c Passing through

We use an ammeter to measure electric current. It must be connected in series in the circuit.

In a **series** circuit, components are connected end to end, one after the other.

In a **parallel** circuit, components are connected side by side.

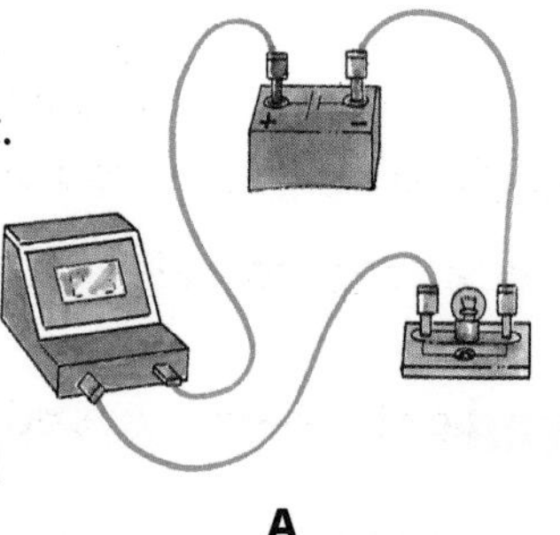

A

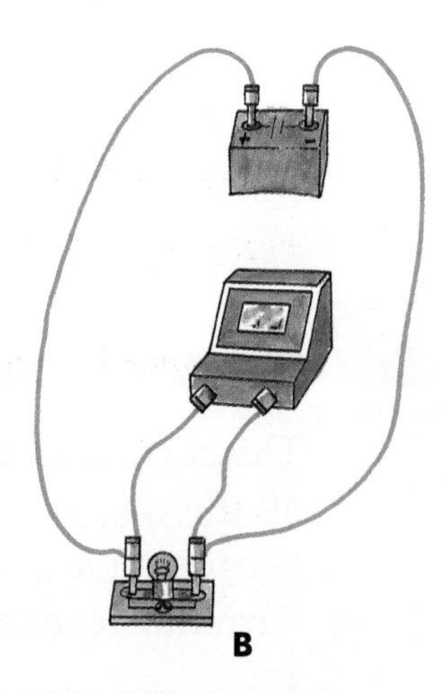

B

1 Which picture, **A** or **B**, shows an ammeter connected correctly?

2 Draw a circuit diagram to show how you would connect together a battery and a buzzer. Include an ammeter to measure the current flowing in the circuit.

battery

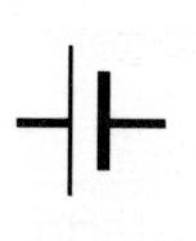

buzzer

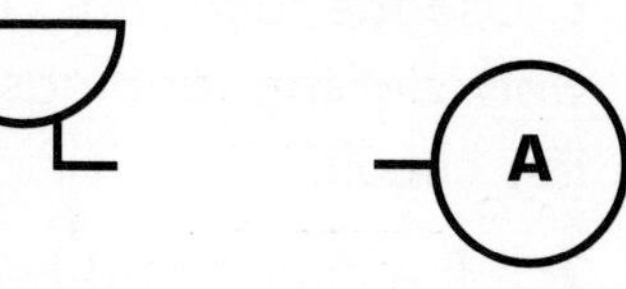

ammeter

Resisting the flow

Electric current has to flow through all the components in a circuit. If a component has a high **electrical resistance**, it is difficult for the current to flow through it.

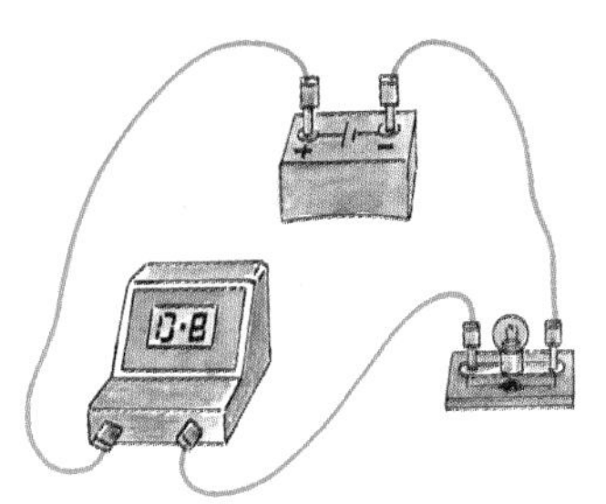

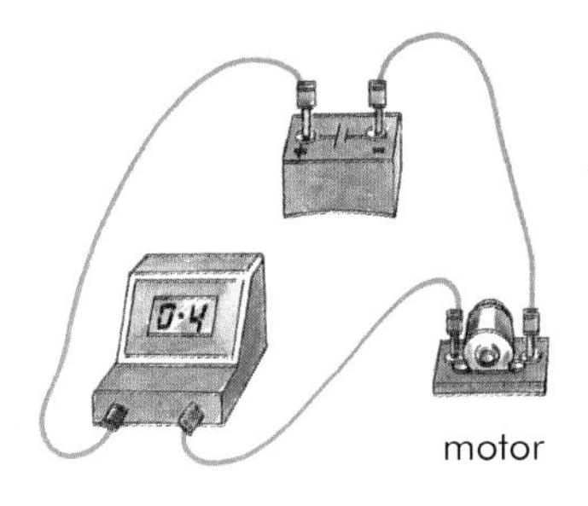

3 Which of these circuits has the bigger current flowing around it?

4 Which component has the bigger electrical resistance, the lamp or the motor?

9d Energy changes

Electric current is useful for carrying electrical energy. The battery or power supply gives the current electrical energy. This electrical energy is changed into another kind of energy when the current flows through components in the circuit.

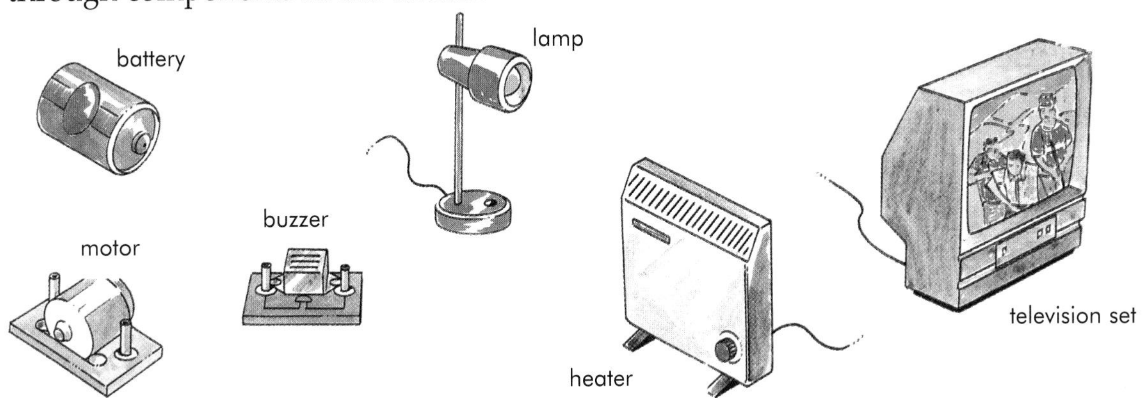

1 Copy and complete the table to show some useful energy changes. The pictures will give you some clues.

Here is a list of forms of energy to help you:

chemical electrical light heat sound kinetic

In a ________	________ energy	is changed to electrical energy.
In a lamp	________ energy	is changed to ________ energy.
In a ________	________ energy	is changed to kinetic energy.
In a television set	________ energy	is changed to ________ energy and ________ energy.
In a ________	________ energy	is changed to sound energy.
In a ________	________ energy	is changed to heat energy and ________ energy.

10a Under pressure

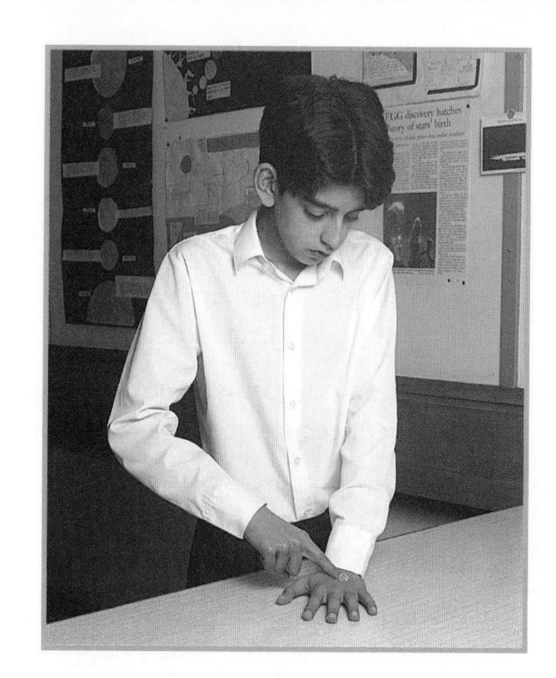

Your skin is useful for telling you about the world around you. It can tell you if something is hot or cold or painful. It can also detect **pressure**.

If you press on the back of your hand with a finger, you can feel the pressure. The harder you press, the greater the pressure.

Into the wood

This nail has a flat head and a sharp point. If you try to push the nail into the wood by hand, your force will not be big enough.

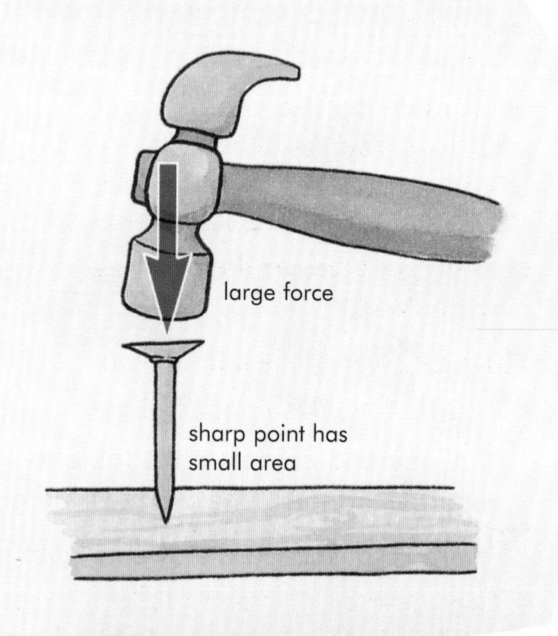

The hammer hits the head of the nail with a big force. The force pushes the sharp point of the nail into the wood. There is enough pressure to push the nail in.

The point of the nail has a very small area. The force of the hammer is concentrated on this small area. A big force pressing on a small area gives a high pressure.

a It is more difficult to hammer a blunt nail than a sharp nail into a piece of wood.

1 Which has the bigger area, a blunt nail or a sharp nail?

2 When is the pressure on the wood more, when the hammer hits the blunt nail or when it hits the sharp nail? Explain your answer.

High pressure, low pressure

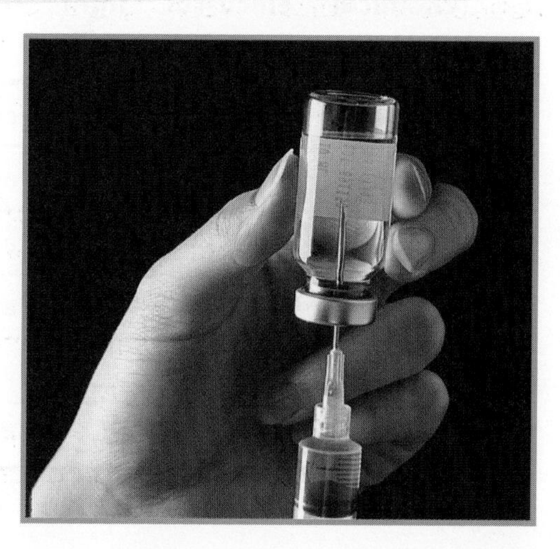

Sometimes we want high pressure, and sometimes we want low pressure.

When the doctor gives you an injection, she uses a very sharp needle. Then she only needs to use a small force to break through your skin. If the needle was blunt, she would need a much bigger force to get enough pressure.

Camels are heavy animals. They walk on the soft sand of the desert, and they are in danger of sinking in. They have large flat feet, so that their weight is spread out over a large area. Then the pressure on the ground is less.

b **1** Who is heavier, the boy or the camel?

2 Use the idea of pressure to explain why the boy sinks further into the sand than the camel.

Treading on thin ice

If you stand upright on thin ice, your weight is pressing down on a small area – the area of your feet. You can make the pressure less by lying on the ice. Your weight is pressing down on a bigger area, so the pressure is not as great.

c How could you use a ladder to help you rescue the boy who has fallen in?

What do you know?

1 Copy and complete the following sentence. Choose the correct word from each pair. There are two correct answers. Can you find them both?

A **large/small** force pressing on a **large/small** area gives a **high/low** pressure.

2 Use the idea of pressure to explain the following:
a It is difficult to burst a balloon by sticking your finger into it. It is much easier using a sharp pin.
b Eskimos wear large, flat snowshoes to help them walk on the snow.
c If you have bare feet, it is more painful to walk on a rough pebbly beach than on a smooth sandy beach.

Key ideas

The **pressure** tells us how concentrated a force is.
A large force pressing on a small area gives a high pressure.

10b How much pressure?

This tractor has wide tyres. The weight of the tractor presses down on a large area, and so its pressure on the ground is small. A high pressure would compress the soil and make it difficult for crops to grow.

Pressure points

Pressure depends on two things:

- the force that is pressing
- the area it is pressing on.

The larger the pressure and the smaller the area, the higher the pressure.

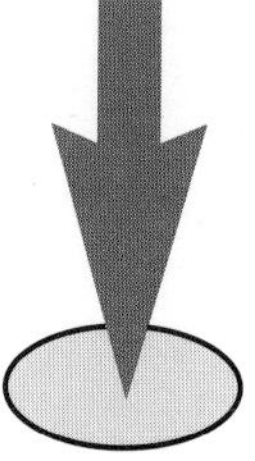

a large force on a small area = high pressure

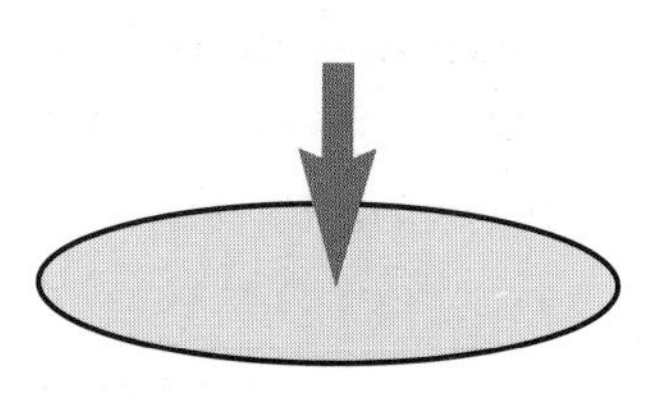

a small force on a large area = low pressure

a Which gives the higher pressure, a force of 10 N pressing on an area of $1\,m^2$, or a force of 1 N pressing on an area of $10\,m^2$?

If we know the size of the force and the area it is pressing on, we can work out the pressure like this:

$$\text{pressure} = \frac{\text{force}}{\text{area}}$$

The table shows the units of force, area and pressure.

Quantity	Unit
force	newtons (N)
area	square metres (m^2)
pressure	pascals (Pa) or N/m^2

On the snow

This sledge presses down on $0.5\,m^2$ of snow. The children and the sledge together weigh 600 N, so the force on the snow is 600 N. The pressure on the snow is:

$$\text{pressure} = \frac{600\text{ N}}{0.5\text{ m}^2} = 1200\text{ Pa}$$

This means that there is a force of 1200 N on each square metre of snow under the sledge.

b If another child weighing 300 N got on the sledge, what would the pressure on the snow become?

On the box

This box weighs 400 N. The pressure on the ground under it depends on which way up you stand it.

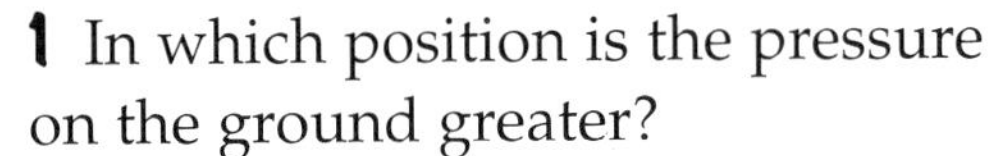

C **1** In which position is the pressure on the ground greater?

2 Work out the pressure on the ground in each position.

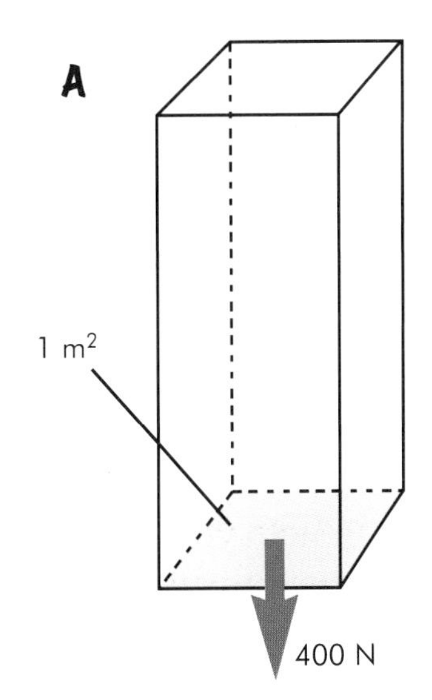

In this position, the area of the box on the ground is 1 m^2.

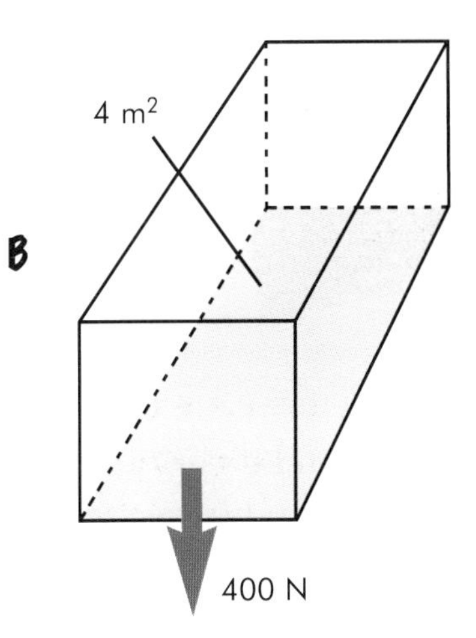

In this position, the area is 4 m^2.

What do you know?

1 James was not quite sure of the correct way to work out pressure. He wrote down three different equations:

$$\text{pressure} = \text{force} \times \text{area}$$

$$\text{pressure} = \frac{\text{force}}{\text{area}}$$

$$\text{pressure} = \frac{\text{area}}{\text{force}}$$

Copy out the correct version of the equation.

2 This packing case weighs 2000 N. Work out the pressure of the packing case on the floor.

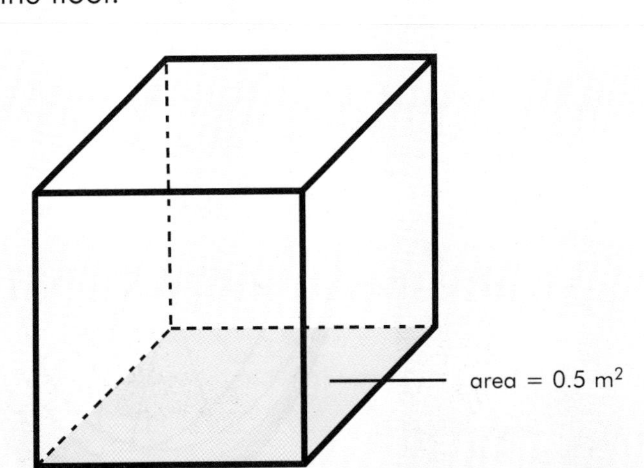

3 This car has four wheels in contact with the road. The total area of contact is 0.1 m^2. The car weighs 5000 N. What is the pressure of the car on the road?

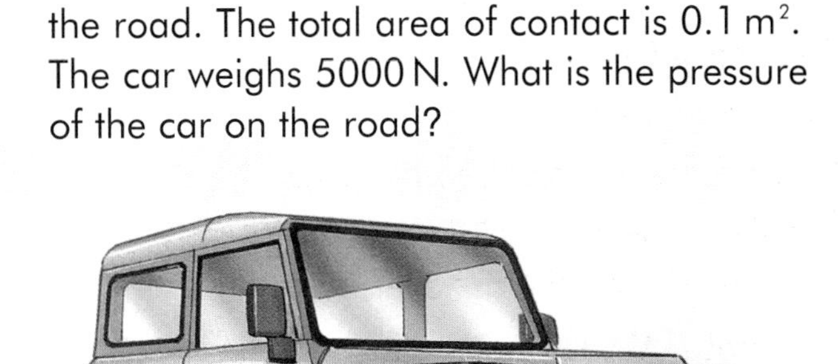

Key ideas

Pressure can be calculated using the equation:

$$\text{pressure} = \frac{\text{force}}{\text{area}}$$

The unit of pressure is **pascals** (Pa). 1 Pa is the same as 1 N/m^2.

10c Lifting and turning

Levers can be very useful. They can help you to do a job which would otherwise be difficult.

This man is using a lever to remove the lid of a large box. The lever increases his lifting force.

Bicycle levers

Cyclists make use of levers. The brake handle has a **pivot**. You pull on the end of the handle with a small force. The lever pulls the brake cable with a bigger force.

If you have a puncture, you may need to take the tyre off your bicycle wheel. It is much easier to do this if you have a tyre lever. You push down on the end of the lever to get as much leverage as possible. Then you can provide enough force to remove the tyre.

a You need a much longer lever to remove a car tyre. Why is this?

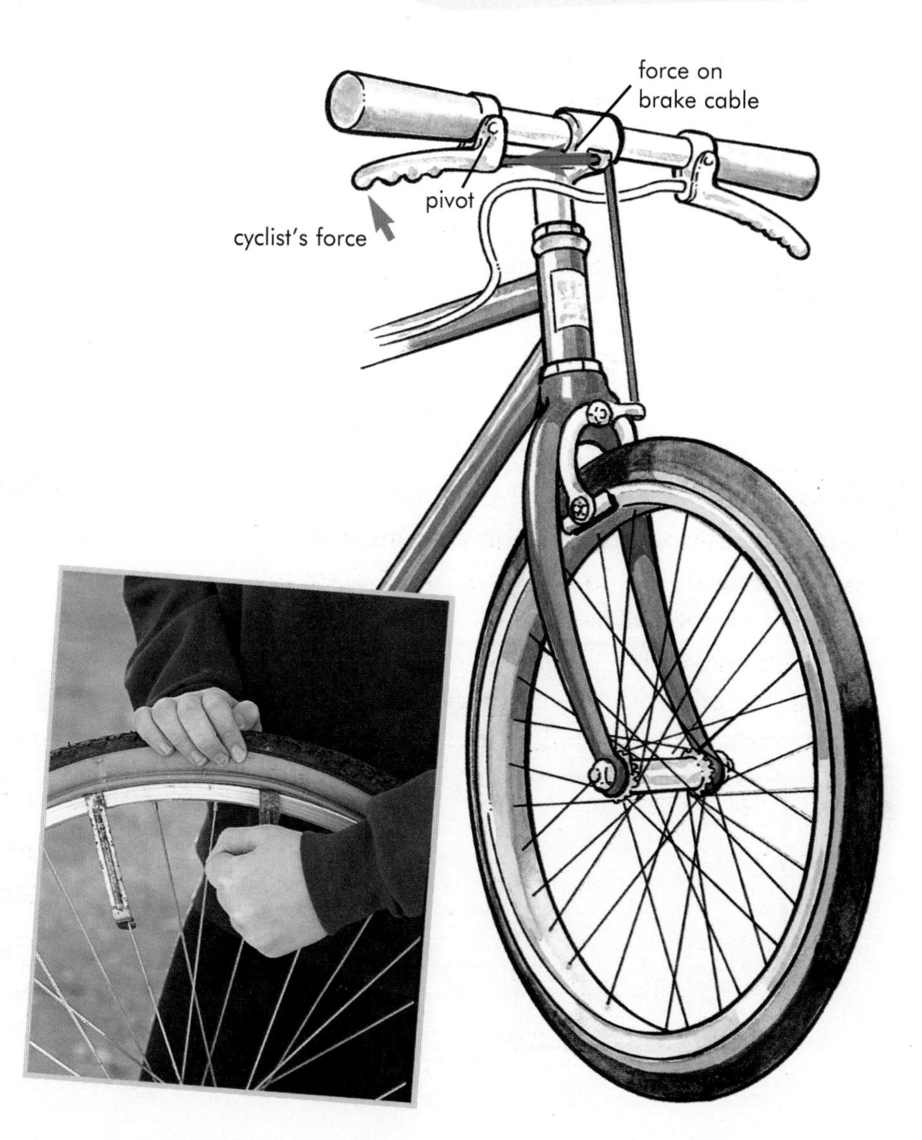

Heavy rock

This woman is trying to lift a heavy rock using a lever. The rock stays on the ground. There are two ways she could get the rock to move:

- She could push down harder. A bigger force has a bigger effect.
- She could use a longer lever. The further the force is from the pivot, the bigger its effect.

See-saw

You can use these ideas to work out where to sit on a see-saw so that it will be balanced.

Fred weighs half as much as Sid, so Fred has to sit twice as far from the pivot.

b Bob is their dad. He weighs 800 N. Where should he sit to balance Fred? Draw a diagram to show your answer.

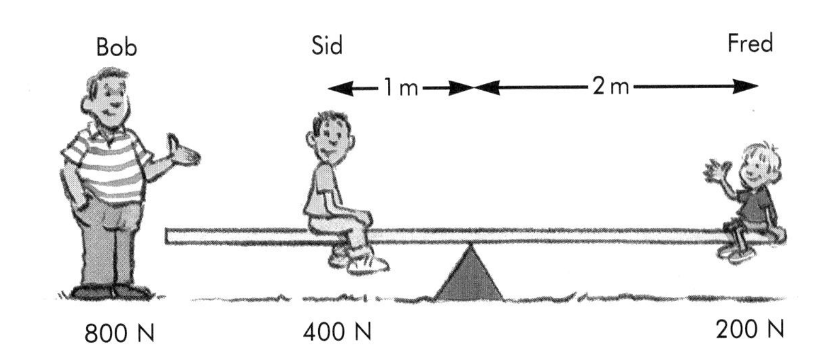

What do you know?

1 This window is stuck. Who is most likely to push it open? Explain your answer.

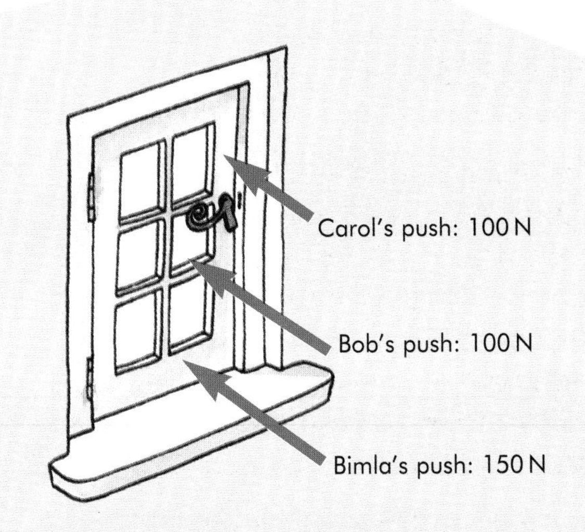

2 A see-saw is a kind of lever. It has a pivot at the middle.

a Jan and Jo are balanced when they sit at opposite ends of the see-saw. What does this tell you about their weights?

b Jenny takes Jo's place on the end of the see-saw. She is heavier than Jo. Suggest some different ways they could balance the see-saw.

Key ideas

You can use a force to make something turn about a **pivot**.

The bigger the force, and the further it is from the pivot, the greater is its effect.

Changing speed, changing direction

A full shopping trolley can be difficult to control. You need a big force to start it moving. You need to push it sideways to make it go round a corner. You need a big force to stop it moving.

A cycle trip

When you set off on a bicycle, you need to push hard on the pedals. Friction makes it difficult to get started. The forces on the bicycle are **unbalanced**.

It is much easier once you have got going. You only need a small force to travel at a steady speed. The forward force balances air resistance. The two forces are **balanced**.

You need unbalanced forces to slow down at the end of the ride. If you pull on the brakes, there is a backwards force to slow you down. The forces are unbalanced, so your speed changes.

You always need an unbalanced force to change your speed – to speed up or to slow down.

a If you stop pedalling your bicycle, you will soon slow down and stop.

1 What force makes you stop?
2 Is this force balanced or unbalanced?
3 Draw a force diagram to show this.

Round the bend

Ice-skating is a skilful sport. There is not much friction on ice, so it is difficult to control where you go. It is quite easy to travel in a straight line, but it is much harder to turn a corner.

A skater must turn her skates sideways if she wants to change direction. Then there is a sideways force which pushes her round the corner.

b Are the forces on the skater balanced or unbalanced?

Here are some other ways to turn a corner. In each case, the forces are unbalanced.

An aircraft tips its wings. This is called banking. Then the force on its wings pushes it around the bend.

If you are standing on a bus, you can feel a force tugging your arm as it goes around a corner.

What do you know?

1 Copy and complete the table to show whether the forces are balanced or unbalanced.

sitting still	forces **balanced/unbalanced**
speeding up	forces **balanced/unbalanced**
steady speed	forces **balanced/unbalanced**
slowing down	forces **balanced/unbalanced**
changing direction	forces **balanced/unbalanced**

2 If you drop a ball on the ground, it bounces back up. Its movement changes from downwards to upwards.
a Draw a diagram to show the force of the ground on the ball.
b When the ball hits the ground, are the forces on it balanced or unbalanced?

3 If you whirl a conker around your head on a string, it does not travel in a straight line. It moves along a curved path, changing direction all the time. What force is pulling on it to make it travel round?

Key ideas

You need **unbalanced** forces to change the speed or the direction of an object.

If the forces on an object are **balanced**, it will move at a steady speed and its direction will not change.

EXTRAS

10b How much pressure?

1 The weight of this explorer is 1200 N. Each of his snowshoes has an area of $0.1 m^2$. Work out the explorer's pressure on the snow when he is standing on:
a one snowshoe **b** both snowshoes.

2 A box weighs 500 N and presses on $1 m^2$ of floor. What is the pressure on the floor?

3 The block on the right weighs 600 N.
a On which face would you place it to make the least pressure on the ground?
b What would the pressure be?

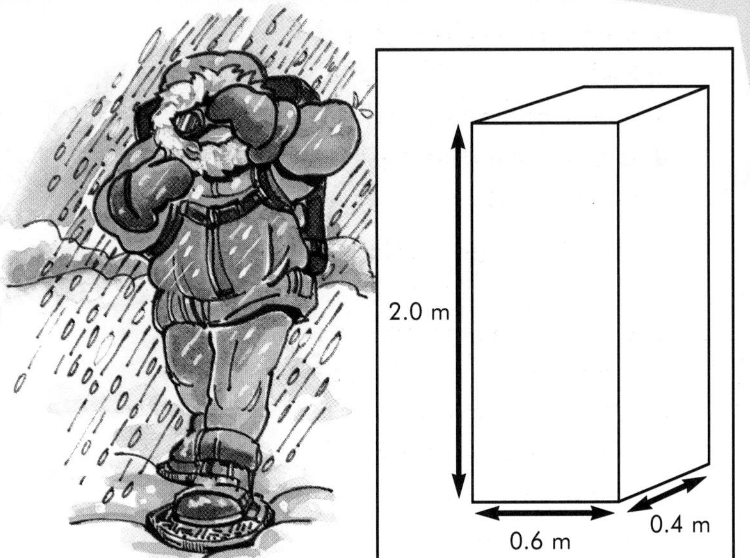

10c The principle of moments

The bigger a force is, and the further from the pivot it is, the greater its effect. We can calculate its effect. This is called the **moment** of the force.

moment = force x distance from pivot

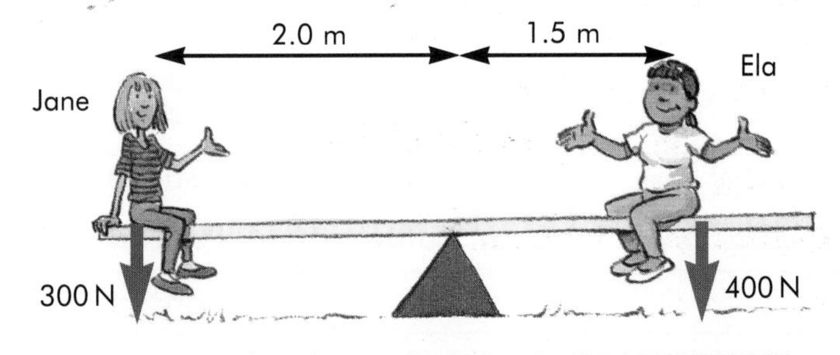

For a lever to be balanced, the moments pulling down on one side must equal the moments pulling down on the other side. The see-saw in the picture is balanced:

Jane's moment = 300 N x 2 m = 600 Nm

Ela's moment = 400 N x 1.5 m = 600 Nm

Ela sits closer to the middle so that the two girls' moments are the same.

1 What force X is needed to balance this see-saw?

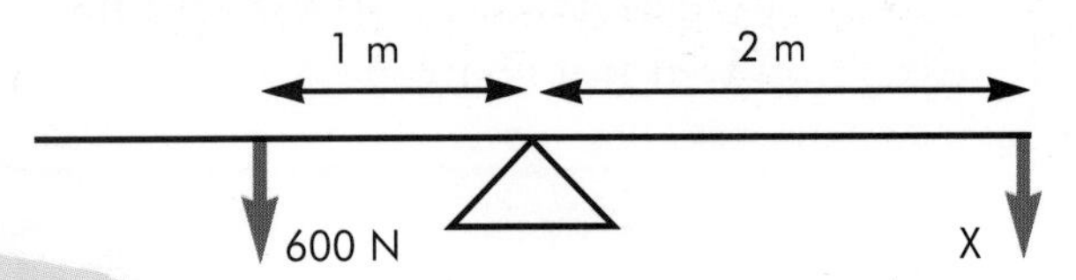

2 Is this see-saw balanced? If not, how could it be balanced?

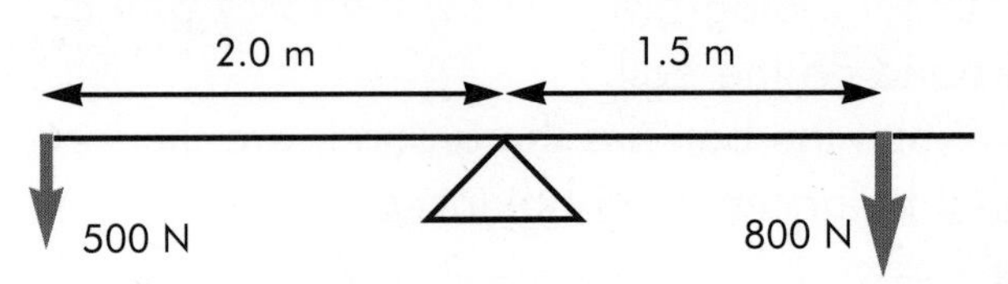

10d Balanced or unbalanced?

1 For each of these examples, say whether the forces are balanced or unbalanced:

a a car setting off from the traffic lights

b someone cycling at a steady speed

c a bus going around the corner

d a ball rolling to a halt on a snooker table.

2 When you are cycling at top speed, you need to keep pedalling. Your force is needed because of air resistance.

a Draw a diagram to show these forces. Are they balanced?

b Explain what will happen if you stop pedalling.

3 Skydivers have to be brave to jump out of an aeroplane. At first, they go faster and faster. When their parachutes are open, they fall at a steady speed towards the ground. Draw diagrams to show the forces on a skydiver:

a just after jumping out of the aircraft

b just before landing.

10 REVIEW

10a Measuring forces

A force is a push or a pull. Here are some important forces:

- **friction** – the force when two surfaces rub together
- **air resistance** – the force when something tries to move fast through the air
- **weight** – the pull of the Earth's gravity on something.

The pictures show how to measure friction and weight.

1 Which picture shows how to measure friction?
Which picture shows how to measure weight?

2 What instrument is used to measure these forces?

3 What unit are forces measured in?

4 Copy and complete these sentences.
a The force of ________ can make it difficult to start something moving.
b The weight of an object is the pull of the Earth's ________ on it.

Mass and weight

Take care not to mix up mass and weight.

- The **mass** of something tells you how much matter ('stuff') it is made of. Mass is measured in kilograms (kg).
- The **weight** of something tells you the pull of the Earth's gravity on it. Weight is a force. It is measured in newtons (N).

Your mass is the same wherever you are. On the Moon, your weight will be less because the Moon's gravity is weaker than the Earth's. In deep space, your weight will be zero because there is no gravity there.

5 This space creature has just been discovered on the Moon. Its mass is 20 kg, and it weighs 32 N. The astronauts are going to bring it back to Earth.
a What will its mass be on Earth?
b Will its weight be more or less than 32 N on Earth?
c What will its mass and weight be in deep space?

10d Speedy measurements

An unbalanced force can make something speed up or slow down. You can find out the speed of something moving by making two measurements:

- the distance it travels
- the time it takes.

Then you can work out its speed:

$$\text{speed} = \frac{\text{distance moved}}{\text{time taken}}$$

1 A runner takes 20.0 s to sprint 200 m. What is her speed?

2 These pupils are measuring the speed of a trolley running along the bench. The timer measures the time it takes for the trolley to move between the two light gates. What is its speed?

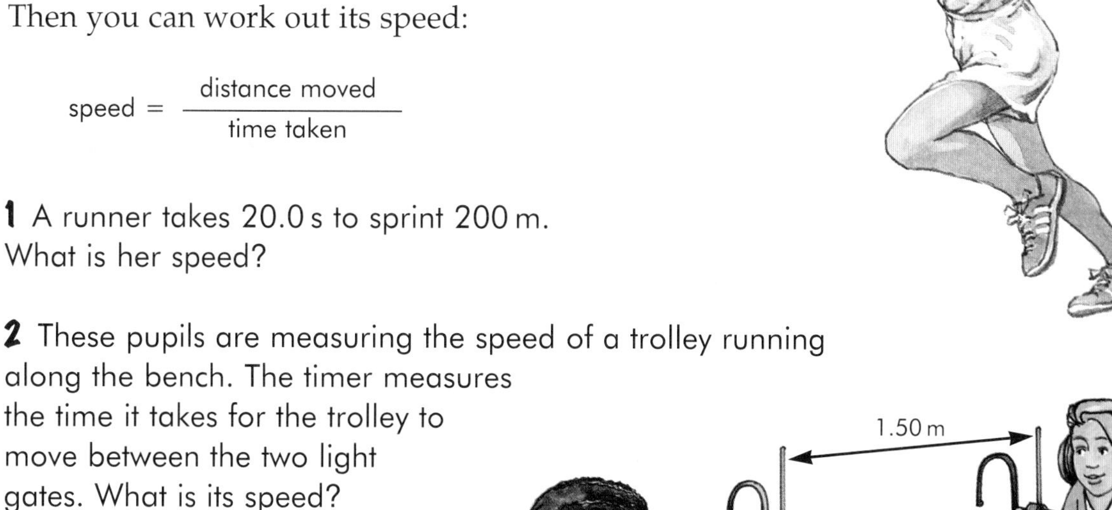

3 Two coaches a day travel the 300 km from York to London. The timetable shows when they leave York, and when they arrive in London.

York *dep*	07.00	18.00
London *arr*	10.15	21.00

a Which is faster, the morning coach or the evening coach?
b What is the average speed of the evening coach?

Glossary

absolute zero
page **49**
the coldest temperature possible, at which all particles stop moving.

adapted
pages **30, 32–3, 40, 41, 46**
an animal or plant that is well suited to its ecosystem is adapted. Cells are also adapted to their function within the organism.

addictive
page **19**
you become addicted to a drug when you can't cope without it, and have to keep taking it to keep feeling normal.

adolescence
page **16**
the physical and emotional changes that take place as your body prepares for adulthood and reproduction.

air pressure
pages **52–3, 61**
the air pushing on you as all the gas particles collide with you. *See* **pressure.**

alcohol
pages **21, 24, 27**
a drug that affects your brain. It can damage your health or kill you in large doses.

alcoholic
page **21**
a person who is addicted to alcohol.

alkali metals
pages **70, 77**
group I of the periodic table, containing reactive, soft metals such as sodium and potassium.

alloy
page **96**
a metal mixture, e.g. bronze which is an alloy of copper and tin.

alveoli
pages **15, 26**
tiny air sacs that make up the lungs.

ammeter
pages **133, 136**
instrument for measuring the electric current flowing round an electrical circuit.

amplitude
pages **108, 115**
the height of a vibration. A sound with a large amplitude is loud.

antibiotic
pages **3, 9, 10, 43**
a medicine that kills bacteria in the body.

antiseptic
pages **3, 9**
a chemical that kills bacteria.

asexual reproduction
page **42**
reproducing using only one parent.

atmospheric pressure
pages **52–3**
another name for air pressure.

atom
pages **48, 66–7, 68, 72–3, 76, 78, 79, 80, 88, 89**
the smallest particle of an element.

atomic number
pages **67, 68, 69**
the order number of an atom when the elements are put in order of the mass of their atoms. The atomic number tells you how many protons are in an atom.

attracting
pages **127, 136**
pulling together, e.g. two objects with opposite electric charges will attract each other.

bacteria
pages **2, 3, 4–5, 9, 10, 13, 43**
micro-organisms that have cells without a proper nucleus. Some cause disease, others are useful.

balanced equation
pages **74, 75, 79**
a chemical equation is balanced when there are the same numbers of each type of atom on the left and on the right.

balanced forces pages **144–5, 147** — forces are balanced when they cancel each other out. The object remains stationary or continues to move at a steady speed.

boil pages **51, 60, 65, 122** — a liquid boils when it all starts to turn into a gas. All the particles become free from each other.

bonds pages **50–1** — elastic forces that hold particles together.

Bronze Age page **96** — the time when people used bronze to make tools, beginning about 4500 years ago.

caffeine page **19** — a drug in coffee, tea and cola that stimulates your body.

cells pages **4, 6, 13, 14, 32–3, 46** — the 'building blocks' that all living things are made of.

characteristics page **29** — special features about a particular animal or plant.

chemical bond page **73** — a strong bond holding elements together in a compound. Different elements can make different numbers of bonds.

chemical equation pages **74, 75, 79, 81** — a way of writing what happens in a chemical reaction, using chemical formulae.

chemical formula pages **72–3** — a shorthand way of showing a compound, by writing the symbols of the elements that are in it, along with how many of each type of atom there are.

cilia pages **6, 33** — little hair-like parts of cells. In the respiratory system, cilia move mucus carrying dirt up away from the lungs.

ciliated epithelial cells pages **6, 33** — special cells lining the tubes of the respiratory system and other parts of the body. They have tiny hairs called cilia, which beat to move mucus or other liquids.

classifying pages **28, 44–5** — putting all living things into groups.

clone page **42** — a group of cells or organisms that are genetically identical. They have all been produced from the same original cell.

compound pages **66, 67, 72–3, 74, 80, 81, 88–9, 91** — a substance made of two or more different kinds of atoms chemically joined together.

condense page **60** — a gas condenses when it is cool enough to turn to a liquid. The particles slow down and move together.

conserved page **135** — when something is conserved, the total amount stays the same. Energy and the current flowing round a circuit are both conserved – they are not used up.

consumers page **47** — animals are consumers, because they eat (consume) food produced by plants.

contract pages **48, 64** — a material contracts when it gets slightly smaller, often when it is cooled. Its particles are moving closer together.

diffusion pages **54–5, 62** — substances mix and spread by diffusion – they are mixed up by the moving particles around them colliding with them.

dispersion pages **103, 112** — splitting a ray of white light into the colours of the spectrum by passing it through a glass prism.

displacement pages **86–7, 91, 97** — pushing a substance out from its compound, e.g. a metal displaces hydrogen from an acid. The metal takes the place of the hydrogen in the acid.

dissolve pages **55, 56–9, 62, 63, 65, 98, 99** — some solids dissolve in some liquids. They seem to disappear but you can get them back later.

drug
pages **18–27**
a chemical that has a particular effect on your body.

ecosystem
page **30**
all the different things that affect an animal or plant's home. The other animals and plants, the weather and the type of soil all make up the ecosystem.

electric charge
pages **76, 127, 129, 130–1, 132, 134**
a positive or negative charge given to an insulating material by rubbing it.

electric current
pages **76, 129, 130–3, 135, 137**
a flow of electric charge.

electrons
page **76**
tiny particles that whizz around the nucleus of an atom. They are negatively charged.

element
pages **66–71, 77, 80**
a substance made of only one kind of atom.

energy
pages **116–25**
this has many different forms, e.g. heat, movement, light and sound.

environmental variation
pages **36–7**
differences between individuals that are caused by the surroundings they live or grow up in.

evolution
page **41**
a theory that says all the different species came about by adaptation and survival of the fittest.

expand
pages **48, 64**
a material expands when it gets slightly bigger, often when it is heated. Its particles are moving further apart.

extinct
page **41**
a species that has died out has become extinct.

fertile
page **29**
animals or plants that can reproduce are fertile.

filter
pages **106–7**
a piece of coloured transparent plastic or glass that makes white light coloured when it passes through.

fittest
pages **30, 31, 41**
the animals or plants that are best suited to their ecosystem and are most likely to survive when conditions are tough are the fittest.

food chain
page **47**
the links between different animals that feed on each other and on plants.

frequency
pages **110–11, 115**
the number of vibrations in each second. A sound with a high frequency has a high pitch.

function
page **32**
the special job of an organism or part of an organism.

galvanised iron
page **93**
steel protected by a thin layer of zinc to stop it rusting.

genes
page **43**
structures in the nucleus of a cell, that carry the inherited information.

genetic engineering
page **43**
changing the genetic information in the nucleus of an organism so that it makes something that is useful to people.

glands
page **7**
places in the body where white blood cells are made. Glands often swell when you are ill.

group
pages **69, 70, 71, 77**
a vertical column in the periodic table, that contains elements with similar properties.

hormones
page **16**
chemical messages that travel in the blood and control changes in your body.

immunisation
page **8**
making your body ready to fight a dangerous micro-organism so that you won't become ill if it gets into your body.

inherited
page **35**
features that pass from parents to offspring are inherited.

inherited variation
page **35**
differences between individuals that are caused by information passed on from their parents.

insulating material
pages **125, 127**
a material that only allows heat energy to escape very slowly is a heat insulator. A material that doesn't allow electric charge to flow through it is an electrical insulator.

Iron Age
page **96**
the time when people used iron to make tools, beginning about 3000 years ago.

key
page **45**
a way of putting animals and plants into the groups they belong to.

law of reflection
page **112**
a law about light rays being reflected. It says that the angle of incidence is equal to the angle of reflection.

lever
pages **142–3, 146**
an easy way of lifting heavy weights.

lightning conductor
page **129**
a copper rod on top of a high building connected to a wire that goes into the earth. It conducts the electric charge away if the building is struck by lightning.

melt
pages **51, 65**
a solid melts when it turns into a liquid. The particles become free to move around in the liquid.

metabolic disease
page **14**
a serious kind of disease caused when reactions in the body cells don't work properly.

micro-organisms
pages **2–9, 13, 15, 23**
tiny living things that can only be seen under a microscope. Bacteria and viruses are micro-organisms.

mitochondria
pages **6, 14, 32, 33**
small structures in cells, in which respiration takes place.

molecule
pages **48, 66–7, 72–3, 79, 80**
a particle made up of more than one atom.

moment
page **146**
the turning effect of a force. Moment = force × distance from the pivot.

mucus
page **6**
a sticky substance produced in the tubes leading to the lungs and other parts of the body. It collects micro-organisms and dust to clean the tubes.

native
page **91**
an element that is found in the Earth's crust as the pure element, not in a compound, is found native or uncombined.

negative
pages **76, 127, 130, 134**
one type of electric charge, which is the opposite of positive.

neutral
page **134**
if something has equal amounts of positive and negative charge it is neutral.

nicotine
pages **20, 26**
a drug in tobacco that stimulates the body but narrows the blood vessels.

noble gases
pages **69, 71**
group VIII of the periodic table, containing unreactive gases such as helium and neon.

nucleus
page **76**
the central part of an atom, which contains protons. It is positively charged.

oxidised
pages **82, 83**
a chemical has been oxidised when it has reacted with oxygen to form an oxide.

parallel circuit
page **136**
a circuit in which two or more components are wired side by side.

particle model
page **48**
the idea that everything is made up of particles. The particle model can be used to explain physical and chemical changes.

particles
pages **48–57, 60, 62, 63, 64**
everything is made up of these tiny pieces that are too small to see, even with a microscope.

pascals (Pa)
page **141**
the unit of pressure. 1 Pa is the same as 1 N/m^2.

peer group
pages **16, 18**
friends of your own age who you are growing up with.

periodic table
pages **70–1, 77**
a table that shows all the elements in order of atomic number. Vertical groups contain elements with similar properties.

pitch
pages **110–11**
how high or low a sound is. A piccolo plays high-pitched sounds, and a tuba plays low-pitched sounds.

pivot
pages **142, 143, 146**
the point around which a lever turns.

positive
pages **76, 127, 130, 134**
one type of electric charge, which is the opposite of negative.

pressure
pages **52–3, 61, 138–41, 146**
how concentrated a force is. A large force pressing on a small area gives a high pressure.

principle of conservation of energy
page **123**
an idea that says that energy can't disappear, or appear out of nowhere. The total amount of energy always stays the same.

producers
page **47**
plants are producers, because they produce their own food by photosynthesis.

products
pages **74, 75, 81**
the new substances formed in a chemical reaction.

proton
pages **67, 76**
tiny particles in the nucleus of an atom, which have a positive charge.

puberty
page **16**
the physical changes that take place as your body grows up and becomes capable of reproduction.

ray box
pages **100, 103, 105**
apparatus that produces a single, narrow ray of light.

reactants
pages **74, 75, 81**
the substances that react together in a chemical reaction.

reactivity
pages **82–99**
how easily a substance reacts. The most reactive substances react the most easily.

reactivity series
pages **85, 86–7, 94**
a list of metals in order of reactivity.

reflection
pages **100, 112**
a ray of light changes direction when it hits a smooth flat surface. A mirror reflects light.

refraction
pages **105, 112**
a ray of light bends when it passes from one substance to another, e.g. from glass to air.

repelling
page **127**
pushing apart, e.g. two objects with the same type of electric charge will repel each other.

resistance
pages **130, 131, 137**
how difficult it is for electric charge to flow through something. Thick wires have a lower resistance than thin wires so it is easier for the charge to flow through them.

respiration
page **14**
a chemical reaction that happens in your cells to release energy. The reaction uses oxygen and glucose, and produces water and carbon dioxide.

saturated
pages **58, 63**
a solution that will dissolve no more solid is saturated.

scab
page **7**
a covering that forms over a cut to stop you bleeding, prevent micro-organisms getting in and protect the new skin forming underneath.

scattering
pages **101, 114**
rays of light move off in all directions when they hit a rough surface.

scurvy
page **12**
a disease caused by a lack of vitamin C in the diet.

selective breeding
pages **38–9**
breeding together particular animals or plants over generations to produce offspring with the features people want.

series circuit pages **131, 136** — a circuit in which two or more components are wired end to end.

sexual reproduction pages **34–5** — making new organisms using special cells from a male and a female.

solubility page **59** — the mass of a solid that will dissolve in 100 g of solvent.

solvent pages **58, 59** — the liquid a solid dissolves in.

spark pages **128–9** — an electric charge which jumps through the air. A flash of lightning is a big spark.

species pages **28, 29, 40–1** — animals or plants of the same type. Animals or plants are from the same species if they can reproduce successfully together.

spectrum page **103** — the colours of the rainbow, that can be separated out of white light. They are red, orange, yellow, green, blue, indigo, violet.

static electricity pages **126, 128, 129, 136** — when an insulating material is charged up by rubbing it.

sterile page **15** — an organism that cannot reproduce is sterile.

stimulates page **19** — a drug that stimulates your body makes your body more active.

Stone Age page **96** — the time before people started to use metals.

symbol pages **67, 80** — a shorthand for the elements. Each element has a symbol of one or two letters.

temperature pages **49, 59, 60, 65, 116–19, 122, 123, 125** — how warm something is, measured with a thermometer.

thermometer pages **49, 116** — a device used to measure temperature.

unbalanced forces pages **144–5, 147** — forces are unbalanced when one is bigger than another. This causes the object to speed up, slow down or change direction.

uncombined pages **90, 91** — an element that is found in the Earth's crust as the pure element, not in a compound, is found uncombined or native.

van de Graaff generator page **128** — apparatus that makes a lot of static electricity. The charge collects on a metal dome.

variation pages **30–9** — differences in features between different species, or between members of the same species.

variety pages **28–47** — the enormous differences between all living organisms.

vibrate pages **48, 49, 50, 51, 108–11, 113, 115** — particles vibrate when they move backwards and forwards, but stay in the same overall position.

viruses pages **2, 4–5, 9, 13** — micro-organisms that cause disease and can only reproduce in the living cells of an animal or plant. All viruses are harmful.

white blood cells pages **7, 8** — cells in the blood that defend against disease.

white light pages **102–3, 106, 107, 112** — light from a very hot object, which contains all the colours of the spectrum.

withdrawal symptoms page **22** — feeling very ill when you try to stop taking a drug you are addicted to.